# PRAISE FOR *SUPPLY CHAIN RISK MANAGEMENT*

'This book is a very pragmatic review of the risks that threaten modern supply chains in our inherently uncertain industry and stresses the increased need for accurate, on-time data. From natural disasters to protectionism, Professor Manners-Bell combines his theoretical knowledge with his operational experience to provide the reader with a comprehensive and very readable assessment of the subject matter.' **Yves Letange, Managing Director, Europe, Turkey and North Africa, BDP International NV**

'In this second edition of *Supply Chain Risk Management*, the author articulately covers all aspects of today's volatile world that impact the supply chain. Reflecting how the risk landscape has changed in recent years, the book explores all the latest and newly evolving threats, including pandemics, climate change, corruption, cargo crime and the various economic, societal and political risks. Strategies for developing supply chain resilience are clearly outlined, including the all-important role of technology. Highly recommended; essential reading for all supply chain management practitioners.' **Mark Millar, author of *Global Supply Chain Ecosystems***

'The second edition of this book is a very valuable addition that will help organizations address the increasingly important and constantly changing topic of supply chain risk. It contains many actionable risk insights that can help you develop your organization's supply chain resilience and improve performance.' **Nick Wildgoose, Global Supply Chain Product Leader, Zurich Insurance Group**

**Second Edition**

# Supply Chain Risk Management

Understanding emerging threats
to global supply chains

John Manners-Bell

First published in Great Britain and the United States in 2014 as *Supply Chain Risk* by Kogan Page Limited
Second edition published in 2018

| | | |
|---|---|---|
| 2nd Floor, 45 Gee Street | c/o Martin P Hill Consulting | 4737/23 Ansari Road |
| London EC1V 3RS | 122 W 27th St, 10th Floor | Daryaganj |
| United Kingdom | New York, NY 10001 | New Delhi 110002 |
| www.koganpage.com | USA | India |

© John Manners-Bell, 2014, 2018

The right of John Manners-Bell to be identified as the author of this work has been asserted by him in accordance with the Copyright, Designs and Patents Act 1988.

ISBN    978 0 7494 8015 8
E-ISBN  978 0 7494 8016 5

**British Library Cataloguing-in-Publication Data**

A CIP record for this book is available from the British Library.

**Library of Congress Cataloging-in-Publication Data**

Names: Manners-Bell, John, author.
Title: Supply chain risk management : understanding emerging threats to
   global supply chains / John Manners-Bell.
Other titles: Supply chain risk
Description: Second edition. | London ; New York : Kogan Page, 2018. |
   Includes bibliographical references and index.
Identifiers: LCCN 2017038972 (print) | LCCN 2017035222 (ebook) | ISBN
   9780749480165 (ebook) | ISBN 9780749480158 (alk. paper)
Subjects: LCSH: Business logistics. | Materials management. | Risk management.
Classification: LCC HD38.5 (print) | LCC HD38.5 .M364 2018 (ebook) | DDC
   658.7–dc23

Typeset by Integra Software Services, Pondicherry
Print production managed by Jellyfish
Printed and bound in Great Britain by Ashford Colour Press Ltd

# CONTENTS

*point 2 (question 2)*

# PREFACE

Since writing the first edition (*Supply Chain Risk*) in 2014, the risk landscape has changed significantly. Some risks, including those which received considerable prominence in the first edition, have diminished in importance, whereas others, some from entirely unexpected quarters, have come to dominate.

For example, piracy was a major problem at the time for shipping lines transiting the Suez Canal. Although the problem has not wholly been solved – the underlying causes for a resurgence in piracy remain – the naval response by the international community almost eliminated the threat. Instead, piracy off the coast of West Africa is now more important – a region where there is no naval presence.

International terrorism, of course, remains a major threat, although at the time of the first edition, Al Qaeda seemed to be the most likely perpetrator. Since then, ISIS (so-called 'Islamic State') has come to prominence, resulting in the destabilization of Syria and other parts of the Middle East. Islamic State terrorism has also been 'exported' to other parts of the world, and although air cargo and shipping has not been targeted (as yet), the hijacking and use of trucks as weapons on crowded streets is a new and worrying type of attack.

After a period of major natural disasters including earthquakes, hurricanes and flooding, the last few years have been quieter in meteorological and geological terms. Likewise, the Rana Plaza factory disaster soon left the media headlines. Although this may result in risk dropping down the corporate agenda for a time, it does not mean that threats to supply chains have lessened. It is to be hoped that corporations have used this period to increase their level of preparedness for the next, inevitable event.

This level of change in the risk landscape illustrates the main thesis of this book. Risk is always there and it is very difficult – some would say impossible – for executives to prepare for any single event. Instead, supply chains need to be made resilient enough to deal with threats from any source, expected or unexpected. Taleb's 'Black Swan' analysis holds as good now as it did for the first edition.

One area which is explored in much more depth in this edition is the existential threat to global supply chains from political forces. Although anti-globalization sentiment has been building for some time, very few people would have predicted the Trump or Brexit results. This is not to say that either will necessarily have negative outcomes for international trade – after all the status quo had resulted in stalled World Trade Organization talks, unpopular and probably fruitless US–EU negotiations to create the TTIP free trade area as well as thousands of new protectionist laws implemented throughout the world.

That being said, more than ever economic liberalism is under severe pressure from all sides. Unless business makes the case more effectively for global supply chains, economies and markets will become increasingly fragmented. This could undermine decades of economic integration and the development of free markets, providing a challenge to the very existence of global supply chains.

# ABOUT THIS BOOK

It is only relatively recently that corporations have started to factor in the cost of external risk to their outsourcing and distribution decision-making processes.

Perhaps for too long, supply chain decisions have been overly influenced by the trade-off between transport and labour costs on one side, and inventory costs on the other. The relatively low cost of international transport and remote labour has led to the development of globalization, while accepted supply chain practice has driven managers to strip inventory to the bone.

In essence this trend has increased supply chains' exposure to a host of new or evolving threats, especially in emerging markets, while removing their ability to maintain their primary function – security of supply – by denuding them of inventory. Many corporations have discovered to their cost that this is a short-term policy which has left their businesses critically exposed.

An easy (and mistaken) response to this new environment would be to rebuild levels of 'safety' stocks. However, as this book recommends, a smarter approach is to focus risk mitigation on the twin goals of supply chain agility and velocity.

The aim of this book is to alert executives, both present and future, to the risks that can impact upon supply chains, of which there are many. It is designed to give the reader an understanding of the nature of risk, and why the subject has developed as an issue in the recent past. It categorizes and explains the various elements of risk before looking at how resilience can be engineered into supply chains (with case studies of best practice). The book then examines the variance of supply chain risk based on sector, explaining why some industries are more resilient than others. Finally, it lays out in detail how supply chains are impacted by economic-driven demand shocks; natural disasters, climate change and pandemics; societal risks including damage to reputation from a failure to take corporate and social responsibility seriously; corruption; terrorism; cargo crime; and piracy. It also examines illicit supply chains. These more often than not utilize the structure, processes and services of established infrastructure networks and logistics providers. In its own way the global distribution of illegal products and substances is highly efficient, although, by increasing the risk of intervention and regulation by the authorities, this threatens all supply chains, licit or illicit.

Finally, a new threat has developed to supply chains: protectionism. The concept of globalization has never faced so much opposition, as electorates in Europe and North America challenge the free movement of goods, capital and people as never before.

The book takes a broad approach to the definition of risk, looking not only at short-term disruptive events, but at systemic weaknesses that threaten not only individual supply chains but the drive towards globalization itself.

# ACKNOWLEDGEMENTS

Once more I would like to thank my colleagues at Transport Intelligence for their help in writing and researching this book.

I am indebted to Ken Lyon for his continued insights into the role that technology and security will play in increasing supply chain resilience.

I am also very grateful to Dr Vincent Shiers, Managing Director of RQA Group, for his contribution to the section on food security.

# Introduction

Within the context of an environment in which natural and man-made catastrophes seem to be increasingly common, the issue of supply chain risk has forced itself onto the corporate agenda of all the world's largest multinationals.

Disasters such as the Japanese tsunami and the Thai floods have not only wreaked havoc in regional supply chains, but they have also had far-reaching consequences for manufacturers and retailers many thousands of miles away in Europe and North America. That a localized flood in Thailand could result in the suspension of an automotive production line in the UK or the United States, demonstrates very clearly the fragility of some global supply chains.

The vulnerability of supply chains has been exacerbated over the last 30 years by strategies aimed at keeping labour and inventory costs to a minimum. Lean inventory strategies, centralized distribution, just-in-time delivery schedules, remote, offshored production, sourcing from developing countries and multiple tiers of suppliers have all improved companies' bottom lines, but not without cost. The fact that many of these costs are deferred until a disaster results in a supply chain failure means that many executives treat them as if they do not exist. This is not the case.

As Bob Lutz, former VP of General Motors, once said, 'Running your procurement purely in a short term, point in time, cost minimization model is like shopping for rock bottom home insurance. It looks real smart until your house burns down.'

However, it would be wrong to describe supply chain managers as playing fast and loose with their businesses in search of a short-term profit. What they have done is to transform measurable 'internal' risks into more difficult to measure 'external' ones. Typically, while company metrics may include inventory-on-hand, stock turns and the like, there are no metrics to measure the resilience of a company's supply chain to potential threats. Consequently, as with insurance, there is a temptation to put off the premiums and 'hope for the best'.

Internal risks are those which arise from holding too much inventory (including redundancy and shrinkage), product defects, long product lifecycles as well as 'process' risks such as high labour costs and the inability to scale production up or down quickly. All of these risks were evident in industry in the 1960s and 1970s, when just-in-case, supply-driven manufacturing strategies were widespread.

External risks are those which can impact upon the supply chain from exogenous sources over which managers may have little or no influence. These can include natural disasters, but also acts of terrorism, piracy or even macro-economic demand shocks. These risks are examined in detail in Chapters 4–9 and in Chapter 12.

By unbundling production stages and outsourcing to suppliers, often based remotely, manufacturers and retailers can reduce internal risks. By keeping production processes in-house and closely bundled within their home market, the opposite result is achieved. The problem is that although high levels of stock involve increased internal risk, they also act as a buffer against external sources of supply chain disruption.

It might be tempting to look at the trade-off between internal and external supply chain risks as a zero-sum game. However, this is not necessarily the case. Nobody is suggesting that years of advances in supply chain management efficiency should be rolled back on the basis that an unforecastable event may disrupt production or supply. Rather it should be the aim of supply chain managers to balance these risks. In this goal, technology will have an important role to play. Latest 'sense and respond' capabilities can enable managers to identify a problem at an early stage, improving their decision-making and consequently enhancing the agility and flexibility of the overall supply chain.

Technology also has a role to play in increasing visibility upstream and downstream. Although many manufacturers and retailers may have strong partnerships with their first-tier suppliers, their knowledge of second and third-tier suppliers and the risks they face may be very sketchy.

Different industry sectors have adopted varying strategies to improve their supply chain resilience depending on product attribute, production methods and customer base. The high-tech sector, for instance, is particularly exposed to external risk as it has been amongst the most enthusiastic adopters of outsourced, virtual manufacturing networks which span the globe. Others, such as the pharmaceutical sector, are more vertically integrated and regional/national in their production strategies. There is a high degree of regulation aiming to ensure that supply chains and production remain uncompromised. The resilience of these different supply chains is dealt with in Chapter 3.

Fundamentally, the main problem that all companies face is that they operate within an environment of less than perfect market knowledge. By assuming that what has happened in the past will continue to occur in the future, managers become complacent, and companies are unprepared for unexpected events.

The truth is that the modern world in which we live is hugely volatile and subject to wild randomness. However, businesses still plan and forecast as if they were operating in a stable economic, societal and security situation.

One of the reasons for this volatility is the way in which networks are now more interrelated than ever. Networks, such as energy, transport, financial and information and communications technology, are intertwined in ways which are not fully understood.

A failure or overloading of one network can have knock-on effects on others. For example, layers of air, sea, road and rail networks interlink at nodes which facilitate the transfer of goods or passengers. If any one of these nodes stops functioning, there is a 'cascading failure' throughout the linked networks.

This is not to say that supply chain managers are powerless in the face of these random and indiscriminate forces. Although it is impossible to predict how and when a supply chain will be disrupted by a disaster, it is possible to engineer 'risk-agnostic' resilience. Visibility, responsiveness and agility will be critical elements in ensuring that supply chains of the future retain their competitive advantage. These issues are dealt with in Chapters 1 and 2.

A transformation in the global political environment has brought a new threat to supply chains. While globalization has long been criticized by some parts of the political establishment for its impact on developing economies, the last few years has seen simmering discontent boil over in the developed world. This has manifested itself in the election of President Trump in the US and in Brexit in Europe, not to mention the growth of non-establishment and populist figures and parties elsewhere. The threat to global supply chains is clear. Increasing levels of protectionism risk disrupting the flow of goods, capital and labour around the world. These developing threats are reviewed in Chapter 10.

Of increasing concern to bona fide shippers is the development of illicit supply chains that piggyback on the existing systems and infrastructure. 'Blood antiquities', drugs, contraband (such as duty unpaid cigarettes) and the illegal movement of rare animals (alive or dead) and their products all use ports, airports, road, shipping, air cargo and forwarding services alongside legal goods. Intervention by security or border agencies threatens the frictionless transit of all goods. Not only this, but the trade in illegal products brings the industry into disrepute. This is dealt with in Chapter 11.

# A framework for understanding risk

01

**OBJECTIVES**

This chapter will familiarize the reader with:

- the nature of threat to supply chains;
- how risks can be either 'internal' or 'external' and how the balance has changed in the past few decades;
- how increasing supply chain complexity and globalization has increased risk;
- methods to quantify risk;
- risk analysis models and understanding of latent threats in the logistics industry;
- the 'Black Swan' concept and how this should be used to create resilience;
- the vulnerability of networks and how they interact;
- categories of external supply chain risk.

## An analysis of supply chain threats

Corporate risk can come from many sources, sometimes related to the internal production and distribution processes and management of a company, and sometimes from outside. There are many ways of categorizing types of risk, but perhaps the most relevant in terms of supply chain is shown in Figure 1.1.

The first two categories ('Internal to the firm' and 'External to the firm but internal to the supply chain network') are largely in the control of the

**Figure 1.1**   Internal and external corporate risks

| | | |
|---|---|---|
| **INTERNAL RISK** | **Process** | Management and value-adding activities |
| | **Control** | Rules, systems which govern how a firm controls the processes |
| **SUPPLY CHAIN RISK** | **External** to the firm but **Internal** to the supply chain network | Demand (downstream) <br><br> Supply (upstream) |
| | **External** to the network | 'Environment' (eg natural disasters, weather or socio-political) |

**SOURCE** adapted from Mason-Jones and Towill (1998)

company, but the latter ('External to the network') is largely outside its control, although better intelligence can improve preparedness for disruption.

In terms of supply chain, the last two categories are of most relevance as they relate to threats which specifically affect the extended networks in which most companies in the modern business environment operate.

This is not to say that internal risks of process and control do not impact upon the wider supply chain. One particular issue stems from a lack of visibility upstream and downstream; for example, a large order not anticipated by a supplier could create a bottleneck disrupting supply. Lack of shared information means that many companies are forecast-driven, not demand-driven, and consequently find it difficult to react quickly to changing market conditions, whatever the cause.

The relationship between external and internal supply chain risk is very close. Increasing inventory levels exacerbates risks of redundancy, wastage, shrinkage, financing, and so on, but mitigates external risks (the impact of a disruptive event on supply).

The reverse is also true; reducing internal risks by, for example, unbundling and outsourcing production to remote suppliers leaves companies exposed to a breakdown in the global logistics system or issues of quality control. For example, the problems which Toyota faced in the United States, relating to a malfunctioning brake pedal design, were blamed on a key supply chain partner. One estimate put the total costs of this disaster to

Toyota at \$2 billion, not including lost consumer confidence (Swanekamp, 2010). With 60–70 per cent of a vehicle manufacturer's inventory managed by the supply chain, the management of these risks is business-critical.

While corporate supply chain strategies have been focused over the past few decades on the reduction of internal risk, there has been little realization that what has actually occurred is essentially a trade-off in risk type, not necessarily a complete risk reduction.

This focus has blinkered many companies to the holistic nature of risk. One piece of research suggests that when outsourcing production (and risk), only 10 per cent of manufacturers undertake any sort of risk assessment (Dittman, 2014).

This lack of due diligence, as it might be called, was evident in the implications for supply chains of the 2011 floods in Thailand. Many global companies had allowed themselves to become reliant on high-tech component manufacturers, which were clustered in a remote region where risk was not fully understood. The high-tech sector that developed in Thailand had many comparative advantages in terms of leveraging a local production ecosystem while at the same time offering low-cost labour. The fact that this cluster developed in a region of South East Asia was not the problem; the issue was that a consolidation of specific competences had been allowed to develop in an exposed, flood-prone location.

**Figure 1.2**    Global supply chain risk – supply chain internal and external characteristics

| Supply Chain Characteristic | Internal Risk | External Risk |
| --- | --- | --- |
| High stock levels | High | Low |
| Lean supply chains | Low | High |
| 'Bundled' in-house production | High | Low |
| 'Unbundled' outsourced production | Low | High |
| Globalized sourcing | Low | High |

# The severity of threat

Given the complexity and global nature of supply chains, it is increasingly difficult to judge what impact an event will have in terms of disruption. Even a localized event may have massive global implications, as shown by the 2011 Thai floods.

Movements in shipping rates, in contrast, are a global phenomenon. They affect all global supply chains, but although serious, have a less catastrophic impact. A geo-political conflict, depending on where it takes place, could have a very serious, disruptive impact at a global level. A supplier bankruptcy, on the other hand, may be a localized problem, and if contingency plans are in place, may not be serious. Of course, the seriousness of each of these threats is very specific to each supply chain as well as the level of disruptiveness of the event in question.

## *Is risk increasing?*

### Rebalancing 'external' and 'internal' risks

External threats to supply chains have received considerable attention following the well-publicized natural disasters in Japan and Thailand. However, understanding of the impacts of these risks is at a very early stage. One survey, undertaken for the World Economic Forum, found that 30 per cent of respondents estimated losses of 5 per cent of annual revenue from supply chain disruption (WEF, 2013a). However, over a quarter of respondents were not able to place any sort of figure on the financial impact.

The risks themselves have not become any more acute. After all, there have always been wars and natural disasters. Rather, it is the evolving supply chain and production strategies of the major global manufacturers that have changed, leading to a rebalancing of the risks inherent in various parts of the supply chain.

One distinction already discussed above is between 'internal' and 'external' risks. For example, in the 1980s, the personal computer sector adopted traditional manufacturing practices involving the outlay of huge amounts of capital in production equipment and inventory. The risks of this strategy were clear, as many of these companies quickly went out of business when their forecasts proved hopelessly wrong. From this period new business models were developed that allowed manufacturers to focus on design and marketing and let their supplier bear the risk of production.

This process has been referred to as 'unbundling' of production. In other words, in this example, 'internal' risks were outsourced to contract electronic manufacturers. This, however, did not leave the original equipment manufacturers (OEMs) risk-free – rather, the 'internal' risks were transformed into 'external', that is, those that are inherent in extended supply chains. The risks have changed in character and, using a medical metaphor, instead of offering a longer-term, chronic threat to corporate health, they are now acute and paroxysmal.

In crude terms, it is possible to say that as inventory holdings have fallen, there has been a proportional diminution in internal risk, but at the same time an increase in vulnerability to exogenous sources of risk. This is not to say that this has to be the case. One of the themes of this book is how to maintain many of the efficiencies that have been achieved in inventory reduction terms while minimizing the increase in external risks.

One example of this relates to the impact of the Japanese tsunami on high-tech supply chains. One consultancy, IHS iSuppli, asserted that the event had had a much smaller effect than would have been expected on the electronics supply chain because inventories had been built up during the prior two quarters as a result of lack of demand in the market (Transport Intelligence, 2011a). It believed that a more widespread disruption was prevented by the level of supplies-on-hand combined with the repair and restart of production facilities and agile moves among manufacturers to shift production from Japan to facilities outside the country.

**Figure 1.3**    Rebalancing of internal and external risk

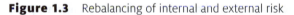

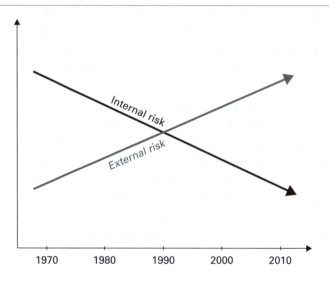

Interestingly – and this may have wider implications for other industry sectors – IHS believes that manufacturers may increase orders to buffer against future supply chain disruptions. If this is the case, maintaining higher inventory levels could become the 'new normal', a calculated measure deployed to mitigate the disrupting effects of natural disasters and other upheavals.

This was also demonstrated by the Chinese automotive sector, which likewise suffered minimal disruption even though several Japanese manufacturers base their production in the country. The reason for this was the lack of adoption of just in time (JIT) delivery schedules, largely because of the poor quality of infrastructure and the lack of a sophisticated supply-side logistics industry that is able to provide these high-value services. This means that Chinese vehicle manufacturers typically keep much more stock on hand than production locations in Japan, North America or Europe.

## Outsourcing and unbundling – risk drivers

The 'unbundling' of various production processes has led many OEMs to evolve into what are, in effect, managers of integrated and complex networks of remote but interlinked suppliers. In some cases this has produced greater levels of risk, and in others it has had the opposite effect. There is no doubt that extended supply chains are more vulnerable to external threats, but on the other hand, such networks have also dispersed risks to a number of markets by reducing centralization of production.

A small supply chain, for instance, with a single production facility is highly vulnerable to external events, whereas a large, complex supply chain with multiple supplier options has the potential to be much more robust through a greater number of sourcing options. Each option may have higher supply chain risk attached, although – and this is the key point – the probability of overall network disruption is less than in a small supply chain (see Figure 1.4).

The move towards more complex supply chains has its own risks, related to a reduction of visibility and the development of sub-optimal networks. With Asia transforming from a production market to a consumer-led economy, this will only add extra layers of complexity into sourcing and outsourcing decisions for Western manufacturers. Timeliness, reliability, information-sharing, quality and design (along with wider benefits resulting from shared labour skills and knowledge) all need to be weighed along with levels of visibility, management control and, of course, external risk.

**Figure 1.4**    Global supply chain risk – probability of disruption

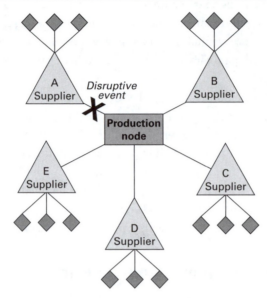

Higher probability of 'some' disruption.
Lower probability of 'total' disruption.

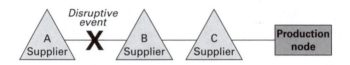

Lower probability of 'some' disruption.
Higher probability of 'total' disruption.

Globalization has also created more risks. Extended supply chains mean longer lead times (and less agile response to market conditions), more handoffs between parties, challenges in ensuring quality control, as well as exposure to currency fluctuations, labour disputes, shipping costs, corruption, thefts, natural disasters and geo-political instability. Increased awareness of these threats has led many manufacturers to look at whether they should be adopting a hybrid strategy of remote production combined with near-sourcing in more stable markets closer to the end consumer.

The cost of transport (on which globalization is predicated) is also overlooked as a major risk. This not only includes shipping rates, which have been volatile over the past few years, but also the cost of fuel, which has been driven up in the past by tension in the Middle East.

The World Economic Forum's Supply Chain and Transport Risk Survey (WEF, 2013a) identified the least effectively managed supply chain components as rated by respondents. The top five are:

- reliance on oil;
- shared information;
- fragmentation along the value chain;
- extensive subcontracting;
- supplier visibility.

As the survey analysis points out, three of these components relate to visibility and control. Improvements in technology can mitigate this type of risk. For example: development of supplier/buyer communities and the use of social media technologies within supply chain communities could be one way in which risks can be reduced; 'sense and respond' technologies allow for greater awareness of the location of products in the supply chain, and hence enable better decision-making/re-routing.

The development of information technologies will play an important role in the mitigation of supply chain threats. There is little prospect that these risks will diminish – some may even increase. Therefore the ability to react to events will become the key competitive differentiator, and technologies that enable an enhanced level of supply chain agility will become highly sought after.

However, the adoption of more technology will also play a role in increasing risks. Increasing reliance on technology will leave supply chains open to 'cyber attacks' or even accidental outages. While technology will lead to greater levels of efficiency, it will also mean that maintaining robust networks will be ever more critical.

Despite this, it is the industry's reliance on oil that is of primary concern to survey respondents. Given the relation between geo-political tension and the price of oil, and the extreme volatility that this causes, it is clear that alternative strategies must be developed. This could entail a rebalancing of the inventory/transportation equation as shippers position stock in closer proximity to end-users. This will increase stock levels, but reduce transport costs. Of course, as mentioned above, this has risks in its own right and these need to be taken into account in a holistic supply chain management strategy. It could also entail a move from global supply chains to near-sourcing of products, especially utilizing less fuel-intensive modes of transport.

The most disruptive supply chain events are those which have not or cannot be planned for. Therefore it is perhaps more useful, rather than look at past events in order to gain some insight into the future, to identify weaknesses in supply chains instead. Addressing vulnerability is the best way to mitigate the impact of a disruption, although there still remains the issue of how much time and money should be invested on each perceived weakness. This approach is called 'risk-agnostic' (although a better term would be 'risk-neutral') as it prepares supply chains for any type of threat.

## Quantifying supply chain risk

It is very difficult to measure the impact of an event on a supply chain and even harder to attempt to forecast the impact of a 'potential' event. In many ways it is much easier to work out the costs of holding inventory in the system (the 'internal' risk), and address this through a cost-minimization strategy. However, as has been discussed, an assessment of whether or not a company is holding the appropriate level of inventory relies on first quantifying levels of risk.

Many companies are good at working round small and frequent disruptions to their supply chains, without any major cost implication. By their very nature, it is much more difficult to predict low-frequency, low-probability 'Black Swan' events, and consequently, making a decision on how much to invest in making a supply chain resilient to these types of events is a challenge.

There are several different ways in which supply chain risk can be quantified. However, one of the simplest ways of measuring risk is by viewing it as the product of the probability of any given event multiplied by its severity (Christopher and Peck, 2004):

Risk = Probability (of a given event) × Severity (negative business impact)

A way of measuring the impact of a disruptive event is by tracking the share price of an affected company. Research carried out by the World Economic Forum and Accenture has shown that a company's share value is impacted by about 7 per cent following the announcement of a supply chain disruption (WEF, 2013a). These disruptions could include natural disasters, production issues, shortage of parts, recalls, and so on. Accenture examined over 62 supply chain disruptions, including the impact of the Japan earthquake and tsunami upon production.

When dealing with risk, manufacturers usually adopt one of three strategies, each of which involves a cost element:

**1** inventory management – build up safety stock;

**2** sourcing – developing contingency strategies for specific suppliers or supply chain links;

**3** 'acceptance' – doing nothing as costs of mitigation outweigh benefits.

Deciding on which strategy to adopt relies on understanding the cost implications of each approach. One pharmaceutical company undertook a cost–benefit approach to working out how it should mitigate supply chain risk. It used insurance and industry data to estimate the frequency and duration of disruptions, and using scenario-planning software, analysts worked out how many weeks a year their production would potentially be affected. They were then able to set inventory holdings at a level which would minimize disruption. Of course, the weakness of this approach was that although it minimized disruption, the strategy imposed huge additional costs on the organization, not only from the financing of the additional inventory, but also from the risks of redundancy of stock.

Modelling exercises also need to take into account the length of disruption as well as the probability. There are other variables: for example, the length of time it takes for alternative suppliers to ramp up production. One other interesting factor that impacts significantly on the extent of disruption is the location of the event within the supply chain. The further upstream it occurs, the longer the disruption to supply. The reason for this is that downstream processing locations act as bottlenecks and take time to fulfil back-orders once upstream supply is switched back on.

When attempting to quantify the impact of supply chain disruption, one technique can be to assess the probability of various events taking place. One project undertaken for a consumer packaged goods manufacturer attempted to do this by first categorizing the major threats into three classes:

- natural disasters;
- external disruptions (such as supplier failure);
- internal disruptions (such as fire or IT failure).

The researchers then used a range of publicly available data, as well as that provided by the company, to attribute probability levels to each event. Not only was the probability of an event assessed, but also the duration of such an event with a minimum, maximum and most likely duration figure being arrived at.

In many respects, effective supply chain management is all about the trade-off of one set of risks against another. Keeping higher amounts of stock in various locations is not necessarily a good response to the threat of disruption as this is not only costly, but in high-tech sectors – for example, where product lifecycles are low – it would be commercially damaging.

Lean supply chains are also a double-edged sword. While they are working efficiently, they have the potential to reduce inventory levels at the same time as maintaining/improving customer service. However, there is no doubt that they are less resilient to external shocks, as they do not provide a safety net when supply chains break down.

In effect, what has happened in the past is that inventory levels have been used as 'insurance' against risk. If there have been disruptions to supply or to transportation, 'safety' stock has allowed production or sales to continue unaffected. Insurance companies that are now entering the supply chain risk market are allowing manufacturers to outsource this risk, while keeping inventory levels to a minimum. However, quantifying the risk for insurance companies (as well as the manufacturer) is a major challenge.

# Understanding the causes of supply chain disruption

## Risk analysis and management

In a highly complex environment, involving the interaction of human, technological and environmental factors, it can be difficult to identify the reasons behind an event that leads to supply chain disruption. In order to help risk analysis and management, two academics – Dante Orlandella and James T. Reason of the University of Manchester – developed what has since become known as the Swiss Cheese Model of accident causation.

The original model was developed in the wake of a number of major disasters, which from a transport perspective included the sinking of the Herald of Free Enterprise and the King's Cross Underground fire. The inquiries into these disasters decided that to understand the causes, it was necessary to understand the context of the event and not just the performance of the employees at the 'sharp end'. This model was adopted and promoted by the air traffic management regulators and air safety investigators.

The model's author was in fact developing earlier work that utilized another medical metaphor to explain how a catastrophic event, such as one of those identified above, could occur. Causal factors could lay dormant (like a pathogen in the human body) before combining with other adverse conditions to breach the human defences. In network terms, the auto-immune system is replaced by the procedures and security put in place as barriers to the threat.

Professor Reason made a distinction between 'active errors' and 'latent errors'. The 'latent errors' could exist in different parts of an organization's structure or processes and, after refining the model, Reason said these weaknesses could occur either at 'organization', 'workplace' or 'person' level (Reason, Hollnagel and Paries, 2006).

There was also a change in terminology. Instead of referring to 'latent errors', the circumstances that could lead to a disaster were termed 'latent conditions'. This recognized the fact that in many cases an error could only be defined as such in hindsight. For example, all organizations have budgetary constraints. It is not necessarily possible to predict that reducing funding for one division will result in a catastrophic failure, although that division may have consequent time pressures and poorer equipment than another. All organizations have these latent conditions – on their own they do not result in catastrophic failure. However, what is required is an 'active failure' that, when these latent conditions align across a network or organization, triggers a disastrous event. This 'active failure' could very well be human error or some sort of violation.

'Latent errors' or 'latent conditions' exist at various levels. Fallible decisions can be made by senior management and line management can be deficient. Active failures can be made by operatives and inadequate defences to such a concatenation of errors/failures can result in a catastrophic event.

Perhaps one of the most enduring legacies of the model has been a change in mindset when allocating blame for a disaster. It is no longer sufficient to blame an accident or catastrophe on simple human error by a single person, as the context in which that person or event occurred needs to be carefully examined.

In fact, some have argued that the pendulum has swung too much in the other direction. There is a tendency to blame management rather than the 'human error' of the operative at the sharp end. Certainly a balance between the two needs to be struck.

## What lessons can be learned for supply chains?

The Swiss Cheese Model is relevant to the logistics and supply chain industry at several levels. First, when analysing the causes of a failure within a supply chain, it could be easy to proportion blame to the 'sharp end' of an operation without fully understanding the weakness of the entire supply chain.

For example, in this scenario, a road freight operator is a day late in the delivery of an important component to a factory. As a consequence, a production line goes down, costing the manufacturer significant amounts of money in lost sales and idle labour. Who is at fault? The obvious party to blame is the trucking company that failed to deliver on time, resulting in a major supply chain failure. This could be due to a breakdown en route, human error in the dispatch department or inability to locate the goods in the warehouse due to incorrect put-away.

However, a more holistic analysis along the lines of the Swiss Cheese Model goes a lot deeper. For example, senior management of the manufacturer may have recently insisted on a 'lean' inventory reduction programme to eliminate 'waste' and bring down working capital tied up in stock-on-hand. Along with that, in our scenario, the purchasing department had come under pressure to reduce costs by outsourcing production to a cheaper supplier abroad. Supply chain managers had instituted a 'just-in-time' delivery schedule with this supplier.

However, there had been significant quality issues with the components produced by the supplier, which had resulted in an earlier delivery of goods being rejected. Instead of using an express parcels company to deliver the urgent consignment, with the added benefit of being able to track the goods in transit, the manufacturer's cost reduction programme had meant that only 'standard' road freight services could be used. The haulier that had been chosen had committed to levels of service that it wasn't able to fulfil, because of the low margins it was making on the contract. Consequently, the shipment arrived late.

In terms of the Swiss Cheese Model, there are some obvious latent conditions that exist in this scenario:

- Senior management had decided on a policy of inventory reduction in order to free up working capital and minimize waste.

- Management had also outsourced production to a low-cost supplier based remotely, as a way of cutting manufacturing costs.

- Logistics managers had negotiated transport costs down and implemented a policy to utilize non-premium services.

In isolation none of these three latent conditions could be seen as 'errors'. In fact, supply chain theory and practice has over the past three decades promoted these measures. However, they have created an environment in which the 'active error' of the trucking company has brought about a major loss to the company.

What is also lacking from this company's resilience is any 'defence' to this failure of supply chain execution. In fact the obvious 'defence', that is, an element of redundancy in supply chain inventory, has been eroded by management.

Other 'defences' could have focused around quality control. To what extent was the supplier's processes and product checked before production was outsourced? The same issue with quality applies to the transport provider. Where were the checks and balances when the logistics contract was awarded? Was the financial health of the haulier monitored?

There is no single point of blame. Was it the untrained driver's fault for failing to finish his delivery schedule? Was it the road haulier's fault for not providing sufficient training? Or was it the customer's fault for negotiating the haulier's rates down so far that it couldn't afford to pay experienced driving staff?

Was it, in fact, the fault of the supplier, whose failure to ship error-free goods in the first place was a major causal factor? Or the line management who chose the supplier – or in fact the senior management who decided on this outsourcing strategy in the first place, without sufficient oversight?

A summary of the supply chain failure event outlined above could be laid out as follows:

---

**Corporate level: organization and management issues (latent)**

- management forced into adopting cost-driven outsourced production strategy without necessary oversight;
- no clear understanding of cost implications of supply chain failure;
- narrow, silo approach to cost reduction undertaken.

**Line management issues (latent)**

- logistics managers overly focused on transport cost reductions, not quality;
- purchasing managers likewise focused on input component costs, not quality;
- freight operator management forced to compete on small margins, resulting in hiring of untrained staff;
- supplier quality control flawed.

**Local issues (active)**

- Driver fails to complete delivery schedule.

**Flawed safety nets**

- quality control programme insufficient;
- supply chain visibility insufficient;
- inventory control flawed;
- freight operator had no telematics or transport management system in place.

## Developing resilience to 'network events'

In his seminal work *The Black Swan* (2007), philosopher Nicholas Taleb asserts that most business professionals assume we live in a world of mild randomness, where events don't stray far from the mean.

Contrary to this view, Taleb argues that, because of tightly integrated markets and networks, we live in periods of wild randomness where small probability events carry major consequences. Intertwined networks – energy, transport, financial, ICT and human – mean that the consequences of failure in one can be critical and unforeseen in another.

From the enormous complexity of the relationships between the various networks outlined, it is obvious that no organization or government could plan for any one catastrophic event. These events are variously referred to as 'high impact–low probability' (HILP) or 'Black Swans'.

However, this is not an excuse to do nothing. Instead, managers and planners should focus on making operations and supply chains resilient to all shocks, not just to those that they believe (usually erroneously) may happen.

In a report on the Icelandic volcano crisis of 2010, research organization Chatham House classified risk into three categories (Lee and Preston, with Green, 2012):

1 'Black Swans' – these are the 'unknown unknowns' that are impossible to predict but that have the potential to do major damage to economies and businesses. While planning for a specific event is impossible, it is possible to build general resilience.

2 'Known and prepared for' – these events have occurred in the past, such as a pandemic or flood, and are expected to happen again in the future, although at a time and place unknown. A large degree of preparedness can be achieved, and the debate is usually about the level of resources that should be committed.

**3** 'Known and unprepared for' – this scenario could involve events that have been foreseen but for which governments or businesses have discounted 'worst-case scenarios'. This is obviously a misjudgement for which there are political or commercial consequences.

## Understanding network failure

Networks have attained critical importance to the supply chain industry. Whereas the simple Swiss Cheese Model discussed above looked at largely internal dynamics and decision-making processes, networks would be described as being external influencers. However, the model also works when exploring the interrelation between networks and their impact on supply chains, and indeed the wider economy and society.

### Energy networks

In the developed world the power grid is essential to every part of the economy and society. In some parts of the world, where it is not in existence or unreliable, contingencies are put in place should it fail. This will include back-up generators, which are widely used in markets such as India.

In a supply chain perspective, electricity is essential for powering warehouses but also traffic signals and even petrol pumps. As well as providing light, it also powers information and communications technology, including mobile networks. The dependence on a reliable energy source makes the supply chain and logistics sector highly vulnerable to power cuts.

### Human networks

Human networks are rarely analysed in terms of risk to supply chains. However, with the logistics and transport industry so labour-intensive, the human angle is clearly a key vulnerability.

How many companies would be able to operate efficiently or at all if half of their workforce did not turn up for work? This would have major implications, especially for grocery retailers, who rely on regular and frequent deliveries to their stores. It would also disrupt supplies on petrol to filling stations, medical supplies to hospitals, the delivery of coal to power stations, and so on.

### Information and communications technology

ICT networks underpin much of the modern supply chain and logistics industry, providing visibility into warehouses, enabling efficient transport management, GPS data, facilitating communications between shipper, logistics provider, end-user, customs and border controls, to name just a few uses. In addition to this, it is essential for air traffic control, traffic management in urban areas and port community systems.

With the industry becoming ever more reliant on ICT, any length of downtime becomes critical to efficiency and safety. As advanced telematics becomes entrenched in vehicle control systems – such as ground-to-air communication and eventually car-to-car (as part of intelligent transport systems) – this vulnerability will only become more important.

## Transport

The term 'transport network' can refer to both the physical infrastructure and the flows of traffic across the infrastructure. It could also be said that there is a further 'organizational' element, with some passengers (those not moving by car) and all cargo being managed by service providers (either air, sea, road or rail). This is important from a risk perspective as businesses moving goods and passengers interact more closely with other networks, such as ICT, in the normal pursuit of their business.

The various networks interact with each other at nodes, as in many cases journeys are multi-modal in nature. For example, the commute to work will often involve a journey to a railway station by car, a train journey and perhaps a bus at the destination. Likewise, air cargo is almost always moved to the airport by road.

The nodes, which are an essential part of passenger and freight movements, are by their nature bottlenecks and highly vulnerable. In the shipping sector in particular traffic is becoming increasingly concentrated on a diminishing number of nodes (ports), which is increasing the risk.

This concentration of risk is also occurring in some prime locations that have developed multiple nodes. For example, Dubai has developed a major port and airport. Louisville in the United States is at a confluence of rail, road and air networks. In Europe, the Randstad region of the Netherlands includes the Port of Rotterdam, Amsterdam Schiphol Airport as well as road and rail networks that link the region with the rest of Europe. The air, road and rail networks are also intensively used by passengers in this highly populated urban area.

The mode most vulnerable to disruption has proved to be air travel. Perhaps because most air cargo travels on the same aircraft as passengers, it is particularly at risk from trends and developments affecting passenger travel as well as its own industry dynamics. For example, the SARS crisis of

2003 impacted on air cargo capacity as passenger flights were cut, due to the downturn in the numbers of people travelling to Asia. This dynamic is of considerable importance to the global economy. It is estimated that about a third of manufactured goods, in terms of value, are shipped by air and 55 per cent of the UK's exports to non-EU countries is airfreighted.

The type of goods moved by air is also important, as these often have a critical impact on other networks. These include medical (equipment and vaccines, for example) and electronic integrated components for telecoms networks.

## How are networks interconnected?

Understanding the wider impact of a disruptive event is made more difficult as it is impossible to view individual networks in isolation. Increasingly networks are interwoven and interconnected in ways that have become increasingly difficult to map or understand.

If, for example, there was a terrorist attack on a part of an urban metro system, it would be likely that the decision would be made to shut down the whole of this particular network. Passengers would exit onto the streets, and many would then use their mobile phones, potentially overloading the mobile telecoms network. Websites would be bombarded with enquiries, and the heavy volumes could bring down the internet. With news spreading, traffic chaos would not just be restricted to the inner urban area but would spread out to orbital roads and the major motorway interchanges. Overland train stations would be overwhelmed by commuters trying to get out of the city early. Economic and humanitarian damage could be considerable. This is not an imaginary scenario as this actually occurred after the 7 July bombings in London in 2005.

Another example relates to the electricity networks and their role in underpinning pretty much every other network in the UK – mobile networks, financial markets, IT, lighting, the traffic signals on the road and rail. With electricity down, garages cannot operate and trucks, cars and ambulances are not able to fill up with petrol. As has been seen in New York during the Superstorm Sandy disaster, when the power goes out, life comes to a halt.

The critical nature of the electricity power supply has not gone unnoticed by malign forces. The technology systems of the main power and distribution companies are consistently under attack – and there was even a threat by one group to black out the opening ceremony of the London Olympics in 2012.

However, a significant crisis came from another source. When tempera-tures fell to below −15 degrees Celsius in the winter of 2010, there was a threat to the infrastructure of electricity sub-stations. It needed large numbers of engineers to physically defrost critical components. This meant that at a time of crisis to one network, additional stress was placed on another – the human network.

The obvious question is, what would happen if the UK had been in the middle of a swine flu pandemic at the time of the severe weather and this meant that half of the engineers hadn't been able to show up to work? This could be termed an 'alignment of vulnerabilities', as identified in the Swiss Cheese Model, which means that when multiple events coincide (and these on their own need not be critical), networks can topple one after another.

# External risk categories

It is possible to divide external threats into five main categories, each of which is dealt with in detail within this book.

## *Environmental*

### Natural disasters

This category comprises a wide range of disruptive events, including extreme weather, earthquakes, tsunamis, floods and even volcanic eruptions. The economic cost of natural disasters was estimated by insurance company Swiss Re at $158 billion in 2016 (Swiss Re, 2016). The supply chain conse-quences are derived from not only the disruption of production but also the impact on transportation services and infrastructure. A World Economic Forum (WEF)/Accenture study found that, following the Japanese tsunami/earthquake, the operating profits of 15 leading multinationals fell by 33 per cent in the subsequent financial quarter directly as a result of supply chain disruption (WEF, 2012).

### Climate change

Within this category, longer-term environmental issues can also be placed. The survey conducted by WEF specifically identified 'rising greenhouse gas emissions' and 'failure of climate change adaptation' as the major issues of concern for company executives. The WEF pointed out that even in the wake of major natural disasters, such as the Japanese tsunami, man-made disasters such as 'mismanaged urbanization' were more likely to be disruptive in the next 10 years than earthquakes and volcanic eruptions.

## Pandemics

Pandemics may not be the first risk identified by supply chain managers, but they are one of the most serious. In the last instance of an outbreak in summer 2009, the swine flu virus killed 392 people, although in fact it could have been much worse. At the beginning of the crisis the UK government was warning of a potential 65,000 fatalities. One assumption made by government agencies is that if a flu pandemic takes hold, up to 50 per cent of the workforce could be affected, with each person who falls sick taking between five and eight days off work (Department of Health, 2013). This would have immediate impact on the ability of the private and public sector to maintain operations, especially in such a labour-intensive industry as transport and logistics. The swine flu outbreak of 2009 provided a very real warning of what could happen and the potential impact on the UK's society and economy.

These risks are dealt with in more detail in Chapter 4.

## *Economic*

In recent years the issue of supply chain risk has been placed firmly on the corporate agenda by a confluence of natural disasters and terrorist actions. However, the focus of risk upon 'spectacular' events means that other causal factors can be overlooked. In fact, the WEF survey referenced above found that the most important network vulnerability identified by respondents related to the cost of oil. Other economic risks are also viewed as highly important – more so, for example, than extreme weather or terrorism.

## Demand shocks

One of the most pressing supply chain risks from an economic perspective is what can be termed 'demand shocks'. An example of this is the disruption caused by the company failure of suppliers following the 2008 recession. This was particularly relevant to the high-tech and automotive sectors, where supplier bankruptcy was widespread. Many of the problems were caused by manufacturers 'switching off' supply from remote suppliers, and although this had a short-term positive effect on inventories and balances, it meant that when demand picked up strongly in 2010, manufacturers were unable to meet demand.

Manufacturers are ever more exposed to currency risks given the globalized nature of their suppliers and customers. Given the debt crises of many economies and the impact this is having on the strength of the euro, dollar and other currencies, this risk is likely to continue in the coming years.

Within this category the WEF survey identified 'chronic fiscal imbalances' as the key risk. This was linked to the possibility of systemic financial failure throughout the world. This would have obvious impacts for supply chains, not least related to the collapse of suppliers and the inability to access trade finance. Volatile currencies are also unhelpful to the development of trade.

## Supply shocks

'Supply shocks' are less obvious, but material threats all the same. The volatile nature of shipping rates could fall into this category. In early 2012 shipping rates on Asia–Europe routes increased by about $1,000 per TEU (from about $650 to $1,650) – a situation that most shippers would find difficult if not impossible to predict.

## Oil

Volatility in the oil market has a direct impact on the supply costs of shippers, whether they operate on a national or international basis. In most developed markets, fuel accounts for around a quarter to a third of transport operating costs and a fluctuation in these costs has a major influence over sourcing and distribution strategy decisions. A surge in the price of oil would certainly rebalance the near-sourcing/offshoring debate in favour of the former and it would also encourage more distributed inventory holding strategies, as opposed to the centralization of stock that most companies choose today.

The risks to supply chains are not necessarily derived from a steady rise in the price of oil – manufacturers and retailers can plan for this eventuality. However, a sudden spike in oil costs caused, for example, by a crisis in the Middle East would be a much more serious threat as this would have major implications in terms of profitability and modal choice.

## Trade disruption/border delays

The success of the World Trade Organization, the advent of the Single European Market and the North American Free Trade Area (NAFTA) has had a major impact in facilitating trade flows and enabling the global supply chain phenomenon. However, as manufacturers and retailers source goods from increasingly far afield, accessing markets without good governance and trade relations, the issue of disruption to trade becomes more significant.

One of the problems that companies face is the unpredictability of such delays. A lack of standardization of documentation and harmonization of trade regulations in Africa is particularly disruptive to the smooth running of trade networks. High levels of bureaucracy increases the probability of errors delaying shipments. Integration into global supply chains relies on not only visibility of supply but also reliability.

Another potential risk to importers and exporters is the incidence of trade wars. The WTO handles a considerable number of disputes a year between members, and the mechanisms that it provides for dispute resolution have been a major factor in preventing more significant breakdown in trading relations. However, tensions, particularly between China and the United States and the EU, continually run high, as protectionist elements lobby governments to protect manufacturing from cheap imports. As markets come under increasing economic pressure, the calls for more barriers to trade will also grow, to the detriment of global supply chains.

## Industrial action

A rise in work stoppages and slowdowns throughout the world is having a significant impact on supply chains. To illustrate the vulnerability of the global transport and logistics sector to this threat, the ports at Antwerp and Rotterdam, Frankfurt International Airport, Brazilian customs agents, Costa Rican port workers and Korean truck drivers have all been on strike at some point in the recent past.

As a result, many shippers now diversify their shipments across several modes and gateways so as not to be completely exposed by any disruption. For example, US shippers (who have a great deal of experience of the impact of industrial action at North American ports) are now better able to divert volumes to unaffected gateways. If there are disturbances at East and Gulf Coast ports, for instance, they can utilize West Coast as well as Canadian and Mexican ports, which are linked to the US heartland via a growing rail and intermodal system.

Work stoppages or slowdowns are amongst the most important supply chain risks that companies need to account for and manage accordingly. However, with the continued economic uncertainty throughout the world, this will prove difficult as labour unions fight to maintain existing jobs in ports and other transportation nodes. This will likely create a vicious cycle as strikes, as seen in the past, can easily cripple an economy – thus further exacerbating an already difficult situation.

These economic risks are dealt with in more detail in Chapter 6.

## *Societal risks*

### Corporate and social responsibility

Supply chains have expanded into many emerging markets where the workforce and the environment are much more vulnerable to exploitation than in the developed world. Companies such as Apple have been accused of taking advantage of low-cost labour and lack of environmental regulations to manufacture their products more cheaply and efficiently than they could in North America or Europe.

The risk emanating from their supply chains in this instance is primarily reputational, although of course if enough consumers were to boycott their products, there would also be a financial impact. For example, considerable damage was done to the brands of several Western retailers following the Rana Plaza fire in Bangladesh in 2013. More than ever, global companies are being forced to take responsibility for their suppliers.

Of course this is easier said than done. In many cases, manufacturers and retailers are not aware of their lower-tier suppliers. Pressure regarding working conditions, the environment and even the use of conflict minerals means that much more consideration is being placed on visibility up the supply chain. In many cases this has resulted in companies undertaking audits of their suppliers for the first time. The indirect benefit of this has been that companies have been able to identify weaknesses in their supply chain, such as single sourcing issues.

These risks are dealt with in more detail in Chapter 7.

## *Security*

### Geo-political tension

There are many flashpoints of geo-political tension around the world: the Korean peninsula; Taiwan and China; various territorial disputes between China, Japan and the Philippines, to name just a few. However, perhaps the most worrying in terms of actual supply chain risk is the Middle East. The Arab Spring created instability throughout the region, with particular implications for one of its biggest economies, Egypt. In addition, sanctions against Iran led to threats by the country's leaders to shut the Strait of Hormuz through which much of the world's oil supply passes. Bellicose announcements by the new Trump administration in the United States could destabilize the region once more.

Terrorism also falls into this category, the most obvious sources being Al-Qaeda, its Somalia-based affiliate, Al-Shabaab, and more latterly the so-called 'Islamic State'. Some analysts believe that the more successful the war being waged against ISIS in Syria and Iraq, the greater the likelihood that the organization will adopt terrorist tactics and export the war to Europe and North America.

Risks to the supply chain come not only from the terrorists (such as the Yemen parcel bombs infiltrated into the air cargo system in 2010), but also from regulators seeking to limit the impact of a terrorist event by increasing levels of security-driven regulations and procedures. Despite seeming counterproductive, it is a typically politically expedient response to a crisis.

## Cargo crime

In parts of the world, a breakdown of law and order has made shipments of goods highly vulnerable to theft by criminal gangs. Even in developed countries in North America and the EU, the problem is very significant. The response of the law enforcement agencies is often weak because of the low priority afforded to the problem by politicians and a lack of responsibility by police; the misdemeanour often straddles different geographies, and in most countries 'cargo crime' itself has no separate legal status. Hence few resources are allocated to tackling the problem.

Shipments are rarely stolen while physically moving (although hijacking vehicles while in motion is becoming more prevalent). Instead, they are most vulnerable in warehouses, airports, ports, intermodal yards or while a driver is taking a break.

## Corruption

Corruption costs shippers billions of dollars a year, and while it is most widespread in markets such as those in West Africa, various forms of it are systemic to the logistics industry right across the world. The best-known form of corruption is the bribery needed to facilitate the transit of goods across international borders. Customs officers are badly paid in many countries, and augment their meagre salaries with this additional form of revenue. Links with organized crime can be strong to make sure that illegal goods are not inspected or seized.

However, much more money can be made by mis-declaring the duties that should be paid by importers, and this often involves large numbers of customs officers at all levels. Either directly or indirectly, shippers have to pay the cost of corruption, and an increasing expansion into emerging markets, either as import or export markets, will increase their exposure to corruption and criminality further.

## Piracy

Piracy can also be a major issue for supply chains, although the true cost of the disruption is largely hidden. For instance, although millions of dollars were paid to pirates off the Somali coast (with ransom activity reaching a peak in 2011), the majority of supply chain costs occurred when shipping lines were forced to divert to longer routes in order to avoid the problem areas. Other costs include increased insurance; security and guards; increased steaming speeds; higher wages for seamen (danger money); not to mention indirect payments for military operations.

A coordinated response by the international community saw piracy in Somalia reduce dramatically. However, new areas of threat have since sprung up – especially in the waters off Nigeria. As this market develops and becomes of greater interest to multinational shippers, the problem is set to grow worse.

These risks are dealt with in more detail in Chapters 8, 9 and 12.

## *Technological*

Technology failure/outage is a major concern to shippers, although as yet there have been few significant incidents (at least that have been revealed). A lot of money has been spent by agencies, such as the Pentagon, in assessing and planning for a 'cyber terrorist' attack, although minor disruption to date has come from power failures or accidents. More reliance in the future will be placed on information and communications networks as the supply chain industry becomes increasingly paperless, and this will only heighten the risks. However, actually measuring the true nature of the threat and robustness of information systems is difficult.

The WEF survey found that, in terms of technological risks, critical systems failures were deemed to have the highest potential impact. However, cyber-attacks were identified as being most probable, either from a state-sponsored, criminal or terrorist source. Other risk events included 'massive digital misinformation', 'incidence of data fraud and theft' and 'failure of intellectual property regime'.

Cyber-crime is dealt with in Chapter 9 as part of a wider examination of criminal activity.

**CASE STUDY** South Africa

A 2011 survey designed to identify the key risks to the supply chain in South Africa has highlighted power outages, theft and labour disputes as the primary concerns. The survey also studied the different types of risk management strategies that are currently in place in the country.

The MIT Center for Transportation and Logistics Global Risk Survey was undertaken in South Africa jointly by the Association for Operations Management of Southern Africa (SAPICS) and IMPERIAL Logistics, in collaboration with MIT (MIT, 2011).

The survey found that extended loss of electricity is five times more likely to occur in South Africa, compared with the world average. Employee theft/executive misdeeds come in four times higher than the international average. Protracted labour disputes are 2.5 times more likely to transpire and disease/infestation 2.3 times higher.

Interestingly, the survey found that, in terms of the top 10 supply chain risk factors, South Africa is more closely aligned to developed rather than developing economies. However, extended electricity loss and major software systems failure are two challenges more commonly associated with developing economies.

South African companies rated raw material supplier failure as the top supply chain risk, followed by finished goods manufacturing failure, product quality failure, transportation carrier failure and economic recession/market collapse. 'Notably, within South African supply chains, companies tend to work more with customers than suppliers in addressing risk management,' said Abrie de Swardt, IMPERIAL Logistics Marketing Director.

In terms of risk mitigation perceptions, South African companies believe in a local response over a central risk response action. This falls in between the North American and European approaches, as identified by the global survey findings. 'By addressing supply chain risk through a centralized approach, a company aligns its strategies to the holistic context. Response at a local level allows site level staff to apply their own actions immediately,' added Abrie de Swardt.

## Summary

The character of corporate risk has changed dramatically over the past few decades. Companies have successfully reduced internal risks by limiting inventory levels and improving production quality. However, external risks have been increased through longer, more complex supply chains that rely on suppliers and transport partners to succeed. The understanding of these types of risks is at an early stage. Supply chains need to be made more resilient to 'Black Swan' events and managers need to adopt agile and adaptive strategies to cope with the unpredictable and volatile nature of the modern world.

## Key points

- Over the past few decades, 'internal' production and inventory risk has reduced while 'external' risk within supply chains has increased.

- Risk is measured as a function of the probability of an event and its likely severity.

- The Swiss Cheese Model of accident causation is commonly used to analyse risk and risk management.

- 'Black Swan' events (those with small probability) are having increasing impact on supply chains because of the interconnected nature of modern networks.

- Supply chains need to be 'risk-agnostic', that is, resilient enough to cope with any eventualities.

- External risks can be categorized as follows: environmental, economic, societal, security and technological.

# Engineering supply chain resilience

02

**OBJECTIVES**

This chapter will familiarize the reader with:

- strategies to prepare for a disruptive supply chain event;
- how to put business continuity management into effect;
- ways in which the risk of business interruption can be offset;
- Cisco's supply chain risk and resilience response within the context of the Japanese tsunami;
- how flexible technology can improve supply chain resilience;
- the role of government to provide a stable and secure framework in which private sector companies can operate.

Work undertaken by the World Economic Forum's Risk Response Network identifies a resilient supply chain as a system that can be returned to its original state after a major disruption (WEF, 2013a). In fact, some analysts go further, suggesting that resilience should include the ability of a supply chain to maintain output at close to potential throughout and in the aftermath of a major shock. To do so not only maintains levels of customer service but also can deliver a competitive advantage over supply chains that are not able to cope with the shock so well.

Of course, engineering resilience is easier said than done. Many executives fear that resilience can only be achieved by compromising system efficiencies, for example by increasing inventory holdings or building redundancy into transport and warehousing capacity. This trade-off goes to the heart of the debate on supply chain risk. Many would argue that the improvements in manufacturing practice that have led to a 'right-first-time' culture have improved quality right the way across supply chains and made them more robust, rather than less so. It could also be argued that unbundling, outsourcing and globalization have led to a diversification of production that mitigates against any single disaster having a catastrophic effect on a company's ability to operate. Developments in technology also allow managers to be much better able to 'sense and respond' to supply chain problems.

However, there is no doubt that lean inventory supply chains, while better able to deal with minor operational incidents, are more prone than ever to catastrophic events. It is the goal of many executives to square this particular circle, and this can be achieved by engineering resilience into supply chains from the outset.

Resilience should be designed into a supply chain by better understanding vulnerabilities and addressing them. One of the best ways of achieving this is through what has been termed 'supply chain intelligence', which involves gaining visibility of upstream and downstream suppliers. By 'auditing' a supply chain, over-dependence on a supplier can be identified and alternatives developed. Levels of unacceptable external risk or long lead times can also be flagged up. In practical terms, this can lead to the development of what could be termed a 'supply chain register'.

Creating visibility relies on a high level of collaboration throughout the supply chain and the creation of an ethos in which a supplier is encouraged to audit its own suppliers. Likewise, there should be a flow of information to suppliers to help them better understand the end customers' demands.

Achieving these levels of information-sharing will allow supply chain partners to more accurately identify appropriate levels of stock, and allow decision-makers to judge the appropriate trade-off between just-in-case and just-in-time production.

Resilience implies an agile supply chain:

- collaboration – active involvement with suppliers and suppliers' suppliers;
- ethos – information-sharing and supply chain intelligence;
- strategy – awareness of emerging trends and issues that may impact on supply chain;
- tactical response – impact on an operational level: demand, supply, process and control risk;
- operations – supply chain event management.

A timely response to an event that impacts on a supply chain is essential to the limitation of damage. The speed of reaction can be described as 'agility' – however, it is not enough for just one player in the supply chain to be agile. For a supply chain to be competitive, it is necessary for multiple parties to have the capability to respond quickly to disruption.

Christopher and Peck describe agility as having two elements: 'supply chain visibility' and 'supply chain velocity'. Visibility of a supply chain involves having a clear understanding of demand and supply (production and purchasing schedules) as well as knowing what inventories are being kept where (Christopher and Peck, 2004). The breakdown of silos within the supply chain is an important goal to provide these levels of visibility.

Velocity – which Christopher and Peck describe as the time lapsed between order from a supplier and delivery – is important in ensuring lean inventories. However, in terms of supply chain risk, inventory acceleration is perhaps more important. How quickly can product delivery be sped up to respond to a particular event in the supply chain? Small batch quantities, reduction of time in which product is held as inventory and streamlining of processes are essential to this concept.

Figure 2.1 shows a simple response to a disruptive event in a supply chain. Managers who have an oversight of the supply chain can respond to the problem by using an alternative source of production, exploiting spare capacity. Levels of safety stock can then be replenished from other sources of inventory. This would then minimize the decrease in production and mitigate losses. However, even in this simple scenario there is an assumption that:

**Figure 2.1**  Supply chain disruption contingency

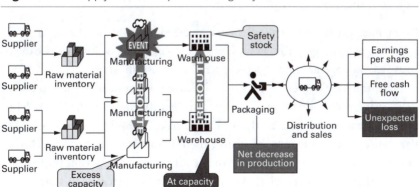

1 Management is in place with the necessary visibility to make informed decisions over production and warehousing.

2 Alternative suppliers are in place, allowing the main customer to switch over quickly.

3 Safety stock levels are sufficient to allow replenishment throughout the supply chain.

# Preparedness and strategies for response

Supply chain disruption can occur at many levels – from localized warehouse disruption (for example, fire or flooding) up to regional/global network failure caused perhaps by a major natural disaster. One of the ways in which companies can formally approach the management of risk is through the adoption of the ISO 31000 standard. Using this standard can help organizations improve the identification of opportunities and threats and effectively allocate and use resources for risk treatment. Although it is not a certification process, it can help provide guidance for internal and external audit processes. Organizations can use it to compare their risk management practices with an internationally recognized benchmark, providing the principles of effective management and corporate governance. The standard helps managers to answer:

- What can happen and why?
- What are the consequences?
- What is the probability of their future occurrence?
- Are there any factors that mitigate the consequences of the risk or that reduce the probability of the risk?

Companies such as Coca-Cola have decided to use the standard in its approach to managing risk in its supply chain operations. It broadly categorizes risk management into 'deployment' and 'sustain' stages.

First, the 'deployment' process includes the identification of significant risks, using a checklist method. This can identify the most urgent risks to the organization. Second, analysis of these risks is required – looking at the risk causes and consequences. Third, there is the mitigation stage. Having identified the risks, it is necessary to identify courses of action that would prevent them from occurring. As this process takes place, each stage needs to be documented and a risk register created that will allow the status and risk treatment plans to be tracked.

After the initial assessment and mitigation phase, a programme of ongoing risk management needs to be put in place. This will review how risks are being managed on a regular basis and identify new and emerging risks using multiple sources of data. Finally, risk awareness can be built into business planning, taking into account risks to overall corporate objectives.

For example, in a scenario presented by drinks manufacturer Coca-Cola, a risk analysis programme would identify potential 'risk events'. This could be the introduction of 'off-spec' carbon dioxide into products. The possible consequences of this would be the necessity to recall and destroy products, resulting in the loss of brand reputation and sales.

Consequently, the possible causes that would trigger this risk event need to be identified. In this example, these could range from external supplier issues with quality, faulty gas filters in Coca-Cola's factories or badly designed piping systems. Having identified these possible causes, a number of quality control initiatives could be undertaken to prevent this event occuring.

At the same time as these, actions to reduce the consequences of a risk event are also put into effect. What this approach does is reduce the 'likelihood dimension' while at the same time mitigate the 'consequence dimension'.

After the identification of the various risk events has been undertaken, a 'risk register' can be developed. This contains the risks, potential causes, consequences and treatments at a specific location. It is then possible to allocate 'ownership' to specific individuals. These registers can then be used to build a bottom-up risk profile over a particular region.

# Business continuity management (BCM)

In addition to the ISO 31000, a further related standard exists, ISO 22301, detailing best practice in business continuity management to which companies can gain accreditation. This involves formalizing a company's response to extreme weather, fire, flood, natural disaster, theft, IT outage, staff illness or terrorist attack. The ISO 22301 management system identifies threats and the critical business functions they could impact. As with ISO 31000, the standard is what is called risk-agnostic: that is, it prepares businesses for all eventualities.

An explanation of ISO 22301 is now described.

# Business continuity management risk standard

### Context of the organization

The first step involves getting to know the organization, both internal and external needs, and setting clear boundaries for the scope of the management system. In particular, this requires the organization to understand the requirements of relevant interested parties, such as regulators, customers and staff. It must in particular understand the applicable legal and regulatory requirements. This enables it to determine the scope of the business continuity management system (BCMS).

### Leadership

ISO 22301 places particular emphasis on the need for appropriate leadership of BCM. This is so that top management can ensure appropriate resources are provided, establishes policy and appoints people to implement and maintain the BCMS.

### Planning

This requires the organization to identify risks to the implementation of the management system and set clear objectives and criteria that can be used to measure its success.

### Support

Since resources are required for implementation, 'competence' is an important concept. For business continuity to be successful, people with appropriate knowledge, skills and experience must be in place to both contribute to the BCMS and respond to incidents when they occur. It is also important that all staff are aware of their own role in responding to incidents.

### Operations

The organization must undertake business impact analysis to understand how its business is affected by disruption and how this changes over time. Risk assessment seeks to understand the risks to the business in a structured way and these inform the development of business continuity strategy. Steps to avoid or reduce the likelihood of incidents are developed alongside steps to be taken when incidents occur. As it is impossible to completely predict and prevent all incidents, the approach of balancing risk reduction and planning for all eventualities is complementary.

**SOURCE** www.iso.org

# Offsetting the risk of business interruption

Business interruption has been defined by one insurer as 'loss due to the necessary interruption of business, operations, and/or services, including all other interdependent operations resulting from physical loss or damage to property...'.

Once a risk has been identified, there are five ways in which it can be dealt with. These can be summarized as:

- avoid;
- transfer;
- share;
- finance;
- insure.

Insuring against losses is highly complex, mainly because different parts of the supply chain process are insured in different ways. Merchandise can be insured while in transit or in warehousing. However, carriers (road, sea or air) may only have statutory liability unless otherwise stated in a contract.

There is also:

- public liability insurance (or as it is known in the United States, errors and omissions) to help guard against negligence claims;
- business interruption (BI) compensates the policyholder for a loss resulting from damage to its own property;
- contingent business interruption (CBI) insurance reimburses a company for lost profits and other possible transferred risks due to an insurable loss suffered by one or more of its suppliers or customers;
- political risk;
- marine;
- trade credit.

A new type of 'all risks' supply chain insurance, which is being developed by companies such as Zurich, provides cover for goods not delivered or otherwise delayed that have a financial impact on a company's operations. Zurich's supply chain insurance is not restricted to property damage and can work with other coverages, such as BI, CBI, political risk, marine and trade credit. It allows a company to transfer supply chain risks for named goods and suppliers.

The insurance company calculates the anticipated loss of profit and/or the increased cost of working in the event of a reduction in supply that caused (or would have caused without the increased cost of working) a reduction in output. It does this by undertaking an assessment of the risk, which is not only useful for insurance purposes but also gives management a better basis to make risk-based decisions.

# Case study of resilience: how does Cisco manage risk?

## Evolution in Cisco's approach to supply chain risk management

Cisco, the high-tech electronics manufacturer, has long been regarded by the business community as having one of the best supply chains in the industry. Cisco regards supply chain resilience as a core business challenge across the enterprise, not just a logistics problem. In its efforts to improve its resilience, the company has gone from a 'reactive approach' in the mid-2000s, through one which embraced 'proactivity', to the position it is in today where resilience is embedded in design and processes. This has involved establishing teams of dedicated 'control tower' staff whose job it is to continually monitor and respond to incidents around the clock.

However, its response to the post-recession demand shocks in 2010 highlighted a number of shortcomings that the company was forced to address. The crisis was caused by the emergence of the global economy from recession, resulting in demand for ICT network products to increase dramatically as companies made investments deferred from the period of the downturn. This demand placed a huge stress on Cisco, and other manufacturers, as the market faced product shortages. Cisco's customers complained that the company could not deliver its products on time or, in some cases, even deliver them at all. Engineers maintaining infrastructure such as data centres faced a wait of up to 12 weeks for basic switching components.

The origin of the problem was with Cisco's suppliers, many of them based in China. According to a statement from Cisco itself, the issues were:

> ...attributable in part to increasing demand driven by the improvement in our overall markets... the longer than normal lead time extensions also stemmed from supplier constraints based upon their labour and other actions taken during the global economic downturn.

In other words, component suppliers laid off workers during the recession and reduced capacity. There was then not enough production capacity to fulfil demand.

The need for Cisco to better collaborate with its suppliers was evident. It also illustrated the need to mitigate risks within its supply chain. The company acknowledged the need for changes and embarked on a mission to regain its status as a supply chain innovator. The company had become bloated with over 8,000 products, with 95 per cent of production outsourced and with more than 90 locations around the world. As such, the company's supply chain organization, Cisco Value Chain Management (VCM), identified areas in which to improve supply chain operations:

- enhance collaboration across supply chain partners;
- build trust-based relationships with suppliers;
- accelerate time to market of new products;
- improve product quality;
- lower costs;
- reduce risk and manage crises more effectively.

Based on the identified areas, Cisco's IT group built a collaborative architectural platform for the company. This platform is utilized throughout the company, including for new product introduction as well as risk management.

To mitigate risks, Cisco has supply chain crisis management teams that are organized by geography and function. These teams monitor Cisco's suppliers and partners, assess the effect on Cisco of a disruption in operations and evaluate each partner's ability to withstand such disruption. If need be, these teams will make real-time decisions if a crisis occurs, such as switching production to a new site or moving to a secondary supplier.

To support the monitoring and assessment stages, company employees collaborate through a common intranet portal. Through this portal, a variety of tools are used, such as crisis response e-mail lists, instant messaging and Really Simple Syndication (RSS) subscriptions, dashboards, videos, and communication services, including phone and Cisco WebEx conferences.

To obtain information about potential crises, Cisco uses a third-party service that specializes in collecting and correlating events from around the world that could affect the supply chain. An internal team manages this information and, when a crisis event is triggered, the team sends notifications to all relevant parties. At this point, all potentially affected parties are brought together to determine the actual effect and next steps for the situation using a variety of conferencing and collaboration methods. Then the team moves on to team activation, management and resolution of the crisis using the Cisco centralized Risk Management Practice Dashboard.

This online application provides a workspace that team members can access to view incidents and potential incidents anywhere in the world, and coordinate a response. It employs the same communication and collaboration tools used in the early stages of crisis response, but extends these efforts from intra-company to inter-company, including supply chain partners, shipping, manufacturing, and more. The system correlates information about all Cisco suppliers, manufacturing partners and logistics providers with maps and real-time information. Crisis response team members can log onto the dashboard and see where the problem is occurring and how serious the risk may be. The team then takes appropriate actions.

After the crisis is over, Cisco undertakes a post-mortem to determine what worked, what requires improvement, and what the early signs of crisis were. This information is presented in a Cisco WebEx conference and then integrated into updated processes based on the post-mortem. These changes are then added to training tools, which take the form of web-based classes, as well as live virtual team meetings.

## Dealing with the Japanese tsunami

In 2011, Cisco's crisis collaboration plan was put to the test when Japan's earthquake and tsunami hit. Within 30 minutes of the initial alert of the earthquake, a dedicated supply chain incident manager was made aware of the event, who in turn alerted the supply chain risk management team leader, team members and the supply chain operations senior leadership team.

Within 12 hours, the primary supply chain incident management team was activated. This team consists of an extended group of operations functional leaders that represent their functional organizations during an incident.

Utilizing business continuity data and processes, all direct suppliers, their associated sites and components and other critical supply chain nodes in the impacted area were identified within 12 hours of the initial earthquake.

Cisco established a supply chain incident management team 'war room' within two days of the initial earthquake to provide a central management point and decision-making forum for all supply chain operations personnel involved in the mitigation effort. In the first few days following the incident, Cisco's incident management team was able to:

- establish contact with suppliers to assess the impact of the incident on site capacity;
- develop a prognosis of their ability to continue to produce;
- identify their ability to distribute components.

The incident management team was then able to develop a snapshot of the supplier impact and status over the entire region. This snapshot was refreshed on a daily basis based on the evolution of the crisis circumstances (for example, the addition of the nuclear exclusion zone around the Fukushima nuclear facility, changing electrical power capacity projections, and so on) and facilitated faster, more informed executive decision-making on mitigation activities and prioritization.

Cisco managers were also able to profile each supplier site from various resiliency perspectives. These included:

- the expected time-to-recover (TTR) for the site;
- back-up power generation capabilities; and
- whether the supplier's components were single sourced or had alternative sites available.

Cisco's supply chain incident management team war room approach, structure and operations were based on their supply chain risk management (SCRM) incident management 'playbooks'. These playbooks create a predefined reference for bringing together the customer value chain management (CVCM) organizational leaders to assess, mitigate and resolve a disruptive supply chain incident. The playbooks define a functional track structure, key contacts related to various types of incidents, templates and other collateral to assist in running and managing an incident response.

In a very short period, the crisis management system was able to assess more than 300 tier 1 to tier 5 suppliers – including site inspections and more than 7,000 part numbers – and complete a risk-rating and mitigation plan. According to management, the largest supply chain disruption in modern times created virtually no revenue impact for the company.

Key to Cisco's response was being able to identify the lack of visibility into the sub-tier supply chain (suppliers that supply tier 1 component manufacturers). Having this as a 'known unknown' was critical to quickly resourcing a team to investigate key impacts and ramifications in this area and to mitigate where possible.

The response team was given an 'open checkbook' by Chairman and Chief Executive Officer John Chambers to seek out new sources of product. Additional teams were set up to locate secondary sources for specific commodities and suppliers. In the end, the company spent around $100 million on mitigation efforts in the wake of the incident.

Things didn't go perfectly. Cisco had underestimated the importance of constantly revising its parts site maps in line with the ever-changing land-scape. It also needed to do a better job of collaborating with manufacturing partners, a lesson that proved valuable in coping with the more recent floods in Thailand.

# The role of flexible technology in supply chain resilience

Partly as a result of the catastrophic natural disasters that have had such a dramatic impact on supply chains in the past few years, companies and governments around the world are now struggling to understand how they can best establish strategies and plans robust enough to cope with similar events in future. The role of flexible technologies will be critical to enable them to not only deal with future disruptions but also gain a competitive advantage.

As discussed above, many companies have very limited knowledge of their exposure to risk and vulnerability because of the poor visibility of their second- or third-tier suppliers. Beyond this, they will have even less understanding of issues such as their transportation providers' reliability, safety record or the reliability of the communications infrastructure between those parties.

In today's supply chains, vast streams of data are created that flow through a range of disparate systems. Many of these systems run the operations inside the largest players in the chain, but are driven by internal IT strategies and protocols that fail to take into account activities outside their domains. Complex technical environments have traditionally required a very structured approach towards management. This is understandable, as the impact of any mistakes can ripple through the organization affecting numerous other systems, with correction being extremely costly in terms of both time and money. This rigid and controlled backdrop has enabled many large enterprises to manage their businesses very well for many years.

However, this approach is now being challenged by organizations that do not have to follow the same constraints. Indeed, the organization may not be a single corporation but a federation of specialist companies acting in concert. These 'networked' organizations will become much more common over the next few years and resemble supply chains in their structure, that is, a group of enterprises working together to deliver a product or service to a customer.

To do so, they will need to have very fluid and flexible information systems. These systems are designed to inter-operate, collaborate and share data with a variable mix of partners. They will also be very accessible to customers, as it is much more efficient to give the customer access to the information they need directly, rather than go through an intermediary. An example of this is the way in which people make travel arrangements – many booking directly with the airline, buying tickets and arranging seating without ever having to speak to a customer service representative.

This inherently flexible approach to sharing and organizing capabilities makes such enterprises very resilient to external shocks. It makes them more adaptive than highly structured organizations and they are assisted by the evolution of technological tools, software and platforms that are very scalable, open to integration and interoperability, and inherently adaptable.

Of course, larger, more established enterprises can also withstand external shocks and disruptions, so long as they have accounted for them in their disaster recovery strategies. They usually have considerable resources to deploy in terms of manpower or financial reserves to cover for 'one-off' events such as natural disasters or national infrastructure failure. So long as these are short-term events and the company can get back to its usual operational state quickly, this is sustainable.

However, if the problem impacts a supplier or trading partner outside of the enterprise and is unaccounted for in any disaster recovery scenario, it is usually very difficult to reconfigure operations to accommodate any new or substitute trading partners quickly. In this scenario, even the largest, most efficient enterprises are in trouble.

The proliferation of communications technologies enabling people to connect and share data, information and experience has overwhelmed the conventional channels between vendors and their customers. As society comes to terms with this increasing transparency, companies are having to reset their expectations and response scenarios. This opportunity to introduce greater transparency into their supply chain operations will provide customers with better information and enhanced customer service. It will also introduce greater accountability into the supplier base. This in itself will be challenging, as it may cut across sensitive supplier relationships and organizational culture.

As supply chains become more extended and customers continue to demand increasing customization and shorter delivery times, conventional hierarchical and functionally segmented organizations will struggle. They will not be able to adapt fast enough to external events and be at a commercial disadvantage to the networked, adaptive value chains provided by the new emerging companies.

Supply chain risk is rising up the agenda of both governments and corporations. However, in some sections of government, the approach to this challenge seems to be moving away from seeking to depend solely on redundancy across every system, towards more agility and adaptability. If their physical and information networks can be reconfigured quickly in response to unplanned events, this will reduce delays and lessen the ultimate impact – or at least that's the theory. Such a philosophy requires not only a fundamental rethink of systems and processes, but also the organization itself.

Large enterprises and multinationals always assume that their sheer size, scale and vertical integration will safeguard them from the negative impact of external events. However, the rush into tightly integrated enterprise resource planning (ERP) systems and related processes actually locked many organizations into an inflexible, rigid existence, intolerant of any rapid adaptation. Such an approach is excellent for controlling highly efficient, internally focused organizations that seldom change. But this is unsuitable as a foundation for fluid, adaptive participation in a value chain network.

# The role of government and commercial companies

Companies in the private sector, of necessity, rely on governments to provide a stable and secure framework in which supply chains can function efficiently and with resilience. This includes good governance, economic competence, societal factors and robust infrastructure.

However, the relationship between governments and the private sector, as regards risk, is complicated. At a basic level, supply chains rely on predominantly public sector infrastructure to move goods around the world. Even if the infrastructure assets themselves are private sector owned and operated, they are most likely to be regulated by the applicable government.

A relevant example of this interaction was the Icelandic volcano crisis. On safety grounds, much of the European airspace was shut down by regulators, largely acting unilaterally, costing the industry and economy many millions of pounds. The relationship between airlines, shippers and governments quickly broke down and was characterized by a lack of information-sharing and mistrust.

Likewise in the Hurricane Katrina natural disaster, private sector companies such as Walmart found that their efforts to help the victims were being more hindered than helped by the response of local and national authorities, who often were working to their own agenda.

On a different level, the UK endured three excessively cold winters between 2008 and 2010. Low stocks of salt and a lack of a centralized plan to deal with the freezing temperatures meant that much of the country's infrastructure was brought to a halt. On occasion, airports such as Heathrow were overwhelmed with snow, and train services were frequently thrown into chaos. In 2010 alone the cost of the disruption was estimated to be £1.6 billion.

It seems that the coordinating authorities sometimes end up as part of the problem rather than the solution. Given the powers that these authorities are vested with, it is of paramount importance to ensure that the same principles of supply chain resilience are deployed by the public sector as much as in the private.

For instance, there is a considerable risk that a proactive public sector approach fails to involve the private sector in its response. This is a mistake – as demonstrated by the Hurricane Katrina response – major grocery retailers have the best distribution structures, which can be utilized for distribution of food and medicines in a national emergency.

In the UK, detailed plans to deal with a disaster are in place – so-called 'Gold Level' planning. However, regulators risk planning for these events in a kind of bubble – failing to understand the level of integration that the public sector has within private sector networks – such as transport, technology, electricity, and so on. This same attitude risks also ignoring the opportunities that engagement with the private sector could exploit. A failure to adopt this approach will mean that the UK's responses to crises and disasters will continue to be characterized by ineptitude and confusion.

The research programme of the World Economic Forum recommended that a four-part multi-stakeholder approach was required to increase supply chain resilience (WEF, 2013a):

- *Policy* – international standards organizations should work together to further develop, harmonize and encourage the adoption of resilience standards.

- *Strategy* – organizations should follow agile and adaptable strategies to improve resilience.
- *IT* – the use of data-sharing platforms should be expanded for risk identification and response.
- *Partnership* – organizations should institutionalize a multi-stakeholder supply chain risk assessment process.

This suggests that governments, manufacturers and retailers, along with the vast array of their suppliers, logistics operators, technology partners and insurance providers, will all play a role in developing the structures and processes needed to increase resilience.

## Summary

Corporations must be prepared for disruption to their business and supply chains at any time, and there are various ways in which resilience can be engineered. Collaboration with partners and suppliers is critical to developing an agile response to disruption in order to maintain output in the aftermath of a shock. Industry standards and models exist that provide a framework for businesses to ensure that risks are identified and responses developed. As well as this, technology is becoming increasingly important to ensure that physical and information networks can be reconfigured quickly in response to unplanned events.

## Key points

- A resilient supply chain is one that can be returned quickly to its original state and preferably maintain output at a steady rate throughout a disruptive event.
- Resilience relies on good communication with suppliers and an understanding of all supply chain partners' requirements.
- Businesses should implement industry standards that create a framework for understanding specific risks that helps prepare a response.

- Cisco, an example of best practice, mitigates risk through supply chain crisis management teams located in key regions, monitoring and assessing risks 24/7.

- The role of flexible technology will be critical in understanding and mitigating risk.

- Governments play a key role in creating a stable environment for resilient supply chains to develop.

# Industry sector resilience to supply chain threats

03

**OBJECTIVES**

This chapter will familiarize the reader with:

- the individual characteristics of risk for the major vertical sector supply chains;

- the impact of catastrophic natural events, economic shocks and industrial disputes on automotive and high-tech supply chains;

- how risk has increased in the automotive sector because of the proliferation of parts in vehicles, especially high-tech components sourced from Asia;

- the high-risk dependency of many sectors on transport because of JIT production strategies;

- the problems caused to consumer goods manufacturers by the centralization of production and distribution strategies;

- the risk to food supply chains from substitution and adulteration of ingredients due to a lack of visibility in the supply chain;

- societal threats to fashion supply chains due to the abuse of suppliers' workers in developing countries.

The characteristics of some supply chains make them more vulnerable to supply chain threats than others. Figure 3.1 illustrates this point. The high-tech sector, for example, relies heavily on global supply chains that are typically high value, lean and unbundled/outsourced. The pharmaceutical

**Figure 3.1**   Global supply chain risk – sector threat resilience

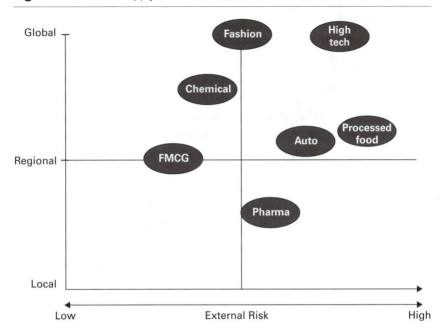

supply chain is much less globalized, and although there are intrinsic risks for the products themselves, the high level of in-house production/distribution mitigates many of these risks. However, with greater levels of outsourcing in this sector, the external risks are set to rise.

The food supply chain is very diverse. At some levels, food supply chains tend to be local, characterized by low product value and, in most cases, have low levels of risk attached. However, as has been seen recently in Europe, processed food products can have very long and complex supply chains that are highly vulnerable to substitution. As will be discussed in more detail below, it has been very easy for some unscrupulous processors to replace more expensive ingredients such as beef with cheaper products such as horse meat.

# Automotive

## *Risk profile summary*

The automotive industry has experienced a difficult past decade. It has faced widespread economic difficulties that have resulted in multiple bankrupt-cies. In addition, manufacturers have seen challenges on both a regional and local level. These include:

- the Japanese tsunami;
- Thai flooding;
- Mexico flooding;
- the economic downturn;
- industrial disputes.

Automotive supply chains have developed a unique set of attributes that have made them highly vulnerable to economic shocks (demand and supply) as well as environmental, technological and security risks:

- A car can have up to 15,000 individual parts – and the failure to deliver just one of these can slow down or halt a production line.
- Supply is becoming more globalized as vehicles assembled in Europe and North America include more high-tech components manufactured in Asia Pacific. High-tech components account for almost half of a vehicle's cost compared with just a fifth in the early 2000s.
- Many of these components are produced in manufacturing 'clusters' in the developing world, increasing vulnerability (for example the Thailand flood disaster and the Japanese tsunami).
- The industry is highly consolidated around a relatively small number of very large assembly plants, for example Honda at Maryville, OH, or the PSA Peugeot Citroen plants at Mulhouse and Sochoux. Supplier parks are developed in close proximity to assembly plants, leading to risk from localized events.
- Automotive supply chains generally employ a 'tiered' supplier hierarchy, with low visibility below tier 1 and tier 2 suppliers.
- Reliance on suppliers can create problems with quality control.
- The customer buying profile is highly cyclical – at risk from demand shocks (as demonstrated in the global recession of 2008–09).
- There is a high level of dependence on future growth in volatile emerging markets.
- There is a high dependence on JIT delivery schedules.
- Low margins are available to logistics providers (especially in the finished vehicle sector), leading to the possibility of supplier bankruptcy and consequent disruption.
- Widespread customization of parts to particular models means that suppliers are often the sole source for a particular component.

According to a survey undertaken by IBM, supply chain visibility is judged by automotive executives as the most important challenge facing their industry, significantly more than in other sectors (IBM, 2009). This has been borne out by the problems faced by auto manufacturers in anticipating the consequences to their operations of such disasters as the Japanese tsunami and the Thai floods. Many companies were not able to judge the implications of the event as they did not have the necessary visibility of lower-tier suppliers. They may well know where their main suppliers are based – but they were not able to identify how these suppliers would be affected. The weeks and months following the disasters were spent trying to find out this information retrospectively and then put in place a strategy to source components from alternative suppliers, if in fact this was possible.

The survey found that the automotive industry is dragging behind other sectors, especially in the effective sharing of real-time demand and inventory data.

For the past 30 years the automotive sector has been at the forefront of the move towards lean inventory and JIT distribution. Given the disastrous economic consequences of 'push'-driven production strategies during the 1960s and 1970s (in contrast with the Japanese 'kanban' or 'pull' manufacturing), this is unsurprising. However, it has left the sector highly vulnerable to supply disruption and this has been exemplified by several high-profile and recent occurrences detailed below.

## The impact of natural disasters on the automotive sector

### The Japanese earthquake and tsunami

The impact of the earthquake and tsunami of 2011 was felt most keenly by the automotive manufacturers with production facilities in Japan. These were shut down for several weeks as companies tried to come to terms with the impact upon their suppliers and supply chains. However, its effects were also felt elsewhere in the world, as several key suppliers of automotive electronics to the global industry were located in close proximity to the disaster. Toyota, Honda and Nissan were most affected, but US and European manufacturers were not immune.

In actual fact, only a tiny proportion of suppliers were impacted by the disaster. However, with the large numbers of components that go into making up a car, even the disruption to a few could lead to supply chain failure.

As an example of the increasing globalization of the auto supply chain, it is estimated that a third of components that are used in assembling cars in the UK are sourced from international markets (Davies, 2015). Those imported from Japan include tyres, seat belts, fuel injection modules, lighting and semi-conductors:

- **Semi-conductors**

  One of the main reasons for a widespread halt in car production immediately after the Japanese tsunami was the impact that earthquake damage had upon a single manufacturer of microchip controllers, called Renesas, based north of Tokyo. Although many auto manufacturers did not source directly from this company, their tier 1 and tier 2 suppliers did, and this resulted in a temporary suspension of production. Once again, problems were caused by a lack of visibility below tier 1 suppliers and the unnecessary reliance on a sole-source supplier.

  Consolidation within the Japanese semi-conductor sector had created a situation where 40 per cent of the world's automotive chip production was undertaken by one manufacturer. NEC, Mitsubishi Electric and Hitachi had merged their semi-conductor into a single entity – Renesas – and its factory was severely damaged by the earthquake. Although production was transferred to other Renesas factories in Singapore and elsewhere in Japan, the fact that the products (and the software needed to design them) are so customized for individual auto makers, meant that supply was severely disrupted for more than four months. Renesas was not the only semi-conductor company to be affected. The factory of Freescale Semiconductors, a US-based high-tech manufacturer, was so damaged that it had to be closed completely.

- **Pigments**

  Another effect of the earthquake was to shut down production of Xirallic pigment – which creates a shinier and more 'glittery' effect in car paints. The only plant in the world that makes these pigments was located near the Fukushima nuclear reactor, owned by chemical manufacturer, Merck. Vehicle manufacturers affected included Ford, Chrysler, Volkswagen, BMW, Toyota and GM. According to reports, a range of paint types became unavailable including Ford's famous 'tuxedo black'. This had an impact on sales and mark-ups.

  One of the interesting points about this issue was that the various manufacturers had no idea that they were all reliant on one supplier. This provided an insight into the lack of visibility below tier 1 and tier 2 suppliers.

- **Electronics**

  Another parts supplier affected was Keihin Corp, a supplier of manifolds and other components to Honda. Even though it was able to get its own earthquake-affected factories back up and running quickly, disruption to upstream suppliers meant that production levels could only reach 50 per cent of capacity. Other suppliers were impacted by the effect of power blackouts and shortages.

One of the worrying aspects about the 2011 crisis was that warnings had seemingly been ignored. In 2007 a much smaller earthquake, this time in the Niigata-Chuetsu-Oki region, shut down the production of Japanese auto manufacturers Toyota and Honda because of the impact that it had upon the supply of engine piston rings and transmission seals. The supplier in question, Riken, was responsible for the supply of 40 per cent of all piston rings to the Japanese automobile industry. Although damage was relatively minor, production was halted for two weeks. The auto manufacturers provided assistance to get the production up and running once more, which minimized downtime.

As a result of the damage, Riken has since established production in other regions so that in future it won't be as vulnerable to localized disasters.

## Thai floods

Japanese car-makers that had just started to recover from the earthquake and tsunami were then faced with shortages of key parts made in Thailand due to the worst floods in 50 years. Toyota and Honda both had to halt production at facilities even in North America because of the effect on their Thai suppliers.

When just two industrial parks – Rojana and Saharat Nakorn – were overwhelmed by floods, 20 components suppliers were affected accounting for 10 per cent of the total volume of components produced in the country.

It was not just a case of the supply of parts. Many manufacturers, such as Ford, had built assembly plants in the country and these were also affected. Thailand is Honda's second largest production base in Asia outside of Japan and its factory at Ayutthaya was badly flooded. Honda produces approximately 5 per cent of its total output in Thailand. Production only resumed in spring 2012 and this had a knock-on effect on production in India that the plant fed. Thirty-two of Honda's suppliers were affected by the floods, including Rohm Integrated Systems, a high-tech manufacturer producing micro controllers, transistors and capacitors, and LAPIS Semiconductor. Toyota had 100 suppliers affected, including its affiliate Aisin Seiki Co, an aluminium die-cast parts manufacturer.

The floods resulted in:

- 300,000 fewer vehicles than forecast being built in 2011 in Thailand;
- suspension of overtime working in Toyota and Honda plants throughout Asia;
- delay of new model launches, such as the next-generation Honda CR-V and Civic;
- suspension of production at Nissan and Mitsubishi plants in Thailand;
- implementation of a three-day week at Honda's plant in the UK.

The Thai floods came at a time when many Japanese manufacturers were switching production to the country in order to take advantage of lower labour costs as well as avoiding the impact of the strong yen.

## Impact of industrial action

The centralized nature of the automotive sector, combined with the levels of trade unionization, has meant that it is often vulnerable to industrial disputes. Labour relations within manufacturing operations are not a focus for this particular discussion of supply chain risk, but it does seem that automotive supply chains, by their lean nature, are particularly vulnerable to transport disruption.

Industrial action cannot only disrupt the transport element of supply chains. The outsourcing process itself can create tensions amongst the workforce, which go to the very heart of how modern logistics operations are managed. An example of this was the threatened industrial action at Jaguar Land Rover's production plant in the UK. The dispute revolved around the differences in pay between staff employed by JLR and those by its outsourcing partner, DHL Supply Chain. This is explored in more detail in Chapter 6.

---

### Examples of the impact of industrial action on supply chains

**9 December 2016**

**Amazon hit by strikes at ABX**

Amazon is once again having problems with its workforce. Previously it was German warehouse staff, now it is US pilots.

On Tuesday (6 December 2016) a restraining order was placed by a US court on the pilots of Air Transport Services Group Inc and its subsidiary ABX Air preventing them taking industrial action. The pilots were planning to stage a strike on Tuesday and Wednesday (7–8 November 2016). Previous 'wildcat' action taken by the ABX pilots on 22 November forced the cancellation of 75 flights. DHL Express has also been affected by the strikes.

The pilots are members of the 'Airline Professionals Association', which in turn is part of the Teamsters Union. Their complaint is that ABX aircrew are understaffed and that the pilots are obliged to work overtime to cover the shortage.

Reports suggest that pilots at fellow Amazon air freight provider Atlas Air also feel that their flight operations are understaffed. The same sources suggest that these third-party air freight suppliers have pay and conditions that compare badly with those received by pilots at FedEx and UPS and this is angering flight crews.

This is potentially a serious issue for Amazon. The fleet of ABX alone is roughly 50 aircraft and removing these from the e-retailer's network would be a significant problem in the weeks leading up to Christmas.

## 10 October 2012

### Largest African economy crippled by series of strikes

Now in its third week, the strike by more than 20,000 truck drivers demanding higher wages has halted the delivery of goods across the country. According to General Motors, 'the transport workers' strike has disrupted material supply activities in our vehicle assembly facility.'

After a three-day strike by the National Union of Metalworkers, Toyota agreed to increase wages by a reported 5.7 per cent. During the strike, the company lost 2,428 vehicles' worth of production, about 14 per cent of its monthly average.

## 12 June 2008

### Fuel strikes bring supply chain chaos across the world

Rising fuel costs have prompted industrial action by hauliers and others in a range of markets around the world, bringing many transport systems to a standstill and severely disrupting the supply of goods.

In Spain, one of the countries hit hardest by strike action, up to 90,000 self-employed lorry drivers are blockading main routes, leading to a shortage of petrol and panic-buying by consumers. Several manufacturers in that country, including Nissan, Mercedes Benz and Seat, have shut down operations due to a lack of parts, and foreign vehicles have been prevented from entering the country. That has led to long vehicle queues at the French border. It is reported that the strike is spreading to neighbouring Portugal.

In response, the Spanish government has promised hauliers a package of subsidies to help mitigate the 20 per cent increase in fuel costs. However, it has stopped short of giving in to demands for a new system of regulated tariffs that would prevent freight companies from undercutting each other.

**SOURCE** Logistics Briefing (www.ti-insight.com)

## Impact of logistics operational failure

Despite being renowned for the sophistication of its logistics, the automotive sector is not immune to a breakdown in operations. In 2004 Caterpillar Logistics Services, the then logistics subsidiary of the US multinational, took over the spare parts business of now defunct UK car manufacturer MG Rover. Cat Logistics had been handling MG Rover's parts business since 2002 from its Desford facility in the UK.

At the outset of the original 10-year contract there were significant problems, although the partnership proved strong enough to overcome them. These difficulties related to the transition from its former logistics supplier Unipart to the new provider, largely caused by the loss of experienced and skilled employees prior to the handover. The resulting bottleneck forced the shutdown of production at MG Rover's plant to allow component manufacturers to drop-ship spares directly into the aftermarket distribution network. At the same time, Cat Logistics was forced to 'parachute' in skilled logistics specialists from other parts of its organization to address the situation.

## Outsourcing of production – quality issues

One of the major challenges that manufacturers face when unbundling and outsourcing production processes is the requirement to maintain standards of quality control. Failure to do so, as Toyota found to its cost, results in major reputational damage as well as the obvious financial consequences.

In September 2009, Toyota recalled 4 million vehicles because of concerns that accelerator pedals could be trapped in floor mats. This was then followed in January 2010 by the announcement that the company was to recall a further 2.3 million cars to fix 'faulty' pedals (Bowen and Kennedy, 2010). Just a few days after this, the production of eight models was suspended in North America and sales of new cars were halted. The crisis then spread to Europe, where another 1.8 million cars were recalled.

One of the major problems of Toyota's response was that it treated the problem as one of 'quality' rather than 'safety'. While the former had mostly a financial cost implication, when it escalated into a safety concern it rapidly became a matter of reputational importance. In the long run this had a far greater impact in financial terms because of consequent loss of sales. In the UK, production at its Burnaston plant was suspended for two weeks.

The pedal itself was made by CTS Corp, a US-based manufacturer that also supplies similar parts to Honda, Nissan and Mitsubishi, but to different specifications.

The incident was put down by some commentators to Toyota's strategy to grab market leadership in the United States from General Motors. This had an impact on quality and resulted in a surge in the number of recalls. Although it is unclear whether the fault can totally be blamed on CTS, there was a strong suspicion that, had Toyota put better quality controls in place, the problem would not have arisen.

Whoever was at fault, Toyota thought it best to take overall responsibility. A spokesman for the company said: 'I don't want to get into any kind of a disagreement with CTS. Our position on suppliers has always been that Toyota is responsible for the cars' (Bunkley and Maynard, 2010).

# High tech

## *Risk profile summary*

As a result of the high-tech industry's quest for cost management and operational efficiency, manufacturing production has moved away from the mature markets such as the United States and Europe and into Asia. Today, the vast majority of all high-tech goods are manufactured in Asia. Although Eastern and Western China are expected to remain the top sourcing locations for many high-tech manufacturers and solutions providers over the next five years, Taiwan, Thailand, Japan and South Korea are likely to see increases as well.

Some manufacturers are going further and moving production and sourcing to other geographic regions, such as South America, most notably Brazil. Many high-tech companies are expanding their manufacturing base in the country so that they can produce PCs locally and avoid high import tariffs. This has resulted in an increase in external supply chain risks, from the perspective of sourcing and transportation.

For the industry sector as a whole, some of the key risks are as follows:

- High-tech goods are primarily manufactured in Asia Pacific and moved long distances to Europe and North America, making the transportation element of the supply chain critical.

- As a result, reliability of transportation is vulnerable to a range of disruptive events – including natural, criminal or terrorist related.

- The high-value nature of the goods makes them a target for theft at various stages of the supply chain, especially en route to port or airport in the country of consignment.

- The introduction of counterfeit goods into the high-tech supply chain is widespread, costing the industry many billions of dollars a year.

- High-tech manufacturers typically keep inventory levels very low so as to avoid the 'internal' risks of a surfeit of unwanted product. This means that any supply chain disruption can have a very major economic impact on revenues and profits.

- Many manufacturers utilize a tiered approach to suppliers, but have very little visibility below tier 1 or tier 2. They therefore have less than optimal understanding of how a catastrophic event could affect their business.

- High-tech products often have a short lifecycle, which makes it critical to get the goods to market in as short a time as possible. Therefore any disruption in terms of transport or production is very serious.

## Supply chain issues

### Economic

One of the most pressing supply chain risks from an economic perspective is what can be termed 'demand shock'. This is not just the direct effects of a downturn in customer demand in terms of volumes, revenues and profits, but the systemic impact that it can have on supply chain structure.

Following the major economic downturn of 2008–09, some high-tech companies decided to 'switch off' many of their suppliers as a result of their dwindling order books. Although this seemed reasonable in the short term as a way of reducing inventories, it also had the effect of driving many of these suppliers out of business. When the upturn came in 2010, the capacity in the supply chain was not there to meet demand. This was certainly the case with Cisco, which, despite having an industry-leading position in the way in which it deals with external threats, found itself ill-prepared for the economic recovery. This example is dealt with in more detail in Chapter 6.

## Supplier visibility

Because of the tiered approach to supplier organization that many of the largest high-tech manufacturers employ, visibility of the supply chain is often opaque. This means that upstream production is at risk from a range of unforeseen events. These include:

- supplier failure;
- supply chain bottlenecks;
- inability to react quickly to the disruption of supply from natural disasters;
- commodity price volatility;
- reputational risks;
- quality control issues.

Although this problem is not restricted to the high-tech sector, its reliance on outsourcing and unbundling of production and the creation of 'virtual' manufacturing networks does make it especially exposed to a lack of supply chain visibility.

In order to address this problem, many companies use consultancies to undertake an audit of suppliers. This includes utilizing scorecards to assess the robustness of key suppliers against a range of criteria, such as assurance of supply and regulatory compliance. This process will include looking beyond tier 1 suppliers to their suppliers and their suppliers' suppliers. Often these results are integrated with other data, such as quality metrics drawn from ERP systems, as well as other third-party databases (such as financial) to assess business resilience.

## Social responsibility

High-tech companies producing goods in emerging markets are particularly at risk from the impact that suppliers' environmental and labour practices can have on their reputation. Apple, which outsources much of its Chinese manufacturing to Taiwanese company Foxconn, has faced considerable criticism about the conditions of its Chinese labour force and the impact that the disposal of waste products has had on the environment. There is no doubt that Western lobby groups have been very successful in ensuring that manufacturers do not feel that they can outsource their moral responsibilities at the same time as their production and logistics. This issue is dealt with in far more detail in Chapter 6.

## Natural disasters and high-tech clustering

As in the automotive sector, two recent natural disasters to affect the high-tech industry were the Japanese earthquake/tsunami and the Thai floods. Their impact was made all the worse because of the 'clustering' of high-tech manufacturers in certain geographical areas. Economically it makes sense for high-tech manufacturers to co-locate; they can draw from a pool of skilled labour, technology 'ecosystems' of associated suppliers develop and they often receive subsidies from governments. However, this also has risk implications from a supply chain perspective. 'Clustering' is very common in the high-tech sector, as can be seen in the development of science parks in both the developing and developed world.

The Japanese earthquake/tsunami affected many industries, but the Japanese electronics sector was among the hardest hit. Output of NAND flash memory, on which new consumer electronic equipment depends, was disrupted, albeit on a temporary basis. Many wafer fabrication plants, supplying the semi-conductor industry, remained closed while aftershocks continued to take place.

In fact, supply chains in the electronics sector, heavily dependent on Japanese production, were affected right across Asia. There were reports of key electronic components being in short supply as leading electronic manufacturers such as Sony, Sharp and Panasonic shut plants.

The floods that hit Thailand in 2011 also negatively impacted the high-tech industry. Thailand supplies about 40 per cent of the world's market of hard disk drives (Wilcox, 2011). Semi-conductor chip manufacturer Intel reported lower revenues and profits due to shortages of hard disk drives in the industry. Because of the closures, Intel's customers were not able to source sufficient volumes of hard disk drives to meet demand, and hence cut down on their microprocessor inventories. Intel said that the shortages continued into the first quarter of 2012.

Intel was not the only manufacturer to struggle. Dell also missed sales targets due, in part, to shortages of hard disk drives. However, management said that it had made strategic purchases of inventory elsewhere in an attempt to overcome this problem. This inevitably came at a cost.

The supply chain problems that high-tech manufacturers are facing have reopened the debate over the wisdom of sourcing from suppliers clustered in such a vulnerable area.

## Substitution and counterfeits

Counterfeits are a growing problem in the high-tech sector. In fact, up to 10 per cent of electronics products globally may be counterfeit; according to consultancy IHS iSuppli, the number of counterfeit electronic parts has quadrupled since 2009. Although the United States and China lead the way in terms of fakes reported, the range of countries of origin where counterfeit products are manufactured is more diverse. Four countries – Malaysia, South Korea, Japan and the Philippines – account for the majority of reports.

According to the US Commerce Department, the majority of counterfeit parts received by original component manufacturers (OCMs) come from brokers. However, a disturbing 21 per cent come from actual authorized distributors (Department of Commerce, 2010).

A year-long investigation conducted by the US Senate Armed Services Committee found more than 1 million suspected counterfeit parts had made their way into the Department of Defense's supply chain and were bound for use in 'critical' military systems. According to the same study, over 70 per cent of counterfeit parts came from China and changed hands several times before being delivered to the final customer. As a result, the US government tightened regulations around counterfeit components in the defence supply chain in 2011, and made it mandatory to establish risk mitigation procedures.

Much of the counterfeit-parts problem can be traced back to the enormous amount of electronic waste (e-waste) generated each year. Upgrades in electronic devices are occurring more frequently. Based on IHS iSuppli figures, 58 per cent of e-waste generated by the United States is shipped to developing countries, but that 'all too often, electronic components such as semiconductors are culled from this waste and then returned to the United States and other developed countries in the form of counterfeit parts' (IHS Markit, 2012).

The need for collaboration and visibility into suppliers' supply chain and their suppliers' supply chain, and so on, is needed for manufacturers to help address this growing problem.

## Transport issues

The dependence of the high-tech sector on just-in-time solutions means that to enable lean inventory supply chains, transport has to be reliable. In the past there has been considerable use of air cargo and express services to reduce stock levels to a minimum, but since the recession of 2008–09, many shippers have preferred to migrate their volumes to lower-cost sea freight. Although this adds considerable time to transit (perhaps in the region of a month on trans-Pacific and Asia–Europe trades), manufacturers have built this into their production and distribution strategies. Reducing visible transport costs has been more tempting, it seems, than reducing less visible stockholding costs.

### Air freight

A particular risk for a manufacturer that is heavily reliant on the air cargo industry is the lack of capacity that can exist at peak times. Over the past few years capacity in the market on a day-to-day basis has exceeded volumes of goods forcing rates down. This has led many carriers to reduce the number of services they operate. This means that high-tech shippers planning major product launches may have to depend on chartering capacity rather than relying on scheduled services. In a worst-case scenario, air cargo carriers can favour major shippers such as Apple or Samsung, who are prepared to pay 'top dollar', switching capacity to these high-volume providers and 'bumping' other shippers. This was rumoured to be the case in autumn 2012, when Apple's iPhone 5 and Samsung's Galaxy Note 2 were launched, although it was denied by the carriers themselves.

### Sea freight

Switching goods to sea freight from air cargo or express services also has risks, beyond the increase in supply chain inventory. While the goods are on the water, there is the chance that an order might be cancelled, and there is also a greater risk of damage to the consignment. Unexpected delays, such as the backlogs at ports, can tip the balance of any cost–benefit equation.

Problems caused by disruption to shipping using the Suez Canal led to major supply chain problems for Sony in the run up to Christmas 2004. A tanker got stuck in the canal, causing serious backlogs and resulting in a container ship carrying supplies of the market-leading games console, Playstation 2, being delayed for two weeks. Stocks in some parts of Europe ran out and Sony was forced to fly in supplies using chartered Antonov cargo planes at huge expense. Product changed hands on electronic auction sites at around four times' retail price.

## Cargo crime

The high-value nature of high-tech goods makes them very vulnerable to theft, either from warehousing, ports, airports or from trucks. In the United States, around half of thefts by value involve electronics equipment. When a single truck can be carrying a consignment of goods valued at $2 million, the temptations for organized crime or driver corruption are obvious. This subject is dealt with in more detail in Chapter 9.

# Consumer goods/retail

## *Risk profile summary*

In comparison with some sectors, the consumer goods industry is nowhere nearly as consolidated or concentrated around localized production clusters and therefore supply chain problems tend not to have industry-wide consequences. However, this is not to say that company supply chains on an individual basis are not just as much at risk.

The consumer goods sector can be crudely categorized as either consumer packaged goods (or fast moving consumer goods) and consumer durables (furniture, toys, white goods, brown goods, domestic electrical, and so on). The former have predominantly regional supply chains while the latter are largely international (and intercontinental) in character.

The difference in characteristics of product means that their supply chains have diverse risk profiles.

### Consumer packaged goods (CPG)

- Manufacturing occurs on a more regional basis, and consequently downstream distribution involves less international (or at least intercontinental) transportation with significantly fewer risks.

- However, CPG manufacturers have centralized production and distribution in recent years, and this has created risk from localized facility disasters (such as fires or flooding); vulnerability to industrial action; and exposure to long-term infrastructure risks (such as congestion).

- Many inbound raw materials to the production process are imported from around the world and these are at risk from volatile prices and delays in shipment.

- The move by many CPG manufacturers towards higher-value goods (such as razors and pharmaceuticals) increases exposure to cargo theft and counterfeiting.

## Consumer durables

- A large proportion of 'consumer durables' are manufactured in Asia (specifically China) and have extended, global supply chains.
- Upstream, while goods are being moved to ports in developing markets, they are vulnerable to disruption, theft or substitution with counterfeit parts.
- Quality control can be difficult because of the long distances involved in the supply chain.
- On the long transit from point of origin to end-user market, goods can be delayed by a range of low probability events, such as natural disasters, storms or even piracy.
- More likely are economic factors, such as rising fuel costs or changing market patterns while goods are in transit for one to two months.

Two specific parts of the consumer goods sector – food and fashion – are dealt with in much more detail below.

### Retailing logistics disasters

Most consumer goods manufacturers' supply chains involve distribution through the major supermarkets. However, despite the sophistication of the retailers' logistics, things, on occasion, can go badly wrong.

J Sainsbury PLC, one of the largest retailers in Europe, provided an extreme example of the critical nature of logistics to corporate success and failure. The retailer faced a financial crisis in 2004, which management partly blamed on its poor supply chain performance. Its disclosure to shareholders gave an insight into how failing logistics systems impacted on the whole company.

Chief Executive Justin King blamed much of the problem on his predecessor for wasting billions of pounds on a new distribution strategy that affected sales and profits at Sainsbury's stores. The three-year 'modernization programme' entailed upgrading a significant proportion of

IT systems, closing 15 older depots and transferring operations into seven new facilities as well as opening four automated depots.

However, management admitted that this initiative severely affected the availability of products on the shelves. It also acknowledged that developing a wide range of products designed to meet the needs of a multitude of consumer groups led to the development of an overly complex supply chain solution that could not be delivered to the required scale. Performance and costs were higher than before these initiatives were implemented.

On top of this, the new automated depots in which the company invested failed to perform at planned levels. This resulted in a new management team being appointed and further changes being made. Distribution centres that had been slated to close, or had already been closed, were reopened in order to ensure availability of product over the Christmas period and manual support was brought in where automated systems were failing. Suppliers were also targeted to ensure compliance with automated processes.

The failures not only impacted on the level of sales. The company was forced to write off £200 million, £120 million related to automated equipment in the new fulfilment centres and £80 million related to the carrying value of stock due to a change in operational approach, disruption in new depot and IT implementation as well as accelerated clearance of excess general merchandise stocks.

# Food

## *Risk profile summary*

- Quality control in terms of health and safety to consumers is absolutely crucial to the industry. This makes threats to supply chain integrity very serious.
- Processed foods have very long and complex supply chains, which means that there is also often little visibility.
- The industry is often under severe cost pressure, reducing some companies' ability and/or willingness to ensure supply chain integrity.
- Recent scandals have shown that it is very possible to illegally substitute cheaper products into the food supply chain.

The consumption of mass-produced, processed food such as burgers or packaged, frozen meals is a characteristic of most developed markets. In fact, this trend has been increasing because of the convenience levels and the busy modern lives that people live. The fact that many meals and products are produced not in the home but in a factory means that considerable trust has to be placed by the consumer in the brands of the companies manufacturing the goods. A consumer has the right to expect the product to be safe and also to contain the ingredients that the labelling says it does.

In order to monitor the industry, governmental food safety and standards agencies are in place to ensure that the consumer is not threatened by products that fall short of food preparation standards, for example. Their remit also extends to ensuring goods conform to a range of other regulatory requirements, including packaging and labelling.

Despite these provisions, a number of food supply chain scandals have shown that manufacturers, retailers and food standards agencies have failed in their primary duty of care to the consumer, especially in the way that they have left supply chains vulnerable to illegal substitution of products.

One of the primary reasons for this lack of vigilance is cost. Over the last four decades, retailers, especially the major supermarkets, have been able to fulfil their customers' need for ever cheaper food by 'industrializing' the food supply chain. Whereas suppliers tended to be reasonably local to their end markets, food chains have become international in organization, and highly complex. There is a large element of what economists term 'comparative advantage' in the way in which food is now produced. The best way to illustrate this is through the examples of 'ready meals' such as spaghetti bolognese or lasagne.

## Food supply chain vulnerability

Vulnerability of the food supply chain is one of the hottest topics in the international food industry. Those vulnerabilities are not limited to breaches of physical security, theft and malicious contamination by ideologues, extortionists, criminals or terrorists. Threats also come in the guise of food fraud: the intentional adulteration of food for financial gain. Examples of the latter can affect large segments of the food industry, for example Sudan dye contamination of chilli powder (dating back to before 2003, with the latest cases in August 2016), cumin spice contaminated by peanut (2014), and the horse meat contamination of beef (2013).

Increasing levels of outsourcing have also exacerbated the risks to the supply chain. 'Economic owners' (the main brand coordinating the supply chain) often have little visibility of the conditions in which the products are manufactured, transported or stored.

In order to enhance the resilience of the supply chains of which they are a part, suppliers, including third-party logistics providers, have an opportunity to support their customers through a variety of risk-mitigating services. For logistics providers this could range from developing innovative new sensor technologies that ensure perishable products remain at the right temperature to providing a holistic strategy to deal with critical product recalls.

## Threats to the food supply chain

### Food fraud and contamination

Vulnerability in food supply chains is not a new phenomenon; the origins of food fraud and contamination can be traced back many centuries. In fact, the Romans recognized that the illegal adulteration of olive oil, a ubiquitous part of the Roman diet, was a real risk to their food supply chain and decreed that each olive oil container should be labelled with information such as producer, point of origin, importer, weight and quality, then sealed to prevent fraud. Today, traceability and food defence systems are certainly more sophisticated, but it could be argued that unless they are effective, they are not much further advanced. Perhaps that is why food fraud is still a widespread issue (Shiers and Manners-Bell, 2016).

Many food manufacturers are now looking to improve the effectiveness of their traceability by examining the practices of their suppliers' suppliers and tracking products during transportation as a way of strengthening their food defence systems and reducing their supply chain vulnerability.

So where do these threats originate in the food supply chain? Almost all food products start with primary ingredients (crops, meat, flavourings, and so on). Even at the start of the supply chain, high-value crops are exposed to threat. For example, post-harvesting of vines may be exposed to the risk of deliberate mislabelling of inferior grapes with superior varieties. Food fraud occurs where consumers (and producers down the supply chain) are misled into paying a premium for an inferior product. Substitution early in the supply chain has been seen with the replacement of Arabica coffee beans with the cheaper Robusta variety. The potential for criminal activity is often a result of a price gap on the commodity market between a premium and a lower-quality variety and the criminals' reliance on the inability of the consumer to discern the difference.

Contamination for fraud purposes is most common at the first stages of the supply chain and the early stages of ingredient preparation. The issue becomes most extensive if an ingredient is tampered with early in the supply chain but the contamination is only detected once finished products are with consumers. This was the case with some of the largest and most widespread product recalls in recent years. Examples include:

- **Peanut in cumin**

  The worst-case scenario is a contamination of a minor ingredient at an early point in the supply chain that results in a danger to consumers. This was the case for the recalls of products containing cumin in the US between late 2014 and 2016. Cumin imported from Turkey was used in a wide range of products, including seasoning mixes, soups, prepared chicken dishes, meatloaf, satay, ethnic sauces and many others.

  While the level of peanut contaminant was very low, the risk to allergenic consumers was considered too great and over 250 products were recalled. The cumin itself probably did not originate from Turkey but, because of poor traceability and incomplete knowledge of the supply chain, the exact origins of the contamination are still to be confirmed. Of course it is possible that the contamination was caused by intentionally adulterating cumin with cheaper crushed peanut shells or the contamination may be the result of cross-contamination in storage, distribution or at primary manufacturing stages.

- **Sudan dye**

  Chilli powder was fraudulently contaminated with the industrial dye (and carcinogen) Sudan Red in India, the intense red colour attracting a higher market price. Unfortunately, the chilli went through an extensive supply chain, being used as a minor ingredient in ready meals, pizzas and Worcester sauce – the latter is also an ingredient in more food products. When the contamination was detected by the Italian food authorities in 2003, it was already too late and the resulting recalls across Europe cost tens of millions of pounds as well as substantial reputational damage to the food industry. Although it was generally accepted that there was no health risk to consumers because of the extremely low level of contamination in the final product, it did not stop headlines such as 'cancer ready meals'.

## The horse meat scandal

The mass market appeal for processed foods means that there are big profits for suppliers that are able to cut costs. One way to do this is to substitute horse meat for more expensive beef in these products.

In January 2013 it was revealed by the Irish Food Standards Agency that horse meat had been found in the products of an Irish supplier to UK manufacturers and retailers. It rapidly transpired that the problem was Europe-wide, and for the first time the public became aware of the complex networks evident in food supply chains.

Well-known food brand Findus was implicated in the scandal when horse DNA was found in some of its products. Findus had placed an order for a range of mince-based products such as lasagne and moussaka with a Luxembourg-based French supplier called Comigel (the company also manufactures Tesco, Aldi, Lidl and Carrefour's own-label frozen meat products). This company in turn had subcontracted the sourcing of mince to another French company, Spanghero, which, via a number of other channels, substituted horse meat for beef supplied by a Romanian abattoir and subsequently mislabelled the product. French authorities investigating said that Spanghero could have made around €550,000 by this process and mislabelling.

It is not just the order and financial trail that is complex – the movement of physical goods also can involve extensive cross-border transits. While in its simplest form product should move from farmer to abattoir to processing plant to retailer, in certain parts of the sector movements of product can be international – even intercontinental – in nature. Low-cost transport, which has had such an impact in revolutionizing production and distribution in other sectors, has also had a major influence on the food sector.

Parts of the processed food market are more at risk than others. For instance, there is far less chance of adulteration in the 'chilled' product section than 'frozen'. Chilled meat products (which command a premium) are usually sourced far closer to the processing plant. The UK's AB Foods, for example, buys meat from cattle within a 30-mile radius of their factories and the supply chain is very simple. Frozen meat products (such as burgers) are much cheaper and, having a lifespan of up to two years, have highly complex supply chains more characteristic of the example above.

The extent of the problem is breath-taking. It has been estimated that 750 tons of horse meat has illegally entered the food supply chain in Europe, adulterating 4.5 million meals. Tests across Europe found that nearly 5 per cent of products assessed contained over 1 per cent horse DNA. In one case, Tesco's own-brand burger contained more than 29 per cent horse meat (Environment, Food and Rural Affairs Committee, 2013a).

Not only is there an issue with mislabelling. Tests found that some carcasses contained a drug commonly used in the treatment of horses – phenylbutazone.

**Figure 3.2**    The horse meat scandal supply chain

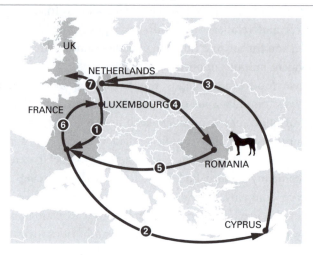

Although chances are that levels of the drug would be so small in any processed meal that it would not be harmful to human health, this obviously impacted on consumer confidence further. Despite this, the issue is not specifically one related to health (the case study opposite regarding Chinese milk powder has far more relevance related to the safety issue). It is one primarily of consumer confidence and the principle that a label should accurately reflect the contents of the product. Without this confidence, trust in the whole supply chain falls apart. It is not just products contaminated with horse meat (offending, it might be argued, cultural sensibilities), but also halal or kosher products adulterated with pork – where religious sensibilities are also brought into play.

## Food regulations

In the EU, legislative efforts have been made to ensure traceability in the food supply chain. Under regulation 178/2002, each player in the supply chain must be able to identify the supplier who provided them with a product or ingredient, and likewise keep records as to the businesses that they themselves have supplied. This is known as the 'one step back, one step forward' approach. On one level it may be concluded that the fact that these directives were ignored at some point in the supply chain, allowing contamination, was an indication of illegal activity. Certainly retailers, industry organizations and many manufacturers were keen to put the scandal solely down to acts of criminality. However, it could also be argued that the complexity and the lack of transparency innate to these supply chains, coupled with cost pressures and the willingness of many parties to turn a blind eye to dubious practices, was the real problem.

## Impact of the crisis

In terms of the impact of this supply chain crisis, it is relatively easy to measure its effects on the industry. According to a report by the UK's House of Commons Environment, Food and Rural Affairs Committee (2013b), frozen burger sales fell by 16 per cent in the aftermath of the scandal. Frozen ready meal sales fell by 13 per cent. In contrast, anecdotal evidence suggested that both sales and prices at butchers – which have far more localized, transparent supply chains than supermarkets – rose.

On an individual basis, a Dutch company was forced to withdraw a 50,000-tonne consignment of meat as it was unable to identify the source of the meat.

Despite the prominence of the horse meat scandal, there is evidence to suggest that these problems are not restricted to Europe. Academics have suggested that similar complexity of supply chains in Australia and South Africa allow for the infiltration of meat substitutes. In South Africa, buffalo and donkey has been found in beef-labelled produce. Both of these types of animal, like horse in parts of Europe, are much cheaper than beef.

## *The Chinese milk scandal*

Fortunately the European horse meat scandal has had no reported impacts on consumers' health. This, unfortunately, was not the case in China in 2008, where there was a far more serious adulteration in the food supply chain, this time affecting milk.

Over 300,000 people were affected by the deliberate adulteration of milk and milk products (including baby formula) by melamine, and it is suspected that at least 11 people died. This toxic substance can be added to food products to increase protein levels – in this instance it allowed Chinese farmers to pass dairy quality tests by adding 'protein powder' to sub-standard milk. Because of the rapid growth in the market, supply of milk had been unable to keep up with demand, while prices were fixed by the government and input costs had risen. It is alleged that dairy farmers, dairies and milk agents were party to these practices and that authorities turned a blind eye, because of corruption.

Given that milk is an important raw material used in many other processed foods, a large number of downstream manufacturers were affected. Cadbury's, Heinz and Unilever recalled several of their product lines and Nestlé was also affected (Wiggins, 2008). Exports to the rest of the world were immediately impacted, with 25 countries placing import bans on Chinese milk products.

Despite the different products and geographies, Chinese milk supply chains and European processed food supply chains share similar characteristics: complexity, cost pressures and lack of transparency. As in Europe, the scandal resulted in testing programmes being reinforced. Deploying 150,000 officials, the complete supply chain was examined – from cattle feed to the dairies themselves.

There have been calls for a reduction in fragmentation in the milk processing industry – it is believed that this could improve standards and supply chain transparency. However, there are major doubts over whether this will ever occur, and, even if it did, whether it would make any difference to the issue of trust.

## Other forms of threat

Beyond the farm gates, the supply chain is made up of a series of alternating steps involving transportation, storage and processing up to the point of sale to the consumer at retail. At each stage there is a risk of tampering, theft, substitution or diversion. More steps in the supply chain can result in an increased risk to the product's authenticity and safety.

While food fraud is more common and has a wider impact when executed early in the supply chain, the entire chain is potentially exposed to risk, although the nature of risks may vary. For example, as the product continues its journey through the supply chain, it gains value and therefore it becomes more exposed to the risk of theft and the prevalence of malicious tampering increases.

### Malicious tampering

The malicious tampering of products is more common in food producers and even at the retail stage, possibly because the perpetrator can see a direct link with their actions and the result on specific consumer groups or companies.

For example, one of the most serious and highly publicized malicious tampering cases occurred in the US in the 1990s involving the contamination of branded Tylenol headache capsules with cyanide. It is believed that the tampering occurred at the retail level and resulted in several deaths.

Other cases of retail tampering have involved the retailer Pick n Pay in South Africa in 2003, when an attempt was made to extort money after someone claimed to have tampered with products on supermarket shelves and contaminated them with poison. Following a product recall, it was concluded that no products had actually been contaminated and the cases were essentially a hoax.

In the UK in 2009, a factory worker was accused of spreading peanuts around a nut-free factory, apparently because of being taken through the disciplinary process. The malicious tampering action was carried out because of a grudge against the company itself. This sort of action, caused by a company's own employees, is a certain risk, but also one that should be controlled and mitigated by effective HR procedures and a positive company culture.

## Theft

The risk of theft of products increases as the products gain value along the supply chain. For example, the risk of theft of bulk rye or barley is low, but the risk of theft of whisky is high. This risk comprises the value of the product in question, how easy it is to transport, opportunity, and prevention and detection measures.

## Food safety and temperature control

When assessing the supply chain vulnerabilities, it is also important to consider the impact of extreme temperatures on products and ingredients. For some products this is not important, but for others – for example meat, dairy, ready meals – it is essential to maintain chilled or frozen supply. This must be maintained during processing, manufacture, storage and distribution. Breach of this cold chain can result in quality-impaired product or even a food safety incident. These factors must therefore be included in the risk assessment of supply chains. It is also not good enough to have complete temperature control, but it is essential to be able to demonstrate it throughout the product's journey through the supply chain to the retailer.

## Securing the supply chain: best practice

To carry out an analysis of vulnerabilities and risks in the supply chain, it is necessary for a food manufacturer to fully understand all the parties involved in producing, storing and distributing their food ingredients. This is not always as simple as it sounds. A key risk is where a supplier outsources the manufacture of an ingredient to a third party, unknown to the food producer. This third party may not have the expected standard of food safety management systems or proper controls in place to prevent food fraud, adulteration or tampering.

Part of the supply chain vulnerability mapping is therefore to collate information from internationally recognized certifications, supplier questionnaires and, where necessary, on-site audits from staff or representatives of the food manufacturer. This applies to all parties, including food processors, distributors and warehouse operators. Effective procurement and robust supplier approval and supplier management then become core elements to minimizing supply chain risks.

A first step is to consider the exposure of each ingredient to the threats identified in this chapter and then rank the risks inherent within the supply chain stages and at each geographical location. For example, if saffron is used as an ingredient, there is high risk of fraud and adulteration with other cheaper spices and dyes. If it is known that one stage of the supply chain involves transportation through war zones or areas of organized criminal activity, the risk level of theft and adulteration for monetary gain can be assessed as high and steps taken accordingly.

# Fashion

## Risk profile summary

- Manufacture of product is predominantly undertaken in Asia and other emerging markets.
- There is often political and social instability in the markets where garments are manufactured.
- Production is vulnerable to disruption from natural disasters (for instance flooding in the monsoon season).
- Transport infrastructure in these markets is also often very poor.
- The long distances moved means that transportation is vulnerable to disruption and delay.
- Outsourcing of production means that relationships and communication are key to mitigating risks in terms of quality control, reliability of supply, and so on.
- Increasing interest in the conditions in which low-paid workers make goods has increased reputational risk for Western retailers and manufacturers.

- Short seasons for fashion items means that the logistics of supply is crucial to businesses' success or failure.

- Many fashion retailers work with very low levels of inventory, using quick response (QR) manufacturing techniques. This places extra stress on the supply chain.

In many respects the international flows of fashion goods and the 'virtual' enterprise networks that have sprung up resemble high-tech supply chains in their complexity. Where manufacturers still exist in Europe, they usually outsource the labour-intensive parts of the manufacturing process to low-wage countries. This is slightly different from retailers buying goods directly from cheaper remote suppliers, as outward processing trade (OPT) is integrated within the manufacturer's internal supply chain. Fabrics, cuttings or semi-garments are shipped to lower-cost production regions where they are made up for re-import into Europe. Poland and Romania in Eastern Europe, Morocco and Tunisia (on the Mediterranean Rim) are amongst the most popular countries where this takes place. Suppliers from these markets have become integrated into European suppliers' evolution towards QR.

Where the QR supplier is located in regions such as Turkey and North Africa – that is, in low-cost areas but with easier access to the European Union – point-of-origin warehousing is often utilized. The customization of garments takes place in the warehouse and they are then cross-docked in the destination markets. This is much cheaper than undertaking the same services in a European warehouse, for example. QR manufacturing can be carried out in markets further afield, but it will usually rely on air freight for effect, thereby pushing up the logistics costs even further.

QR manufacturers must be able to:

- manufacture to shorter product runs with short lead times;
- produce trial runs in limited time;
- ramp up production to full runs in a short period;
- ensure quality;
- ensure fast delivery.

The most successful fashion retailers have been those that manage high-rotation products in small quantities. They also are able to purge their stores of non-selling stock, as it is expensive to store low-rotation garments and there is the opportunity cost related to not being able to stock best-sellers. Therefore there is a growing need for reverse logistics operations right the way through the season and not just at the end, as used to be the case. It may then be possible to redistribute these goods to other stores, rather than sell them at a discount.

As in the high-tech sector, many of the risks, therefore, come about because of the outsourced and remote nature of production, often in developing countries. Efforts by companies such as Spanish retailer Zara have been focused on driving out 'internal' risks, that is, reducing inventory and product lifecycles and doing this in a smart way without driving up labour costs by over-reliance on European suppliers. This has meant of course that transport is critical to the fashion logistics supply chain.

The fashion industry is also at risk from upstream bottlenecks or disruption affecting commodities. For instance, climatic conditions affecting the cotton harvest could have serious implications for the supply of raw materials. Because such conditions tend to impact upon whole regions, the effect is system-wide. This is perhaps one issue that is unique to this particular sector.

Sourcing clothing and textiles from foreign markets also carries with it other risks that are not as evident in other sectors. One of these is the impact of quotas. Quotas exist to limit the amount of goods that can be imported from a certain market. When volumes exceed a certain level, punitive tariffs are applied. This obviously complicates supply chains, as retailers have to plan around these volume restrictions.

In recent years, consumer demands have made the business of supply chain management even more challenging. Commentators report that retailers are no longer able to rely on consumers accepting fashion items reflecting the four distinct seasons (winter, spring, summer and autumn). Instead there are far more in-season changes, meaning that a fashion item may have a shelf life of only a few weeks before consumers move on to new colours, designs or textures. At a micro-level, but still highly significant, is the role that celebrity can play in influencing consumer tastes. Successful retailers are able to replicate the style of a dress worn by the Duchess of Cambridge, for instance, and ensure that it is in their stores within days, using QR manufacturers in Southern or Eastern Europe. This leaves the retailers still attempting to forecast demand and source goods on a quarterly basis trailing in their wake.

Not every retailer has managed the change from locally sourced fashion to global supply chains successfully. In the early 2000s UK retailer Marks & Spencer struggled initially to migrate from its traditionally UK-focused sourcing strategy when pricing pressures forced it to source from low-cost markets. It was not able to maintain a just-in-time delivery schedule to its stores, quality fell and the range of goods on offer looked increasingly incoherent because of the large number of suppliers and designs used. This eventually impacted severely on the company's bottom line.

To reverse this trend, the retailer established a new supply chain strategy. To reduce complexity it focused 75 per cent of its sourcing on a smaller number of key suppliers with whom it built personal relationships and who supplied the company directly, cutting out agents. The product design (taken in-house) and forecasting were directly integrated into supply chain management. Product became far more responsive to customer demands and suppliers became better able to fulfil this demand in a timely fashion.

To further reduce risk, M&S has built relationships with its tier 2 suppliers, improving reliability of raw material supply to its garment manufacturers.

M&S categorizes risks in a slightly different way from other retailers or manufacturers. They are divided into 'acceptable' and 'non-acceptable'. For example, market volatility, changes in fashion, popularity of certain materials, and so on, are looked upon as being acceptable risks – the normal risks of being in the fashion business, so to speak. However, poor management of the supply base, lack of financial stability of the supply base, political risk and the inability to develop a robust and achievable strategy are viewed as 'non-acceptable'.

# Pharma/healthcare

## *Risk profile summary*

Globalization, government legislation and the rise of generic drugs have caused a rethink in how pharmaceutical drug manufacturers operate their businesses. Pharmaceutical drug manufacturers are facing increasing financial pressures to manage their operations more effectively as they face patent expiration of major drugs and the growth of emerging markets such as India, China and Brazil.

Emerging markets such as China, India and Brazil offer opportunities for drug manufacturers for sales of products as well as outsourcing. Many manufacturers are moving into Asia and South America, resulting in cases of operational cuts in the more traditional locations in Europe and the United States.

These changes present many opportunities for profitable growth, but they have also increased the industry's risk profile, not least from the perspective of counterfeiting:

- Many parts of the pharma supply chain are now being outsourced, both in terms of production and logistics. This diminishes the amount of control that manufacturers have over ensuring supply chain integrity.

- Increased production and distribution of pharma goods to emerging markets has exposed supply chains to risk from the perspective of criminal interference.

- Large amounts of money can be made from substituting drugs with counterfeits.

- The distribution of drugs is complex, often involving many wholesalers and distributors. This reduces visibility and often leads to large amounts of inventory redundancy.

- Regulations in emerging markets are complex and subject to frequent change, making compliance challenging.

The trend of relocation of production from high-cost to low-cost manufacturing regions can present risks in itself if it is not handled effectively. Manufacturer Smiths Medical undertook such a relocation of plants from the UK and Germany. Unfortunately this resulted in a temporary supply disruption and sales declined by 1 per cent. The major changes in the structure of the internal supply chain also resulted in a faster utilization of buffer stocks and a slower ramp-up of production than was required to satisfy demand.

## Changing product attribute

Growing global demand for complex drugs is increasing demand for cold-chain solutions, meaning they require refrigeration during transportation and storage. Further, these products may also have a short window of viability, which makes rapid transport essential. Logistics spend for cold-chain products will be driven by increased volumes of products and with faster pharmaceutical market growth in emerging economies.

Airlines have increasingly developed products to make the transit of pharmaceutical products more reliable. For example, British Airways World Cargo's offering, 'Constant Climate', provides an SMS text update service messaging customers at key milestones through the air freight journey. For Constant Climate Active shipments, the exact temperature inside the unit and the condition of the battery are included in the update.

Other airlines have expanded their cold-chain services to utilize dry ice and battery-powered containers to actively regulate temperature levels, regardless of ambient conditions. Customers are able to access online tracking and receive notification alerts via e-mail or mobile phone.

Ocean carriers are also announcing cold-chain solutions for the pharmaceutical industry. For example, APL announced the SmarTemp system for monitoring onboard refrigerated containers via satellite communications.

Packaging technology is continually evolving. Express carriers are now able to carry frozen shipments for the life science industry using packaging that allows products to remain frozen at temperatures below –150 degrees Celsius for up to 10 days, unlike dry ice shipping, which often requires re-icing during transit.

## Supply chain visibility

Because of various government regulations and security issues, the pharmaceutical manufacturer must have as much visibility into its supply chain as possible. However, as the manufacturer expands its operations throughout the world, it becomes difficult to connect to not only its primary suppliers but also to its suppliers' suppliers. According to some manufacturers, the primary method used to gain visibility into suppliers' practices is a periodic audit. Many still manually aggregate the data.

Many industry executives are also concerned about the willingness of suppliers and distributors to provide information to address regulatory requirements. Hurdles exist in implementing the necessary technology, including cost, the difficulty of implementation, lack of industry standards and lack of regulatory requirements and guidance.

Progress is being made as a variety of industry consortia have been established to address these issues. Many logistics providers offer visibility solutions that could benefit manufacturers. They also have introduced specific industry solutions to address visibility of products while in transit, particularly for those products that require temperature monitoring. For example, DB Schenker offers an RFID (radio frequency identification) solution to monitor products' temperature as well as to track the cargo from origin to destination. Both FedEx and UPS offer barcode solutions.

## Cargo crime

Theft of pharmaceuticals that are in the process of being stored or transported is a very major problem for the industry; based on data from FreightWatch International, 13 per cent of all cargo thefts in the United

States involved pharmaceuticals. Not only are there major implications in terms of costs, but even more worryingly, there are issues for patient safety once the drugs re-enter the supply chain (FreightWatch International, 2013).

The major concern is that after the goods have been stolen, they are unlikely to be kept in appropriate conditions, such as in temperature-controlled facilities. Many such goods can be distributed via illegal online pharmacies. Reputable logistics companies have made the point that if there were higher levels of regulation – such as the TAPA (Transport Asset Protection Association) accreditation scheme – it would be far more difficult to deliver these goods on a cross-border basis. Customs or other enforcement agencies would be able to target their attention on consignments carried by logistics companies that did not have necessary validation.

It is not only theft of product that is a problem. Many pharmaceutical companies have reported an increase in the theft of packaging, which can then be used to more effectively pass off counterfeit drugs to retailers and consumers.

## Conclusion

The unbundling and outsourcing of production processes as well as the transportation and storage of products to third-party logistics providers has increased the level of risk in the supply chain for manufacturers. Consequently it has created the necessity for manufacturers and retailers to engage and invest in supplier relationships to ensure that controls, checks and balances are in place at every stage of the extended value chain.

This represents a considerable responsibility for third-party suppliers, including those providing global supply chain and logistics services.

As governments and consumers become far more aware of the origins of the products they buy and the conditions in which they are moved and stored, the issue of supply chain vulnerability will become ever more critical.

According to Dr Vincent Shiers of RQA Group, a consultancy advising the food industry on supply chain security, questions that manufacturers and supply chain companies must be able to answer include:

- What defence processes are in place and are they sufficient?
- Where are the supply chain vulnerabilities?
- What are the plans in the event of a product recall?
- Are there robust reverse logistics capabilities?
- What impact would fraud or tampering have on customer trust and brand equity?

## Summary

Each individual vertical sector supply chain has its own risk profile depending on, inter alia: levels of complexity; product lifecycles, cyclicality and seasonality; internationalization of distribution channels; and exposure to developing markets. While automotive and high-tech supply chains were hit badly by economic shocks and natural disasters, processed food supply chains were compromised in Europe by the substitution of horse meat for beef and in China by the use of toxic chemicals in baby milk. Meanwhile, fashion retailers were rocked by the Rana Plaza incident in which many workers were killed while manufacturing goods for some well-known global brands. In all these cases, the root problem was the lack of supply chain visibility and management preparedness to deal with unexpected events.

## Key points

- 'Tiered' supplier networks in the automotive sector reduce supply chain visibility and leave the sector vulnerable to a range of shocks.
- Global supply chains in the high-tech and automotive sectors expose manufacturers to events (such as natural disasters) in the developing world.
- High-value goods (such as electronic equipment) are targets for cargo crime.
- Low-inventory environments are less resilient than those that have built-in redundancy.
- Increasingly complex supply chains in the processed food sector are vulnerable to substitution of products with lower-cost alternatives, potentially creating public health issues.
- The fashion industry has been criticized for its lack of visibility and action over the conditions for workers in outsourced suppliers' factories, creating reputational risk.

## *Acknowledgement*

I would specifically like to thank Dr Vincent Shiers for his expertise and contribution to the sections on food supply chain vulnerability and threats to the food supply chain.

# Natural disasters and pandemics

04

**OBJECTIVES**

This chapter will familiarize the reader with:

- the types of natural disasters that can occur;
- the biggest natural disasters that have occurred in the past two decades;
- how the public response to Hurricane Katrina highlighted shortcomings in planning and execution;
- the impact that the Japanese tsunami had on high-tech and automotive supply chains, worldwide;
- how the Thai floods of 2011 impacted on global supply chains;
- the potential devastating results that a global pandemic could have on the transport and logistics industry.

## The impact of natural disasters on supply chains

Natural disasters are those that can either result from geo-physical events (such as earthquakes and tsunamis), hydrological (floods), meteorological (tornados, hurricanes, storms, blizzards, and so on) or climatic (heat waves, droughts, and so on). Potentially they could also include space-related events such as solar flares or meteor impact. Obviously in some cases disasters are a combination of multiple categories, in which case the severity of the disaster can be exacerbated. An example of this is Hurricane Katrina – a storm that not only resulted in enormous damage in its own right, but led to the breach of the levees protecting New Orleans from the Mississippi River, causing massive flooding.

Events throughout 2016 provided a cross-section of the disasters that fall into this category. It was estimated by insurer Swiss Re that natural catastrophes accounted for $150 billion of economic losses in that year, caused mainly by earthquakes, floods and wildfires.

In economic terms, the United States is most at risk from meteorological-related disasters because of the location of important economic centres in sub-regions prone to severe weather events. In the past, these have included events such as: Hurricane Matthew in 2016, which resulted in estimated losses of $8 billion; Hurricane Sandy in 2012, costing $70 billion; and, of course, Hurricane Katrina (see below). Hail and thunderstorms can also have devastating impact. In 2016, these cost the US $3.5 billion through crop and property damage. Climatic disasters also have a major impact on the United States. Heat waves can lead to severe crop failures (Swiss Re, 2016).

Outside of the United States, many parts of the world are vulnerable to earthquakes. Even relatively minor earthquake tremors can result in large economic losses. Of course, measuring in humanitarian terms (numbers of casualties, for example), disasters in Asia can far outweigh those in the developed world. However, as they affect predominantly poor areas, the economic damage in dollar terms is low.

In total cost terms, the nine mostly costly recent natural disasters are shown in Table 4.1.

**Table 4.1**   Major recent natural disasters (by economic cost)

| Rank | Year | Natural disaster | Total cost |
|------|------|------------------|------------|
| 1 | 2011 | Tohoku earthquake, Japan | $309 bn |
| 2 | 2005 | Hurricane Katrina, North America | $200 bn |
| 3 | 2008 | Sichuan earthquake, China | $146 bn |
| 4 | 2012 | Hurricane Sandy, North America | $71 bn |
| 5 | 2011 | Thai floods | $46 bn |
| 6 | 1992 | Hurricane Andrew, North America | $32 bn |
| 7 | 2008 | Hurricane Ike, North America | $30 bn |
| 8 | 2010 | Chile earthquakes | $25 bn |
| 9 | 2004 | Hurricane Ivan, North America | $20 bn |

**SOURCE** World Bank, Swiss Re, various (2017)

The catastrophic earthquake in Sichuan province, China, stands out not only for the vast cost of reconstruction, but also for the fact that its impact was highly localized. For global supply chains, the most costly events were the Japanese tsunami of 2011 and the Thai floods. This was because the impact was largely on the upstream distribution – disrupting the flow of goods and production around the world.

The greatest impact of the hurricanes in North America was largely on downstream distribution. Retail and consumer supply chains were severely affected, thus leading to a humanitarian disaster.

Many people believe that the frequency of hydrological and climatic disasters is becoming greater because of the effects of climate change. This has resulted in a response by governments and businesses that has already had material consequences for supply chains. Although the impact of natural disasters is dealt with in this chapter, the broader and long-term risks (and in a few cases, benefits) are discussed at length in Chapter 5.

## The Hurricane Katrina disaster

### The public sector response

Hurricane Katrina, which hit New Orleans in August 2005, had a massive impact on the city, resulting in the flooding of around 80 per cent of the urban area, much of which was below sea level. After moving through the Gulf of Mexico, the hurricane strengthened to a Category 5 storm but weakened slightly and came ashore as a Category 4 storm with winds of 145 mph. The city, with a population of around 500,000, had already been evacuated. In total Hurricane Katrina caused 1,324 deaths – 1,096 in Louisiana and 228 in Mississippi. More than 273,000 people were displaced and 300,000 homes were destroyed.

The US government and its agencies, specifically the Federal Emergency Management Agency (FEMA), came under intense criticism for its slow response to the crisis and lack of effectiveness. Many of the criticisms were directed at the poor logistics management practices that FEMA employed to deal with the supply in the response stage (although the agency was also criticized for its lack of preparedness and ineffectiveness in the recovery stage).

FEMA's initial reaction to the hurricane forecasts was good, according to subsequent assessment of the disaster management. It established a National Response Coordination Center (NRCC) in Washington, DC, and Regional Response Coordination Centers (RRCC) in Atlanta, Georgia, and Denton,

Texas. Emergency Operations Centers were set up in Alabama, Mississippi and Louisiana. In terms of logistics, FEMA opened operational staging areas that received quantities of ice, water, ready meals and other commodities.

However, when the disaster broke, the agency was overwhelmed by the scale of devastation. Roads and bridges were destroyed, making air and water transport the only means possible to distribute aid. Communications were also disrupted because of the destruction of infrastructure including phone lines, cell phone masts and satellite antennae. This hampered the relaying of situational and operational reports up the chain of command.

As the disaster unfolded, FEMA's response started to unravel further. It failed to implement a delivery system capable of distributing goods to victims and emergency services. Its lack of asset visibility system meant that neither FEMA staff nor those from other responding agencies knew where critical supplies were being held or when they would be delivered. In Mississippi, less than 50 per cent of the products ordered by field staff were received. Part of the problem was lack of availability in supplier inventories and the lack of transportation capacity available, largely due to inadequate contingency planning. There were also problems with coordination between FEMA and the states involved in the emergency that led to confusion in establishing priorities, duplicated efforts, mismanagement and widespread inefficiencies.

At the time of the disaster, FEMA operated seven logistics centres across the country. These warehoused essential supplies such as baby formula, tents, blankets, sheeting, water, ready meals as well as emergency generators. In the distribution of these goods to the affected area, FEMA worked with the Department of Transportation to contract suppliers as well as with a range of other public agencies.

One of the main problems identified by subsequent reviews of its response was the lack of asset visibility. In anticipation of Hurricane Katrina, only a quarter to a third of FEMA's vehicles were fitted with tracking devices – according to the agency the funds did not exist to fit out its entire fleet. In many cases, trailers were hired from third parties, and tracking devices for these first had to be deployed and then recovered. Because of software deficiencies it was not possible to tell whether they had unloaded their consignments or changed cargo after they had left base, even for those vehicles that were fitted with them.

Another problem that FEMA faced was the inefficiency of the suppliers it contracted to undertake deliveries. It struggled to meet its own logistics performance measures (a response in 72 hours), even though these were woefully inadequate in terms of the emergency it faced. A response of less than 24 hours would have been more in keeping with the requirements of the situation and public expectation. As a large proportion of its transportation needs were outsourced, FEMA was dependent on the operating practices of its suppliers. There were complaints, however, that transport providers refused to deliver at weekends and holidays; there was a lack of commitment to make a delivery when roads were partially blocked or in poor weather conditions. One solution to this problem would be a larger in-house fleet, although this has significant cost implications as natural disasters cannot be forecasted and for large parts of the year these assets would be underutilized.

Since the crisis, FEMA has taken steps to increase the distribution of its inventory throughout hurricane-prone areas, especially along the Gulf Coast. By moving supplies closer to the possibly affected areas, the problem of its fragile transport network should be mitigated.

Despite a hurricane in the New Orleans area being eminently predictable, the government failed in its duty to plan for such an incident. High levels of bureaucracy, low management skills and a weak distribution strategy resulted in an inept response to the crisis. In certain respects, FEMA actually made the problem worse, by making wrong decisions based on inaccurate information. This contrasted with the private sector response, which was robust, well planned and effective.

## The private sector response

FEMA's uncoordinated, under-resourced and ineffective response to the catastrophe was shown up by an unlikely source – giant US retailer Walmart. While the agency – and indeed the US government – appeared to be caught in the headlights, overwhelmed by the scale of the catastrophe, the private sector company was able to move with much greater levels of flexibility and agility to move supplies to the affected area. Walmart was not the only retailer responding effectively – Home Depot and Lowe's were also exemplary in the way that they handled the crisis. However, its contribution to aid efforts was the most significant.

Within a few days of the hurricane, Walmart had made $20 million in cash donations, moved 1,500 truckloads of free merchandise, and provided food for 100,000 meals. Ahead of the landfall of the hurricane, the retailer had already loaded 45 trucks at its Brookhaven, Mississippi distribution centre. These were dispatched and were delivering in New Orleans the day after the hurricane hit. Walmart's emergency control centre standing staff of six was joined by senior management and rose to about 50 dedicated to overseeing the response. (Home Depot had also anticipated the landfall of the hurricane and had set up a 'war-room' at its headquarters in Atlanta three days beforehand.)

Using its own weather forecasting software, Walmart was able to track the path of the hurricane and plan accordingly for damage to its own retail premises. All this was happening at least five days ahead of the hurricane's landfall.

The retailer, of course, has many advantages over the supply chain of the government agency:

- It has total visibility of its distribution network, allowing it to track and trace its vehicles and their shipments.
- It has a fully owned transportation network, ensuring that management of assets and drivers is efficient.
- It has a dense distribution network already in place, including huge distribution facilities.
- Management is strong and coordinated.

The response was strong and effective. One mayor of an affected city stated that, 'the only lifeline… was the Wal-Mart stores. We didn't have looting on a mass scale because Wal-Mart showed up with food and water so our people could survive' (Leonard, 2005).

Walmart was not immune to the problems that were encountered by FEMA. Its inventory management system in the region was rendered unusable because of power failures. However, employees were able to relay information up the chain of command using satellite phones, which had been issued specifically for this contingency in the days ahead of the storm.

The flexibility of this approach allowed products such as mops, brushes and bleach to be dispatched when it was realized that house flooding was going to be a major problem. Walmart was also fast-moving in reopening its stores. Although 126 stores were shut down at the height of the crisis, along with two distribution centres, within 10 days all but 15 were open.

## Hurricane Katrina: impact on transportation and economy

Although the humanitarian aspect of the disaster obviously attracted most of the media attention, there was a major economic impact to the city and region due to the disruption to port activities. The Ports of New Orleans and nearby South Louisiana handle the largest volumes of bulk tonnage in the world and about 15 per cent of all US exports. Both ports are critical in the facilitation of grain and foodstuff exports from the Midwest as well as oil and petroleum products from the Gulf of Mexico. Trade with Latin America is particularly important.

Rail transport was critically impacted by the damage caused by the hurricane, with operator CSX the most affected. Two-thirds of its track was damaged between New Orleans and Mobile, Alabama, and five bridges were made inoperable between Biloxi, Mississippi, and New Orleans. The operator estimated that reconstruction costs were $300 million.

CSX responded to the situation by re-routing its trains onto competitors' tracks, and in many cases sending them around the affected region to the north. This had cost implications of its own, both in terms of additional operating costs and also in lost time for shippers.

The effect of the disaster post-Katrina was also felt acutely in terms of transport jobs. It is estimated that around 3,500 port workers lost their jobs in the aftermath of the storm, with a loss of wages of $136 million (Dolfman, Wasser and Bergman, 2007).

There were other indirect consequences. Oil output in the Gulf of Mexico was shut down, driving the cost of a barrel of oil for a time to over $70. This had a temporary impact on supply chain costs across the world.

The period of acute disruption in terms of parcels delivery was felt for three weeks. Twenty-one days after the event, UPS resumed service to parts of New Orleans' Central Business District and sections of the French Quarter. Outside New Orleans, UPS had reopened 21 of its 22 affected facilities in the region and restored delivery service to every zip code in Mississippi and Alabama. The company also resumed daily air flights into and out of Louis Armstrong New Orleans International Airport.

## Superstorm Sandy: impact on the transportation sector

In humanitarian terms, the effects of 'Superstorm Sandy' were nowhere near as bad as Hurricane Katrina. However, it had a major economic impact, not least because of its disruption of transportation.

'Superstorm' Sandy had tracked its way across the Caribbean, causing substantial damage in Haiti, Jamaica and Cuba before crossing the Eastern Seaboard of the United States on 29 October 2012. In total 24 states were affected, with some of the worst damage being experienced in New York City, where a storm surge led to extensive flooding.

If that was not enough, on the western end of the storm, up to three feet of snow fell in parts of West Virginia, Virginia and North Carolina. The storm's effects could also be felt as far south as Atlanta, Georgia, as winds were recorded gusting over 55 mph.

In anticipation of the storm, ports, airports, rail, bridges and subways shut down. The Port of Virginia closed, but reopened the following day. However, the nation's third-busiest cargo container seaport, New York–New Jersey, remained closed for several days. The port closed at midnight on 29 October but, because of electrical problems, wind and flood damage, it was slow to reopen. Port Elizabeth was the first to reopen, followed by Port Newark Container Terminal and the Global Terminal in Jersey City. By 6 November all terminals had reopened. The storm disrupted shipping right along the Eastern Seaboard, a significant issue as it occurred in the middle of peak retail season.

Over 16,000 flights were cancelled because of the storm. New York's three main airports closed, forcing flights to be re-routed to other airports. The problems express carrier DHL faced were typical of the type of disruption caused by the storm. It was forced to hold all shipments for New York in Cincinnati until the airport reopened. UPS shut down its package sorts at its Philadelphia air hub for two days. Because of that, inbound flights from Europe, which normally would land at the Philadelphia air hub, landed in Louisville. UPS gateways at Newark and JFK near New York City were shut down for the longest period.

CSX's rail network closed from Richmond, Virginia, to Albany, New York. The company halted traffic originating on other lines travelling to most points between Boston and Philadelphia as a means to reduce congestion. Meanwhile, Norfolk Southern tracks were flooded in some locations; not only did it face floodwater, but also snow in West Virginia.

For the trucking community, most bridges reopened quickly as well as primary roads. However, many secondary roads remained closed as debris such as fallen trees still blocked the roads.

One of the consequences of the extensive power outage that affected the region was that many petrol stations were forced to close. This was a major problem for emergency services, relief organizations and the private sector as a shortage of fuel impacted upon mobility. In response, a logistics-related relief organization, the American Logistics Aid Network, worked with the American Automobile Association (AAA) and OPISNet, a fuel price reporting network, to generate and disseminate reports showing which stations were pumping fuel.

## The Tohoku, Japan earthquake and tsunami

The impact of Japan's 2011 earthquake and tsunami on global supply chains was dramatic, with production across a whole range of sectors badly affected. The Japanese electronics sector was amongst the hardest hit. Output of NAND flash memory, on which new consumer electronic equipment depends, was disrupted, albeit on a temporary basis. Many wafer fabrication plants, supplying the semi-conductor industry, remained closed while aftershocks continued to take place.

More surprising were the effects on other industries. The Japanese automotive sector traditionally has a highly localized supply chain, with mechanical component manufacturers located next to major assembly plants. Although these supplier parks weren't affected, production was halted all the same.

One reason why production at many of these automotive plants was compromised is the increasing number of electronic components in new motor vehicles. Now a significant part of the value of new cars, electronic component sourcing differs from that of mechanical parts. Increasingly, the more complex assemblies are sourced globally, with physically small yet important and expensive products often moved by air freight from distant production locations. This illustrates an emerging trend in the automotive supply chain.

Plants beyond Japan suffered as well. For example, Toyota's plant in the UK shut down production because of uncertainties over component supply. Renault's Samsung plant in South Korea also slowed output because of problems accessing its supply chain, part of which it shares with Nissan. In fact, supply chains in the electronics sector, heavily dependent on Japanese production, were affected right across Asia. There were reports of key electronic components being in short supply as leading electronic manufacturers such as Sony, Sharp and Panasonic shut plants.

However, things could have been worse. More widespread disruption was prevented by global supplies of flash memory on hand having built up over the previous two months. Manufacturers were also able to shift production from Japan to facilities outside the country.

Japan also has a large chemical sector, much of which is located on the coast. Many of these facilities were damaged, with Dow Chemical reporting one of its facilities flooded.

# Tsunami: Impact on automotive manufacturers

## Toyota

Toyota, Japan's largest automotive manufacturer, was worst affected by the disaster. Its Japanese factories were shut for a month in the immediate aftermath of the earthquake, and for the next three months produced only a half of normal volumes.

In the United States, 150 stock-keeping units (skus) were left in short supply, which meant that production was initially operating at just 30 per cent of capacity. This increased to 70 per cent in June and returned to normal by the end of 2011. Factories in Europe and China were also affected.

## Nissan

Renault-Nissan had problems with 40 of its key suppliers in addition to its own Iwaki engine plant. The parts' shortage resulted in its US and Mexican factories being shut for a week. Priority was given to production of its best-selling models, but volumes of cars delivered to the US markets slumped in the aftermath by more than three-quarters.

## Honda

Honda suspended production of three of its most popular models in the United States in addition to closing its Japanese facilities. Volumes produced at its UK, Indian, US and Canadian plants dropped by 50 per cent.

## General Motors

It was not only the Japanese auto manufacturers that were impacted by the disaster. GM suspended production at a facility in Louisiana because of an interruption of supply to air flow sensors produced by Hitachi. This had a knock-on effect at an engine plant, where there were temporary lay-offs.

## Chrysler

Chrysler seems to have been the least affected by the supply chain disruption. It faced parts shortages four to five months after the event and brought its annual plants shutdown forward to June from July in order to allow suppliers to catch up with orders and managers to identify alternative sources. It was also impacted by the shortage of pigments.

> **Ford**
>
> Several of Ford's plants were closed for two weeks, including those in Taiwan, the Philippines, China and South Africa, because of a shortage of parts. Factories in Europe and the United States (Louisville) were closed for a week. The company also had problems with sourcing Xirallic pigments.

## The Thailand floods: impact on high-tech supply chains

In 2011 Thailand suffered one of the worst floods in five decades. The floods began in July, but steadily worsened throughout October, and were mainly limited to northern and eastern areas around Bangkok. However, these affected areas were home to hundreds of manufacturing facilities that were completely flooded.

Japanese car makers that had just started to recover from the earthquake and tsunami were faced with shortages of key parts made in Thailand. Toyota and Honda both had to halt production at facilities even in North America because their Thai suppliers were flooded.

The hard disk drive manufacturing sector was particularly affected; Thailand is the second largest market for production of hard disk drives after China. Toshiba, the fourth largest producer of hard disk drives, halted all of its production in Thailand. Seagate was less impacted and did not have to stop production because its factories were in the northeast, where flooding was less severe. Shortages of supplies lasted into the first quarter of 2012, and prices, at their height, increased 20–40 per cent (Wilcox, 2011).

As a result of the disruption, semi-conductor chip manufacturer Intel warned that its revenues and profits would be lower than expected because of shortages of hard disk drives in the industry. Because of the closures, Intel's customers were not able to source sufficient volumes of hard disk drives to meet demand, and cut down on their microprocessor inventories.

Intel was not the only manufacturer struggling. Dell also missed sales targets in its quarterly results due, in part, to shortages of hard disk drives. However, management said that it had made strategic purchases of inventory elsewhere in an attempt to overcome this problem. This inevitably came at a cost.

Thailand supplies about 40 per cent of the world's market of hard disk drives. The supply chain problems that high-tech manufacturers faced reopened the debate over the wisdom of sourcing from suppliers clustered in such a vulnerable area.

## The Eyjafjallajökull volcano

The eruption on 14 April 2010 of Iceland's Eyjafjallajökull volcano (the second eruption in a month) caused havoc throughout Europe and beyond because of clouds of ash that were blown across Europe, resulting in the decision by air traffic control regulators to shut airspace on the grounds of safety. The impact of this first eruption in 190 years continued even after airspace restrictions were lifted.

The regulators' decision to shut down airspace in Britain, Norway, the Netherlands, Germany, Austria, Belgium, Denmark, Finland, France, Germany, Latvia, Luxembourg, Poland, Slovakia, the Czech Republic, Bulgaria, Sweden and Switzerland cost airlines some $200 million per day from cancelled flights and caused the European economy to suffer significant losses in lost business.

The obvious reaction by logistics planners was to use other modes of transport for intra-European movements, such as roads and short sea shipping. The main problem was handling inter-continental traffic. As a contingency, freight forwarders and airlines set up hub activities in airports in southern Europe. For example, UPS flew some freight to Istanbul and moved it into Europe by road. Other providers used North African or even Middle Eastern airports. The issue with using facilities in the Mediterranean, however, was one of capacity. It was impossible to move the combined volumes of the Northern European airports through a handful of airports in Southern Europe or North Africa.

The supply chain consequences were felt further afield than in Europe, and nowhere more acutely than in East African markets. Here perishable air cargo, such as fresh fruit and flowers, backed up at airports and, given the lack of appropriate temperature-controlled storage facilities, much of it was ruined. This caused considerable hardship to exporters and their employees.

All flights to and from Europe were affected on all routes and many were cancelled. Specifically for the trade 'Far East westbound', this situation impacted on already tight capacity and led to additional bottlenecks. Some carriers in China stopped accepting cargo because of unavailable warehouse space at the airports, and grounded most flights.

**Figure 4.1**     Map of air space affected by ash clouds from Eyjafjallajökull

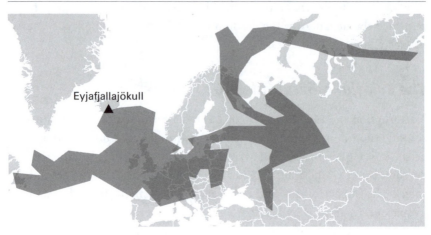

**CASE STUDY**  Gap's approach to natural disasters

Global fashion retailer Gap assesses risk at an enterprise, brand and asset level. The company has developed a framework to manage risk, including social, regulatory impact and climate change. On each of the major risk factors, it maps its own preparedness against the potential size of the impact. The risks are measured on the basis of financial, material and reputational impact. Gap has a wide range of facilities. These include retail outlets, data centres, call centres as well as Gap International Sourcing hub and spoke facilities.

   At the enterprise level, risk is monitored on an ongoing and annual basis and any change is reported to the board. At an asset level, Gap deploys business continuity planning (BCP) teams, which, amongst other issues, address the potential impact of extreme weather events.

   One initiative being developed is at the textile mill stage, where ways to reduce the levels of water, energy and chemical usage are being assessed.

   Each year Gap undertakes an annual risk assessment that involves interviewing 70 senior managers. Based on the findings, the internal audit team summarizes the most important risks to the enterprise. Gap's social and environmental responsibility team, with direct links to Gap's CEO and its Executive VP of Supply Chain, works with the Environmental Council, which meets quarterly to identify and prioritize risks. Other events are dealt with as they arise.

In terms of meteorological events, Gap uses the predictive and actual models developed by the National Oceanic and Atmospheric Administration (NOAA), which enable Gap, combined with the utilization of GoogleEarth, to track emerging weather threats.

BCP also relies on Gap's San Francisco-based headquarters incident command structure (SFHQ ICS), which is particularly important in the tracking of hurricanes in relation to store locations. This information is then disseminated throughout the organization to prepare as well as deal with the impact of severe weather on staff and facilities.

It is the role of the BCP to produce company-wide programmes that address preparedness, emergency response, crisis management and business recovery. The company has in place incident command structures that provide the tactical capabilities in the run-up to and during any serious business interruption. This will include plans and documentation, as well as training, which will allow for the better protection of the business, its reputation, assets and employees.

Specifically in terms of extreme weather, Gap has acknowledged that adverse conditions have the potential to disrupt its operations in stores or its supply chain. Over the past two years it has seen disruption from flooding, tropical storms, hurricanes in the United States, typhoons in Asia and tornados. In particular, its retail operations in Japan were affected by the earthquake and tsunami of 2011. This was not only because of physical difficulties, but also because of the impact of depressed consumer spend in the country.

## Summary

It can be seen from the case studies above that natural disasters can occur in any region of the world at any time. Unfortunately in most cases the examples highlighted demonstrate the lack of preparedness shown by governments and, with a few exceptions, by supply chain companies. Often the sheer extent of a disaster can overwhelm authorities, laying bare poor communications and lack of coordination between different governments, agencies and other parties involved in the recovery effort.

Some events are predictable – such as hurricanes in the south-eastern US or floods on flood plains in Asia. Others are more difficult or even impossible to predict, such as the eruption of Iceland's Eyjafjallajökull volcano. However, as outlined in Chapter 1, this does not mean that all parties involved should not take steps to mitigate risks and build a resilient response to whatever situation may arise.

# Pandemics

While the likelihood of a global pandemic should not be overstated, there are serious concerns that modern supply chains are uniquely vulnerable to disruption from such an outbreak. These worries focus on two distinct issues. First, and in humanitarian terms less importantly, a widespread outbreak would have an immediate and severe impact on the financial performance of all companies that operate within any sort of extended supply chain.

At a macro-economic level, the logistics industry, whose growth is directly proportional to economic activity, would be affected by a slowdown in global demand and global supply. It should be noted that this may occur in any case because of fear of a pandemic, even if in reality a widespread outbreak fails to materialize. Examples of this were seen in Mexico, where the swine flu outbreak of 2009 was first identified. The authorities cancelled sporting events, and people avoided non-essential socializing, with a corresponding impact on the trade of hotels, bars, restaurants and clubs.

The Mexican government also suspended production at many industrial locations, in order to prevent the disease being transmitted throughout the workforce. This impacted upon supply chains, particularly those of US manufacturers producing components in the country. The Mexican government estimated that GDP fell by 0.3–0.5 per cent and was responsible for delaying the recovery from the global recession of the time. Luckily the global pandemic did not spread to the extent that many governments and health agencies feared.

One of the main problems for the industry (and wider economy and society), if the pandemic had become significantly worse, would have been the spread of disease to drivers and other logistics staff. Those manufacturers that were able to keep working would find that they could not move outbound goods. Most, however, would find that lack of spare parts delivery and inbound materials would lead to the suspension of production, especially since many manufacturers now keep only a few hours' inventory on hand and rely on a continuous supply of components throughout the day. In such a scenario, governments might also take the step of closing borders to prevent people from spreading the virus internationally and this would directly disrupt the movement of goods.

The air cargo industry is especially susceptible to the fear of a pandemic as much as the reality. Even if no ban is imposed on air travel, passengers may choose not to visit infected regions. As so much freight is transported in the holds of passenger aircraft, capacity would be severely affected should airlines reduce or suspend services completely.

Aside from the economic impact of a pandemic, there is the risk that supply chains may not prove robust enough to deal with the humanitarian consequences of such a widespread disaster. The supply chains that have been engineered to suit the needs of business may prove too fragile to face the stress of a major disruptive event such as a pandemic. In effect, modern supply chains may prove to be part of the problem, and not the solution.

Consumers are increasingly dependent on sophisticated supply chains to provide them with a whole range of essential everyday products, the most important being food, fuel, pharmaceuticals and medical peripheries. Over the last two decades the industry mantra has been to drive down stock levels through techniques such as just-in-time deliveries. This has placed increasing reliance on the physical distribution element of the supply chain, to deliver the goods when and where they are required. If transport systems break, so do supply chains. Although of course this has always been the case, these days the margins for error are much smaller.

To illustrate this point, a 2004 study undertaken by Heriot-Watt University examined the vulnerability of the UK's economy from disruption to its road freight network (McKinnon, 2006). The study involved the development of a fictitious scenario that envisaged a stoppage by all heavy goods vehicles for at least a week. Although the authors did not specifically develop the scenario with a pandemic in mind, a disease that affected a large proportion of the population would inevitably have an impact on the movement of goods vehicles. The UK government has itself modelled a national framework response based on a worst-case scenario of 50 per cent of the population falling ill and it may be supposed that mobile workers – drivers – could find themselves disproportionately affected because of their necessary movement around the country.

Within their scenario, the authors believed that the effects of a stoppage on the consumer would be felt almost immediately, with fast moving consumer goods and food items running out in supermarkets very quickly. Retailers would be unable to replenish these stocks from their regional distribution centres. Within a week fuel supplies would run out at petrol stations, making mobility difficult or impossible, and there would be localized disruption to power and water supplies as spare and critical parts failed to be delivered.

The Heriot-Watt study did not specifically deal with the impact of a pandemic on supply chains. However, if it had done so, the authors may well have considered that its effects on healthcare services would have been even more extreme than those they suggested. As it is, they foresaw that hospitals and surgeries would be limited to emergencies only, with hospital laundry, food and waste being impacted in the short term.

The UK is particularly vulnerable to such a stoppage because of its success in reducing the amount of inventory held at various points of the supply chain. In 1986 the number of times that manufacturers, retailers and wholesalers rotated their stock was 7.2 per annum. By 2001 this had increased to 10.5. Grocery retailing is also characterized by high frequencies of deliveries. One estimate puts the number of deliveries of fresh food to a typical supermarket as over 11 times per week.

The UK may be more highly exposed to such a crisis than other countries because of its dependence on the low inventory supermarket chains for a large proportion of the food and essential goods it consumes. Other markets in Europe have a higher predominance of 'hypermarket' stores, which keep a much greater proportion of goods in stock on the premises. However, there is no doubt that the trend towards JIT delivery, and the adoption of other supply chain management techniques, is increasing the risk of such a disruption to all economies.

It is possible to conclude that the supply chains that provide the backbone to the modern global economy may well prove to be its Achilles' heel, should there be an incidence of a global pandemic of disastrous proportions. Stocks that ran down quickly would be impossible to replace, magnifying the hardships faced by consumers. However, the situation is not totally bleak. Until there is a complete breakdown in physical distribution, the complex supply chains that have been developed over the years will prove the most efficient way to distribute products, including medicines, to those areas in most need. In the aftermath of Hurricane Katrina, which hit New Orleans in 2005, it was the retailer Walmart that attracted praise for its agility and speed in distributing relief supplies in the affected region rather than the slow and sclerotic reaction of governmental organizations.

## Summary

Natural disasters, including hurricanes, flooding and earthquakes, have had a critical impact on the supply chain and logistics industry over the past two decades. Globalization has encouraged manufacturers and retailers to source products from developing markets, where labour is cheap. However, this has increased their exposure to disruption from geo-physical, hydrological or climatic events. Localized disruption can have a catastrophic impact when 'clusters' of industry suppliers are affected, as seen in Thailand and Japan. However, it is not just developing countries that are at risk. Major hurricanes and storms in the United States had a major economic and humanitarian impact, exacerbated in some cases by the failings of the government response.

## Key points

- Natural disasters can be categorized into geo-physical, hydrological, meteorological or climatic events.

- The largest hurricane to hit the US in recent years was estimated to cost the country $200 billion and demonstrated a lack of planning by the government.

- The private sector response was far more effective, with major retailers, such as Walmart, showing governments how a humanitarian response should be undertaken through planning and flexible logistics operations.

- Lack of supply chain visibility at a lower-tier level resulted in localized events in Asia disrupting production right across the world.

- Pandemics could severely disrupt transport and logistics operations because of the labour-intensive nature of the sector.

# Climate change and emissions policy    05

**OBJECTIVES**

This chapter will familiarize the reader with:

- the types of disruption that can occur to logistics and supply chains because of climate change;
- how transport infrastructure projects in many parts of the world are being made 'climate-proof';
- the high-risk areas and many specific problems faced in North America, Europe and Asia in terms of infrastructure vulnerability;
- the logistics opportunities that climate change could provide in some regions, such as the opening of the North East Passage in the Arctic;
- strategies employed by retailers and manufacturers to adapt to climate change;
- latest emissions regulations and changing public policy;
- specific regulations being introduced to limit vehicle access to cities in Europe, the Americas and Asia;
- what this will mean for logistics and supply chain operations.

## Climate change

Many of the disasters identified in Chapter 4 relate to weather conditions such as hurricanes, storms and the associated flooding. Most scientists believe that these meteorological events are becoming more frequent in occurrence because of climate change, whatever the underlying cause of this may be. Recent intergovernmental conferences have affirmed the need for governments around the world and, crucially, businesses to commit to reduce their carbon emissions, this being a likely cause of global warming.

Consequently, many companies have put in place overarching plans to implement carbon mitigation strategies through initiatives such as greenhouse gas emissions reduction. Mitigation strategies take many forms, including maximizing product energy efficiency, reducing and eliminating sensitive materials from products, or providing recycling options for customers. It could also involve improving transport and logistics efficiencies, including streamlining transportation networks to reduce transit times, minimize air freight, and reduce emissions. Packaging can be designed to minimize box size and to increase recycled content of materials along with recyclability.

Although this is a commendable long-term approach to reducing the greenhouse gases that may be responsible for climate change, it is only sensible for companies to identify and prepare solutions that make their supply chains more resilient to the challenges that extreme weather conditions, including floods and drought, are already having.

## Climate change adaptation

'Adaptation' has been defined by the Intergovernmental Panel on Climate Change (IPCC) as the initiatives and measures to reduce the vulnerability of natural and human systems against actual or expected climate change effects (IPCC, 2014).

The impacts of extreme weather are varied and can include the following:

- Increased rainfall leads to flooding, which also threatens the integrity of road and railways as well as bridges.
- Storm surges and high winds affect the whole range of transport infrastructure.
- Rising sea levels affect coastal road/rail infrastructure as well as ports and airports located close to the sea (for example Hong Kong Airport).
- Increased temperatures can lead to the melting of tar and bitumen, degrading road surfaces. This means that there are increased maintenance costs.
- Increased temperatures can also result in the warping of bridges, rail tracks and other structures.
- Extremely low temperatures lead to the creation of pot holes as water in cracks expands and contracts. This also means greater costs in terms of repair.

- Excessive heat also has an impact on 'hot and high' airports. The higher the temperature, the longer the runway needed for an aircraft to get airborne. Consequently at some airports in periods of extreme temperature, aircraft are required to reduce their payloads and may even be grounded.

- Increased severity of snowstorms and ice can disrupt airports as well as road and rail services.

- Extreme temperatures can affect the performance of engines on motor vehicles as well as train engines and mechanical features of rolling stock. They can also result in points failures on rail networks, leading to widespread disruption.

- High winds can close bridges and damage overhead electric cables on railways as well as bring down trees blocking roads.

- Lightning strikes can impact on information and communication systems such as mobile phone networks.

To address these issues, climate-proofing projects may need to be undertaken, or in a very worst case, facilities abandoned.

Effective adaptation could take the form of using more heat-resistant materials in road surfaces or rail tracks that are better able to cope with contraction and expansion in extreme temperatures. It also could be as simple as increasing the size of drainage ditches alongside roads or increasing the camber to ensure water runoff is efficient. The design of resilient transport infrastructure will be an important issue to take into account in the future.

The needs of operators that use the infrastructure will also need to be taken into account by governments. In the case of snow and ice, it may be that better clearance plans are developed and more money is invested in snow ploughs to clear roads, railways and airports or that stocks of grit are always kept on hand by local authorities. To deal with storm surges and flood water, investment will be needed in river defences and levees.

It would seem that, although most governments are aware of climate change as a potential threat to much of their transport infrastructure, few policies are being adopted to address this threat. Little research has been undertaken that can provide data on the costs of making transport infrastructure climate-change-proof, compared with doing nothing.

However, this is starting to change. In one project in Bangladesh, the costs/benefits of raising the proposed road embankment level from 0.5 metre to 1 metre was taken into account and found to be cost-effective. A methodology developed by the Institute of Development Studies has helped with this process (IDS, 2009). Proper impact assessments of future climate change are clearly required when looking at potential transport projects, and incorporating enhanced standards is one option that can be considered. However, although this is useful for new infrastructure, it would be more difficult to climate-proof existing bridges, roads, airports and ports.

## North American vulnerability to climate change

One of the main reasons why the United States is so highly exposed to the effects of climate change is the large number of people and economic centres located near the coast. Many of these areas are regularly impacted by natural events such as hurricanes in the Gulf of Mexico. As populations are forecasted to grow in coastal areas in the coming years, and as these events become more severe and more frequent, the potential for catastrophic consequences obviously increases. It is estimated by the US Census Bureau that 53 per cent of the population live in counties with coastal areas, despite these areas making up just 17 per cent of the US land mass. Population density is also higher in these areas than elsewhere in the country.

The situation will be compounded by rising sea levels, which many experts now believe are inevitable. This will leave these high-density population areas more vulnerable to storm surges. In terms of transport infrastructure, the US Transportation Studies Board (TSB) believes that 60,000 miles of roads are already exposed to periodic storms and wave action (Committee on Climate Change and US Transportation, 2008).

The TSB judges that the following transport nodes are at risk:

- Six out of the top ten US freight gateways (by value of shipments) are vulnerable to a rise in sea level.
- Seven of the top ten ports (by tonnage) are located on the Gulf Coast and exposed to storms.
- Oil and gas industry (production and shipping) is located in the Gulf and is vulnerable to disruption.

As an example, the port of Gulfport, a major competitor to the Port of New Orleans, was almost entirely wiped out by a storm surge caused by Hurricane Katrina in 2005.

It is not just coastal areas, though, that are at risk. Increased levels of precipitation, and also increased intensity, can produce flooding, especially throughout river systems. For example, in 1993, the so-called 'Great Flood' disrupted road, rail and marine traffic across the Mississippi and Missouri

Rivers, impacting an area from St Louis to Kansas City and as far north as Chicago. A more recent flooding event is detailed below.

It is not only flooding that is foreseen as a problem. It is also being predicted that some areas of North America will endure periods of much drier weather, especially inland. This could reduce river levels to the extent that river traffic is not able to operate. The St Lawrence Seaway is one inland waterway at risk; in 2000–01, levels fell to their lowest in 35 years. One measure of adaptation to this will be increased dredging required to keep the river system open for freight.

The Mississippi River is also at risk. In 2011 it flooded, whereas the following year levels fell dramatically as a result of one of the worst droughts in over 50 years. The river is a primary transportation means for much of the US's agriculture, petroleum, steel, coal and other bulk commodities. In fact, according to the American Waterways Operators, about 60 per cent of the United States' grain exports and one-fifth of its coal are transported along the nation's inland waterway system (Ti, 2011b).

At one point during the drought near Memphis, Tennessee, the river fell to about 13 feet below its normal depth. In Vicksburg, Mississippi, it was more than 20 feet below and overall the river was 55 feet below 2011 flood levels. As a result, barge, tugboat and towboat operators had to change how they moved goods up and down the river. Many had to lighten loads for fear of getting stuck. As the drought worsened, the river got narrower and shallower forcing barges to sail more closely past each other, often slowing their speeds. In some sections of the river, only one-way traffic was able to move through (Transport Intelligence, 2012).

The result of lighter loads and slower speeds caused by low river levels will likely drive up transportation costs, making waterways less competitive against road. If these extremes of weather make using rivers less economic (floods followed by droughts), there is likely to be a switch to road traffic, which could have environmental implications of its own.

## US floods impact on barge, truck and rail traffic

Because of heavy rains in May 2011, the Mississippi River experienced one of its worst floods since 1927, and the waters did not completely recede until mid-June. The river, an important means of transport for bulk cargo such as grains, coal, timber and iron, transports about 550 million tons of cargo annually. On a typical day, about 600 barges move along the river, with a single vessel carrying as much cargo as 70 tractor-trailers or 17 railcars. Over 60 per cent of the United States' grain exports are transported via the river to the port of New Orleans. The flooding seriously disrupted waterway commerce, delaying barge traffic and forcing some cargo to be trucked overland.

To reduce pressure on the levees, the US Coast Guard closed a 15-mile stretch of the river to cargo vessels. The economic impact of this was estimated to be at around $300 million a day. Parts of major highways, such as Interstate 40 in Arkansas, were closed to traffic because of the flooding. Truck carriers were detoured to longer routes through Arkansas and around Memphis, Tennessee.

Railroad companies also experienced delays. Sections of BNSF's track in Missouri were closed for several days. Both Union Pacific and Norfolk Southern commented that disruptions from the flooding reduced their May freight volumes.

## Specific impacts of climate change in North America

The retreat of permafrost in Alaska has resulted in the subsidence of road and rail infrastructure. It is also affecting runways, which are numerous throughout the sparsely populated state. Ice roads that connect many settlements have shorter seasons before they melt.

In the rest of the United States, droughts will create the conditions for wildfires, which could have an impact on transiting roads and railways. Water levels in the Great Lakes are expected to reduce, meaning that ships will be unable to carry loads as heavy as today. This will result in costs increasing for Canadian shippers in the region by between 13 and 29 per cent by 2050, depending on how far the water level falls. Dredging would offset some of these capacity issues but would itself have implications in terms of cost and environmental damage.

Also at risk are the middle reaches of the Mississippi, where there are no locks or dams. Dependent on the underlying river flows, droughts could critically damage the river as a viable mode of transport.

Some already 'hot and high' airports in the United States will be affected by temperature increases. A study found that a Boeing 747 could lose about 17 per cent of its payload capacity at Denver, Colorado, airport and 9 per cent at Phoenix, Arizona, airport by 2030 because of temperature increases.

A change in precipitation type will also be disruptive in some parts of North America. In California, for example, it has been found that there would be major implications for infrastructure if existing levels of snow start falling as rain. The additional runoff would have the effect of undermining roads and railways and result in more landslips and floods.

A rise in sea level could result in the silting up of certain waterways. One such waterway at risk is that using the inshore waters of the Gulf Coast. Some research has shown this passage could disappear completely as sediment rises, 'barrier islands' are submerged and land subsides.

## Impact of climate change on Europe

In Europe particular attention in terms of the impact of climate change has been paid to inland waterways. Europe's main river in terms of shipping is the Rhine. It is already very prone to flooding as well as on occasion to diminishing water levels due to drought. In 2013, flooding closed the river to barge traffic for about five days on sections from Koblenz in Germany to Basel in Switzerland, disrupting, inter alia, oil and chemical shipments. Not only does disruption to shipping impact upon customer service, but the capacity constraints that it creates also push up rates.

This contrasts acutely with the situation in 2011. Then a prolonged period of drought in the region meant that water levels fell to a point where the use of barges was unviable.

A study by EC-funded agency ECCONET (Effects of Climate Change on the Inland Waterway Networks) concludes that there will be little disruption to intermodal barge traffic from rising temperatures until the end of the twenty-first century (Heyndrickx and Breemersch, 2012). This is not to say that extreme weather does not already have an impact. The study found that in drought years, the cost of intermodal barge transport rises by 6–7 per cent compared with normal years. However, this is just part of the normal pattern of the weather.

Another European-funded research project, 'WEATHER', which reviewed over 1,000 damage reports produced in six countries, as well as an assessment of available transport operators, estimated that weather-related events cost the transport industry €2.5 billion a year between 1998 and 2010. There were a further €1 billion of indirect costs borne by other sectors as a result of the disruption to transport (this includes freight and passenger). Other projects suggest that this may be a conservative estimate if accidents and other externalities are taken into account.

During this period rail transport was the worst affected sector, with Eastern Europe and Scandinavia impacted by hydrological events. In the future Britain may well be amongst the most vulnerable countries in Europe because of flooding. Road disruption was spread right across the European region, although mountain areas were particularly vulnerable.

For the region as a whole, climate change is expected to result in greater levels of snow in Northern Europe, whereas Eastern and Central Europe (as well as the Alpine region) will warm up. The Mediterranean region can expect stronger winds and hotter temperatures, with heat waves becoming more intense and prolonged.

The 'EWENT' project suggested that rail is likely to be the worst affected of all the modes (Leviäkangas and Saarikivi, 2012). However, it is worthwhile putting these additional costs in the wider context of technological and economic development. This suggests that climate change in most parts of Europe will have little impact on wider supply chain costs. Overall, it has been found that those countries with weak infrastructure, ageing transport assets and dense populations and congestion face faster rising transport costs as a result of climate change.

## Impact of climate change on Asia

In South East Asia, climate change is likely to manifest itself in increased summer precipitation and increased frequency and intensity of tropical cyclones, while in northern Asia, for example on the Tibetan plateau, heavier winter precipitation of snow is expected. In Central Asia, precipitation is expected to reduce, leading to more periods of drought and heat waves.

Climate-proofing of certain transport infrastructure projects in Asia, such as the design of Avatiu Harbour in Cook Island and coastal infrastructure projects in Vietnam, has been undertaken. Depending on the climate change models, sea levels are expected to increase by 18–59 centimetres in the region. Islands in the Indian Ocean as well as the Pacific Ocean are expected to be the most affected.

Other examples of climate-proofing have been the increased height of bridges to take into account surges from rivers in spate following downpours.

Bangladesh, Vietnam and the Pacific Islands are considered to be at most risk from climate change because of their low-lying topography (Regmi and Hanaoka, 2009). Examples of severe weather events in Asia in the last 11 years include:

- Aceh flood, Indonesia, 2006;
- Cyclone Nargis, Myanmar, 2008;
- Typhoon Morakot, Taiwan, 2009;
- Thai floods, 2011.

Steps can be undertaken to reduce the impact of the floods, but in many parts of the region a lack of resources has frustrated attempts to improve initiatives such as flood defences. However, some efforts have been made to treat building materials, for example, to make bridges or road foundations more resistant to flood water. Roads themselves have been raised above flood water levels to allow transportation to continue even throughout a sustained period of flooding.

## Benefits of climate change

Climate change is not an entirely negative factor for supply chain risk. In some parts of the world, risk could actually diminish as a result of climate change. In parts of Canada and the United States, there will be fewer costs related to the removal of snow and ice. This will also result in fewer chemicals and salt being applied to roads, aircraft, runways and other infrastructure, which will have a positive environmental benefit.

Rising temperatures would mean that the St Lawrence Seaway would remain ice-free and open for longer and this would also be the case with the Great Lakes. Ports and ships will suffer less from icing and less down time.

The retreat and weakening of the Arctic ice cap will have benefits for shipping lines by opening up a new route to the Pacific.

---

### The opening of the North East Passage presents new shipping options

Europe is one of China's largest trading partners, with trade valued at approximately $500 billion in 2012. In 1869, the Suez Canal revolutionized trade between Europe and Asia, as previously ships had to travel the length of Africa. Now, another alternative is developing thanks to the warming climate: the North East Passage.

Several shipping operators are already looking at the passage; in 2014 a Chinese line, Cosco, deployed a freighter from Dalian through the Bering Strait en route to Amsterdam. Transit time is anticipated to be about 12–15 days less than if the freighter travelled by way of the Suez Canal.

The drawback of this route is that it is only navigable two to four months of the year because of the ice, and each year, despite concerns over global warming, levels of ice coverage vary. Forty-six ships utilized the passage in 2012 compared with just four in 2010. However, this had fallen to only 19 in 2016.

It had been thought that up to 15 per cent of Chinese foreign trade could use the Arctic route by 2020, a figure that is looking overly optimistic. Even with the ice receding at faster rates, with over 19,000 ships passing through the Suez Canal each year, it will be many years before the North East Passage rivals the Suez Canal in terms of traffic. However, the recent tensions in the Middle East as well as concerns of piracy off the coast of Africa have increased concerns of supply chain security along this route. On the other hand, travel through Russian waters could also present risks because of possible instabilities in the Russian economy and its political environment.

Regardless, the possibility of an additional trade route between Asia and Europe is welcome news in the shipping community and one that will offer an alternative choice for shippers for this important trade lane.

## The adaptation of retailers and manufacturers to climate change

Analysing responses to the Carbon Disclosure Project, an organization that works with 3,000 of the world's largest corporations to minimize carbon emissions, it is possible to identify the supply chain initiatives that are currently being undertaken by global manufacturers and retailers.

### Upstream – raw materials

One major concern for manufacturers and retailers is the impact that climate change would have on the availability of raw materials. This was an issue flagged up especially by retailers of fashion, including Nike, Gap and Debenhams, who commented that changes in seasonal patterns of rainfall and temperature could impact on their ability to source raw materials from certain markets, particularly cotton and leather. They also identified that water availability could become an important issue. Walmart also recognizes this threat, stating that a decrease in agricultural yields would impact on its supply and customer base.

### Distribution centres

Logistics operations can also be impacted by the more frequent and intense periods of severe weather. Debenhams commented that a number of its facilities were at risk from direct consequences of storms, such as flooding and power cuts. Those companies with facilities in coastal areas commented that they could be vulnerable from a rise in sea level. Nike stated that its consolidation facilities in ports could be at risk from increased flooding due to rising sea levels.

Increasing temperatures could also result in the greater use of temperature-controlled warehousing and distribution, increasing transport costs. Walmart monitors the temperature in all its facilities, which it says is providing it with the necessary data to be able to prepare for this eventuality.

Nike has a very proactive approach to ensuring that its properties, retail and logistics, are protected as much as is feasible from the impact of extreme weather events. It ensures that all properties are built and maintained to a standard it refers to as 'Highly Protected Risk'. This includes making sure that facilities are located outside of flood plains.

## Downstream distribution

Distribution to customers either through companies' own retail outlets or through parcels/freight delivery networks has also been identified as at risk from climate change. Nike commented that its multiple marketing channels gave it the flexibility to respond to disruptive events and that its diverse product lines would also mitigate impact. Transport networks can be more frequently disrupted by snowstorms, as well as flooding and other hazardous weather events.

**CASE STUDY**  Dell's response to climate change

PC manufacturer Dell does not have a specific risk management function dedicated to climate change. Rather it is part of a holistic approach to identifying and dealing with risk right across the corporation. 'Major risks', which it defines as those that can have an enterprise-wide impact, or affecting multiple organizations throughout the company, are dealt with at a corporate level. Lower-level risks are more often dealt with within a business unit.

Dell's development of a climate change strategy is framed by a broadly based assessment of risks, and responsibility for a response lies within its 'Global Operations' and 'Manufacturing and Supply Chain' functions.

Management has developed a specific programme, its Business Continuity Resiliency Plan (BCRP), which provides a detailed playbook and is implemented by either Dell's Facilities team (for property assets) or by the Dell Worldwide Procurement team (in the case of supply chain disruption).

Dell's Facilities team is also tasked with undertaking a comprehensive risk analysis of the location of new facilities, taking into account climate change risks. It also undertakes due diligence of acquisitions from the same perspective. The extent of Dell's oversight doesn't just extend to its own operations. It also insists that its suppliers have in place their own business continuity plans.

Dell's climate change strategy is part of a wider response to its corporate and social responsibilities. Dell has a Sustainability Operating Council, which has overall responsibility for coordinating and communicating its sustainability provisions.

One of the major issues that has been identified by Dell is its reliance on single-source or limited-source suppliers. It has highlighted the risk that an event, triggered by extreme weather, for example, could have on its ability to maintain production as well as fulfil customer demands. As a company totally reliant on its supply chain, disruption to its suppliers, manufacturing locations and the information technology infrastructure that underpin its networks could be devastating in reputational, operational and financial terms.

Dell says it maintains these single-source relationships either because multiple sources are not readily available or because the relationships are advantageous because of performance, quality, support, delivery, capacity or price considerations. However, as the company itself admits, if the supply of a critical single – or limited – source product or component is delayed, it may not be able to ship the related product in desired quantities or configurations, or in a timely manner. Even where multiple sources of supply are available, qualification of the alternative suppliers and establishment of reliable supplies could result in delays and a possible loss of sales, which could harm operating results. Dell obtains all its components from third-party vendors, many of which are located throughout the developing world. A significant proportion of its products are assembled by contract manufacturers, primarily in various locations in Asia.

One potential risk that Dell has highlighted is the impact of rising sea temperatures, which it says could be a causal factor in the increasing frequency of storms and hurricanes. These do not just affect supply chain performance and production capabilities but, in the case of catastrophic events, can also impact upon customer buying behaviour.

Rising air temperatures can also result in greater electricity demand in order to keep production facilities cool. This in turn could result in a greater number of power shortages or outages, not to mention higher energy costs.

Dell specifically mentioned that it was impacted by the Thailand floods of 2011, which resulted in a significant shortage in the supply of hard disk drives (HDD). Although Dell's own facilities were not affected, one of its main suppliers – Western Digital – ceased production at two of its factories for a period. This resulted in HDD shortages and a rise in costs (by $150 million) affecting the high end of Dell's product range. This meant that the company missed profit targets, and when it announced its fourth quarter results in February 2012 following the floods, its share price dropped by 5 per cent. Dell was not the only company to be affected – the share prices of Hewlett-Packard, Lenovo, EMC Corp. and Acer also fell.

# Pollution and 'diesel bans'

## Emissions regulation, 'diesel bans' and the impact on supply chains

Air pollution in cities is an increasingly important issue being addressed by governments and city administrators. According to the United Nations' Climate & Clean Air Coalition, 9 out of 10 people around the world live in an environment where pollution levels exceed World Health Organization limits.

Diesel emissions are regarded as a primary source of pollutants and have been blamed for the premature deaths of 3 million people a year (Harvard, 2016). This has led an increasing number of city authorities to place controls and even ban diesel engine vehicles. Political momentum is gathering pace. The Institute for Public Policy Research has stated that 'it is likely that diesel cars [and trucks] will have to be completely phased out... over the next decade in order to reach compliance with safe and legal levels of air pollution.'

It seems that public policy has changed significantly in the past few years, from exclusively concentrating on the reduction of $CO_2$ emissions to a focus on the reduction of particulates. What this has meant is that types of fuels that were once regarded as a good alternative to carbon-emitting petrol have now come under scrutiny themselves. Foremost of these has been diesel engines, which, although producing low-carbon emissions, generate particulates that can result in breathing problems and are also considered carcinogenic. Diesel engines produce the following toxic pollutants:

- Non-methane hydrocarbons and nitrogen oxides – together these contribute to the formation of ground-level ozone and smog.
- Dust/soot particulates are a severe health hazard. Soot particulates, which are produced by diesel combustion, are now regarded as a cancer

risk. In the case of electrically powered vehicles, on the other hand, dust emissions are produced entirely during power generation and distribution. While most dust emissions are dissipated into the atmosphere at great height (for example from power plant stacks), the distance travelled by airborne diesel soot particulates from exhaust tail pipe to the human being who inhales them is much shorter.

● Sulphur dioxide – which can lead to respiratory diseases.

However, the impact of regulations and bans on diesel-engined vehicles on supply chains and the wider logistics sector is yet to be fully understood. Cities compete globally on the basis of their efficiency, and despite politicians stating that the harmful effects of pollution must be eliminated, none will want to do so at the expense of jobs. This could be the outcome if urban supply chains become burdened with regulation and delays, with logistics costs rising significantly. At present, most urban areas are supplied by distribution centres located remotely in areas of low-cost labour, low land prices and good land availability. Meddling with supply chain structures could have many unanticipated consequences.

Typically regulations on urban freight operations have included:

● restrictions on delivery times;

● routing schemes that regulate when and where goods vehicles can go;

● loading/offloading zones;

● weight and size restrictions;

● arbitrary day bans on vehicles (such as odd/even number plate measures).

In December 2016, the mayors of Paris, Mexico City, Madrid and Athens made the commitment to ban not only diesel-engined trucks but also cars from their cities by 2025. They say that they will at the same time incentivize the use of alternative fuels and electric vehicles (Guardian, 2016). However, a number of measures in cities around the world have already been implemented to regulate the use of vehicles. These include:

## *Europe*

### Denmark

● Copenhagen's low emissions zone (LEZ) for HGVs (over 3.5 tonne) has existed since 2008, requiring minimum Euro IV standards.

● Vans or cars are not affected.

## Finland

- Helsinki has an LEZ affecting buses and waste trucks, requiring a minimum Euro standard of engine.
- Lorries longer than 12 metres are restricted.

## France

- An LEZ came into force in Paris in 2015.
- Vehicles registered before 1997 are banned; by 2020 the ban will extend to cars registered before 2010.
- Trucks registered before October 2001 are banned from city streets during weekdays.
- There are monthly road closures.
- Major thoroughfares have been pedestrianized.
- Other French cities are in the process of following Paris's lead.

## Germany

- National legislation has been passed empowering towns and cities to ban diesel-engined vehicles (cars and trucks) that don't meet Euro 6 standards (mandatory for all diesel vehicles since 2015).
- Many German cities already have an LEZ, utilizing a coloured 'sticker' system to denote the type of engine (Euro standards).
- The Bundesrat has called on the EU to ban diesel – and petrol – engine vehicles completely by 2030.

## Ireland

- Although there is no LEZ in Dublin, Ireland's capital city, lorries with five or more axles are banned between 7am and 7pm from a specific area.
- A permit scheme exists for deliveries to the city on specific routes.

## Italy

- A low emissions zone ('Zona Traffico Limitato') exists in Rome's city centre.
- Euro 0 engines are not allowed within the zone and Euro 1–6 are allowed only on weekdays if they belong to residents or have a delivery permit.

- Other controls exist within other concentric emissions zones.
- Milan also has an LEZ, which restricts Euro 3-engined HGVs and those longer than 7.5 metres.
- From 2017, Euro 4 engines (without particulate filters) will be banned from the city centre.
- The area will be enlarged in 2022.

## Netherlands

- The Dutch government is planning to ban the sale of all new petrol and diesel vehicles by 2025.
- Amsterdam's LEZ has been in place since 2008, requiring HGVs to have Euro 4 or Euro 5 engines.
- Number plate recognition scanning is used to enforce the regulations.
- Vans will be included (Euro 2) from 2017.

## Norway

- The Norwegian government is planning to ban the sale of all new petrol and diesel-engined vehicles by 2025.
- Oslo is looking to ban the use of private cars by 2019.

## Portugal

- Lisbon has an LEZ, introduced in 2011 and enlarged in 2012.

## Spain

- Madrid has no LEZ but does limit access to certain parts of the city centre.
- Barcelona has no LEZ, although the old city has a weight and speed limit for vehicles and there are bans for non-resident vehicles at certain times of day.

## UK

- A congestion charge has been in place since 2003.
- London's LEZ was introduced in 2008.
- Vehicles registered before 1 October 2006 entering a designated zone have to pay a charge.

- The UK government has also developed plans to allow clean air zones in Birmingham, Leeds, Nottingham, Derby and Southampton.
- The London Lorry Control Scheme is another initiative, designed to minimize noise pollution rather than air pollution.

It seems that most countries in Europe have already instituted controls on vehicles (including trucks) entering urban areas. For example, LEZs have been established in at least some of their major cities. However, there is very little consistency in the forms of regulatory measures imposed within these zones. Some ban certain types of engine standard while others impose a charge on them. There is also little consistency in the ways in which the regulations are imposed. Some use a 'sticker' system, others use more sophisticated number plate recognition technology.

What is clear, though, is that most countries have already undertaken what could be regarded as the most lengthy and difficult first step: to win political approval to establish zones within which emissions regulations on vehicles can be applied. This paves the way for the more draconian legislation that many politicians seek – the outright ban of diesel-engined vehicles entering a city.

Such complete bans rely on there being an alternative solution. For this to happen there has to be considerable progress in the development of alternative fuels – electric, natural gas or biofuels, for example.

## Asia

Reducing traffic emissions and their impact on public health was identified as a key policy objective by the Association of Southeast Asian Nations (ASEAN) in 2010. Despite this, in many countries the problem has got worse.

### Japan

Tokyo became the first city to ban certain types of diesel engine in 2001. The law required that older vehicles needed to be retro-fitted with filters on their exhausts. This was followed by the creation of an LEZ in 2003. However, in 2014 this policy was relaxed as diesels had become much cleaner and, running contra to sentiment in many other countries, the government introduced subsidies for 'clean' diesels.

### India

In Delhi, the government operates an 'odd–even' licence plate system in order to cut traffic levels on alternate days. Public bodies have also been told to stop buying diesel-engined vehicles, although this ban does not apply to private individuals. Air pollution levels often reach 40 times the World Health Organization recommended levels.

## China

Because of high levels of congestion and traffic pollution in China, cities such as Beijing, Shanghai, Guangzhou and Suzhou have looked closely at the experience of London and Singapore. Traffic-restricting measures were introduced for the 2008 Olympic Games and these have been developed over the years. A ban on Euro 1 engines applied to vehicles moving inside the '5th Ring Road', and this was extended in 2009 to the '6th Ring Road'.

At present Beijing is in the last year of its Five-Year Clean Air Action Plan (2013–17), which was put in place to prevent pollution levels exceeding those of 2013 and reduce particle density by 25 per cent. New vehicle registrations have also been limited to prevent them from reaching 6 million by 2017. Authorities are also actively considering a ban on coal transportation in Beijing.

Large trucks are banned in Guangzhou from 7am to 9pm, although special permits are available for daytime deliveries.

## Singapore

Authorities in Singapore have taken steps over the years to address traffic levels, not only because of their economic impact but because of the public health implications:

- Since 1998 there has been an electronic road pricing programme in place. Users are charged during peak hours to limit traffic in parts of the city.

- The government places quotas on types of vehicles and Certificates of Entitlement (COE) are auctioned. Only about 15 per cent of the population owns vehicles.

## Hong Kong

Despite widespread congestion and pollution, especially in the central business district, and three consultations (1985, 2001 and 2009), Hong Kong's government has yet to introduce any charging schemes. Plans to implement a scheme, originally due for 2017, have been pushed back, linked with other infrastructure projects that have been delayed.

Legislation will mean that new trucks must adopt the Euro 6 standard with effect from 1 January 2018. Plans are in place to remove all Euro 3 commercial vehicles (and earlier engines) by 2019.

## Philippines

With half of the Philippines' population living in urban areas, the country has a major traffic and pollution problem. A range of policies has been adopted to try to reduce traffic, such as promoting alternative forms of transport, but no LEZs or diesel bans have yet been put forward (although certain municipalities operate 'car-free' days).

## Indonesia

Traffic congestion in Jakarta is extremely severe, with major implications for public health. The government has been planning for some time to introduce electronic road pricing (ERP) in the city, but progress has been slow. Problems include the quality of existing roads, opposition from residents and commuters, inadequacy of law enforcement resources and alternative transport systems.

# *Americas*

## United States

During the last administration, the environment became an increasing priority and the Environmental Protection Agency (EPA) published standards for vehicle emissions. California has some of the most stringent air quality rules in the country, which go beyond these, although the Trump administration may attempt to overturn this state's right to continue setting its own clean vehicle rules.

There have been plans mooted to ban the registration of diesel-engined vehicles in Washington, DC, although this would not stop diesel trucks from entering the city from elsewhere.

The Port of Long Beach in California represents one of the few regulated zones. In 2012, a programme banned older, more polluting trucks from Port terminals and today almost all of the 13,000 drayage trucks servicing the Port terminals are 2007 or newer models. This has reduced pollution by more than 80 per cent (Mongelluzzo, 2012).

The Port of New York and New Jersey attempted a similarly aggressive approach, planning to ban pre-2007 diesel engines. In 2016 this was watered down in the face of opposition from trucking companies, who protested at the additional costs involved in replacement. Now only 1994 and 1995 engines (as well as earlier) will be banned from 2018.

In New York itself authorities are nervous about introducing stringent regulations. In 2015, when anti-pollution regulations were being updated (first introduced in 1970), freight operators were encouraged to invest in lower-emission trucks through a fee-waiver programme, rather than through banning older types of engine.

However, New York (as with other major cities in the US) does have a number of other controls:

- designated truck routes;
- plans and pilot-trials for 'off-hours' delivery (7pm to 6am);
- reducing emissions from non-road equipment (such as temperature-controlled trailers).

## Mexico

As one of the cities to agree a ban on diesel-engined vehicles by 2025, Mexico City already has advanced plans for the implementation of an LEZ to reduce air pollution. The city – part of a wider conurbation comprising 25 million people with approximately 4 million cars – is situated in a valley, which has exacerbated the problem of pollution. The city already implements so-called licence plate bans, which allows the authorities to regulate the number of days individual vehicles are allowed within a proscribed area. This works by prohibiting vehicles whose licence plate ends with a certain number from entering the city between certain times (usually 5am to 10pm). This scheme is referred to as 'Hoy no circula', or 'Don't drive today', although there are exemptions for tourists.

## *The impact of bans*

A ban on diesel-engined vehicles would obviously completely disrupt the transport operations of companies delivering within large parts of the most economically active regions of the world. Politicians who make pronouncements while running for office have found that the reality of prohibiting trucks in urban areas is far more problematic than they may have first thought.

Presently electric vehicles are not sufficiently developed to provide a practical alternative, and the costs would be prohibitive. It may be at least 10 years before electric vehicles are able to replace diesel trucks in any great quantities. There is not only the issue of the technological development required, but also (perhaps most importantly) the impact that a large-scale migration from combustion engine power to the use of grid energy would have on national power-generation strategies. In many countries, electricity grids often struggle to provide the power required for existing use without the enormous additional demand of new electric trucks and, of course, cars.

However, there are ways in which logistics in inner city urban areas could be made more efficient. One such option often suggested is through the development of more urban logistics centres (ULCs) (otherwise known as urban consolidation centres), or cross-docking facilities. ULCs are designed to:

- reduce the number and loaded/unloaded mileage of vehicles in the inner city area;
- increase the intensity of use of vehicles by ensuring greater utilization rates.

ULCs consolidate consignments from a range of shippers for delivery in a more efficient way to end-recipients in urban areas. It would then be possible for regulators to insist on the type of vehicle that was used to undertake the final delivery. Obviously this could involve the use of electric vehicles.

ULCs generally are either privately or publicly owned, and in the past have had mixed success in their application. One of the primary problems is that in many cases it is difficult to see in whose economic interest these centres work. They add in an extra stage in the supply chain, which often results in delays as well as the cost of the operation of the centre. In some cases there is a clear benefit. Consolidation centres work well when a retail centre operator can insist through leasehold obligations that goods to shops within the centre are handled off-site. This prevents the high levels of potential congestion that could occur within a confined area.

However, outside of this controlled environment there are few benefits or reasons for retailers or manufacturers to work together. It would seem that there needs to be investment by public bodies to kick-start the initiative through perhaps a public–private partnership financing model. However, this then relies on transport planners to develop solutions that fit the needs of a huge number and range of economically interested parties – a job that many believe would be completely unworkable.

## Real estate consequences

Around the world, the property market for the logistics and distribution industry has been influenced by the benefits of centralization of inventory holdings. This of course relies on the trade-off between (low) transport costs and (high) inventory costs. In addition, real estate and rental costs are very important.

Consequently, modern warehousing premises are often located equidistant from a number of economic centres, next to good transport links, in areas where land prices are low and in greenfield sites – certainly not in urban areas where, in any case, it is often difficult to get planning permission.

Any diesel ban would create the need for large numbers of consolidation centres located on the main arterial routes into an urban area. These routes are already often characterized by competing land use needs, not least housing.

The additional stage, and consequent delays, in the supply chain created by consolidation would mean that there would also be a requirement within the urban area for additional holdings of inventory to ensure that just-in-time deliveries could be maintained. These would be much smaller units.

**CASE STUDY**  Sogaris

Sogaris is a publicly owned organization (owned predominantly by Ville de Paris, Hauts-de-Seine, Seine-Saint-Denis and Val-de-Marne) that was set up in the 1960s to manage and reduce the flow of goods vehicles into and around Paris.

The organization employs a three-zone approach within its urban logistics strategy:

- wider urban area in which logistics facilities are located at points of entry for road, rail and intermodal barge;
- the development of multi-modal consolidation centres (including data centres, fulfilment and offices) for more densely populated areas;
- urban delivery centres for inner city requirements, including stock-holding.

It holds more than 545,000 square metres of warehousing space and is developing a further nine sites.

## Conclusion

Emissions from diesel engines are obviously a major public health issue. However, banning them entirely, as many politicians and campaigners are calling for, would have a significant impact on the economies of the major cities around the world and consequently on the citizens they are trying to protect.

While policies have been put in place (with varying degrees of success) to provide alternatives to car owners, both petrol- and diesel-engined, in the urban environment, little consideration has been given to how goods can be moved in and out of a city without the use of diesel trucks. For example, large electric goods vehicles are still not an option; the battery technology is not capable of providing a viable alternative to diesel in terms of range and power.

The good news, however, is that this is changing. The emissions problem may well be solved within the next 10 years if alternative fuels can be developed. At the same time, the 'sharing economy' will provide many opportunities to better improve the efficiency of logistics in an urban context and perhaps this should be the primary concern of administrators.

Other initiatives that stop short of a ban are also being examined. Collaboration between carriers may be an option if the benefits can be demonstrated.

The result if bans are introduced could be very costly for supply chains, plus, no doubt, a waste of taxpayers' money if consolidation centres are underutilized. Opposition from the industry would be intense and many politicians would also consider the impact on their constituents in terms of jobs and increased prices.

And there is also the question as to whether a ban on diesel trucks is proportional to their contribution to the problem. Using statistics supplied by Transport for London, 17 per cent of nitrogen oxides were generated by LGVs or HGVs in London in 2010. Diesel cars were responsible for 11 per cent, and, in comparison, petrol cars 7 per cent. Looking at particulates (PM 10), road freight vehicles generated just 13 per cent (diesel cars 12 per cent and petrol cars 16 per cent) (GLA, 2010). No doubt since that time an increase in engine efficiency and the introduction of Phases 3 and 4 of the LEZ has had a positive impact.

## Summary

Climate change is having a major impact on weather patterns and sea levels. Governments and corporations are planning to adapt to these changes so they can safeguard transport and warehouse infrastructure from extreme temperatures, increased rainfall, storm surges and high winds. Transport and production facilities are at greatest risk in coastal regions, and this applies equally to developed as well as developing countries. At a localized level, governments are also focusing on the impact of toxic emissions from diesel engines on public health. This is leading to an increasing level of regulation, especially in urban areas, and this has the potential to severely disrupt city logistics strategies.

## Key points

- Climate change has long-term implications for the level of risk in supply chains.
- Governments and corporations are actively studying ways in which supply chains and logistics operations can be made more adaptive to the effects of climate change.
- Many parts of the world, even in developed countries, are highly exposed to increased frequency of natural disasters and rising sea levels.
- Government regulation is increasing. The implementation of 'diesel bans' in many large cities is becoming a reality.
- City logistics strategies could be highly disrupted by such regulation, leading manufacturers, retailers and logistics suppliers to reconsider the way in which they serve urban areas.

# Economic risks to the supply chain

**OBJECTIVES**

This chapter will familiarize the reader with:

- the impact of 'demand shocks' on supply chains, with reference to specific case studies;
- how currency fluctuations can be particularly disruptive to cross-border commerce;
- various 'supply shocks', such as shipping rate and oil price volatility;
- the role that trade restrictions and trade 'wars' can play in disrupting the international movement of goods;
- how industrial unrest in the labour-intensive transport and logistics market is a growing risk, not least in sectors affected by the growth of e-commerce.

A Supply Chain and Transport Risk survey undertaken by the World Economic Forum and consultancy company Accenture (WEF, 2013a) identified that, in terms of perceived threat, economic events are more significant to company executives than many other risks, including corruption, piracy or pandemics.

The survey identified the following economic risks:

- demand shocks;
- volatility in commodity prices;
- border delays;
- export/import restrictions;

- currency fluctuations;
- energy shortages;
- ownership/investment restrictions;
- shortage of labour;
- industrial unrest.

# Demand shocks

Demand shocks – the surge or collapse in demand for products and services – are a significant risk for supply chains because of the difficulty of forecasting their onset and the impact (positive or negative) on production and supply. The 'Great Recession' of 2008 was the most severe negative demand shock of recent years, born out of the United States' subprime mortgage crisis, falling house prices and a collapse in consumer confidence.

One of the reasons why demand shocks are now so critical to supply chains (and one of the reasons why risks have increased) is the changing character of manufacturing. The unbundling and outsourcing trend has resulted in much higher levels of intermediate goods being shipped between companies and across borders, before being assembled by a supply chain principal, such as an OEM.

A sharp drop-off in demand results in a crisis throughout the supply chain, resulting in supplier failures (see Cisco case study below). For the principal player in the supply chain, this results in increasing costs, as capacity is affected because of the time it takes to arrange alternative suppliers. The situation is aggravated by the nature of intermediate goods. Unlike commodities, which can be more easily sourced from a range of suppliers, the products need to be customized to customers' needs. In some particularly severe cases, production can be brought to a halt.

In fact, the financial crisis that caused the last recession went to the very heart of supply chains. Suppliers were starved of working capital as banks sought to reduce their loans' exposure as companies' assets fell in value. Credit facilities were often cancelled despite the merit of a particular investment case.

Consequently many companies suffered from both a demand shock and also a 'supply of money' shock as their credit rating fell and banks reined back on lending because of capital adequacy rules introduced by central regulators. Cross-border loans were considered particularly risky, again striking at the heart of the remote, fragmented manufacturing model adopted throughout much of industry.

Some markets were more impacted than others. Japanese manufacturers, for example, which rely heavily on the above manufacturing model because of high production costs in their domestic market, were highly affected, as were the Asian economies that relied on supplying Japanese manufacturers. Hubert Escaith, Chief Statistician at the World Trade Organization, suggested that Japanese companies were both 'importers' and 'exporters' of demand shocks because of their central position in international supply chains. Escaith estimates that for Japan and the United States, the increase in production prices due to a failure of their Asian suppliers averaged 2 per cent. However, Chinese companies, which have a lower exposure to upstream cross-border supply chains, were less affected (Escaith, 2009).

That is not to say that Chinese suppliers are totally protected from financial crises. There have been several occasions in the last decade when Chinese government policy has suppressed lending, which causes a demand shock in its own right. The latest of these was in the summer of 2013, when the country experienced what could be described as a 'minor' financial crisis. The country's central bank reduced the quantity of finance available, resulting in a degree of panic as 'private' banks and other loan-making institutions scrabbled to refinance their short-term loans. As a result, short-term interest rates shot up. The move was interpreted as an attempt by the central bank to reduce the growth in credit in the economy, something that has been expanding at an extraordinary rate over the past five years.

The Chinese banking system is overwhelmingly state-owned and therefore a banking collapse in the classic sense is never likely to arise. However, this move represented the inevitable end of an unsustainable economic trajectory.

**CASE STUDY**  Cisco's troubles typify supply chain challenges

In June 2010, the Council of Supply Chain Management Professionals (CSCMP) asserted that the sharp destocking experienced during the recession had disrupted supply chains and that many organizations had to resort to emergency measures to cope when demand picked up. This, according to the Council, was behind much of the boom in air freight seen in the previous few quarters as manufacturers desperately sought to source components and support increased production. What emerged were some examples of such supply chain stress.

Take Cisco, a huge company built on the design of the hardware that makes up the infrastructure of the internet. For much of 2010 Cisco was in crisis because of the malfunctioning of its supply chain. Its customers complained that the company could not deliver its products on time or, in some cases, even deliver them at all. Engineers maintaining infrastructure such as data centres were facing a wait of up to 12 weeks for basic switching components.

The origin of the problem clearly lay with Cisco's suppliers, many of them based in China. According to a statement from Cisco itself, the issues were 'attributable in part to increasing demand driven by the improvement in our overall markets… the longer than normal lead time extensions also stemmed from supplier constraints based upon their labour and other actions taken during the global economic downturn'. In other words, component suppliers laid off workers during the recession and reduced capacity. Consequently there was not enough production capacity to fulfil demand.

It was also very interesting to see the reaction of customers to the worsening supply situation. According to Cisco, this led customers '…to place the same order multiple times within our various sales channels and to cancel the duplicative orders upon receipt of the product, or to place orders with other vendors with shorter manufacturing lead times.'

In its statement Cisco said that, 'Our efforts to improve manufacturing lead-time performance may result in corresponding reductions in order backlog. A decline in backlog levels could result in more variability and less predictability in our quarter-to-quarter net sales and operating results.' This might be taken as typical 'squirrelling' behaviour, where customers increase inventory levels in an environment of uncertainty. The result is lumpy demand, with wild swings between shortage and overstocking.

The economic stress being visited upon supply chains led in turn to a failure to manage inventory properly. This in turn affected the management of transport. Or in the words of Cisco:

> We have experienced periods of time during which shipments have exceeded net bookings or manufacturing issues have delayed shipments, leading to nonlinearity in shipping patterns. In addition to making it difficult to predict revenue for a particular period, nonlinearity in shipping can increase costs, because irregular shipment patterns result in periods of underutilized capacity and periods in which overtime expenses may be incurred, as well as in potential additional inventory management-related costs (Cisco, 2011).

In other words, this statement meant Cisco, an erstwhile poster child of supply chain excellence, faced immense challenges in its logistics.

# Currency fluctuations

The last few years have been particularly difficult for global shippers in terms of currency fluctuations. The extension of supply chains into multiple currency zones means that shippers have increased their exposure to shifts in exchange rates. One problem is the obvious impact on input costs that an appreciating currency can have. However, an indirect impact on global supply chains can be the shift in sourcing decisions that this can prompt.

At a macro-political level, currencies can create tensions that have consequences for global trade. After the recession of 2008–09, the finance minister of Brazil described the competitive devaluation between major economies as a 'currency war'. Particularly important has been the Chinese currency peg to the US dollar, which has kept Chinese goods very competitive. A number of other nations, even those with huge trade surpluses, such as Switzerland, Japan and South Korea, have moved to depress the value of their currencies by selling them on the international markets.

This sort of behaviour provokes anger in the United States and has, in the past, prompted draft legislation designed to impose sanctions on countries it feels are responsible (mainly the Chinese) by way of retaliation. The US Treasury Secretary of the time, Timothy Geithner, described China's currency policy as a 'dangerous dynamic'.

Since 2010 the quantitative easing policies pursued by many countries in the West have devalued their own currencies, and this has eased tensions with China.

The fall in the value of the pound following the Brexit referendum result will eventually lead to higher input costs, although inflationary pressures in the British economy are still not high. This may indeed lead to the restructuring of supply chains as importing goods becomes more expensive, resulting in a boost for UK manufacturers. However, where products are exclusively or largely produced abroad (such as consumer electronics), price rises are inevitable.

# Supply shocks

## Shipping rates and capacity

Shipping rates are a significant element of total costs for many products. In fact, the manufacturing strategies of many companies are predicated on the low cost of transport that allows them to take advantage of low labour costs in remote parts of the world. Consequently, any upward surge of input costs not only has a short-term impact on the price of goods, but can also influence long-term production strategies.

There has been significant volatility in shipping rates over the past six years. From around $880 per TEU at the end of 2011 on the China/Europe trade lane, shipping rates surged to $1,353 the following year. After years of slow decline ($1,161 per TEU in 2014), they then suddenly went into free fall, as low as $629 in 2015 (UNCTAD, 2016). The shipping lines have been trying to increase their rates regularly, but excess capacity in the market, which has outstripped demand, has made these attempts futile.

A shortage of capacity and disruption to delivery schedules are also hazards for the shipper. When shipping lines attempted to cut costs, many turned to 'slow-steaming' as a way of reducing their spend on fuel. Reducing speed by 10 per cent cuts the overall fuel needed for the voyage by just under a fifth. Rotterdam's Erasmus University found in a study that the industry could save $67 million by cutting speeds to 20 knots (Van der Lugt and Streng, 2013). The flip side of this is that inventory costs increase considerably. The study found that inventory costs rose $170 million, based on price-per-hour waiting time.

In terms of risk, although these extra costs are clearly related, it is uncertain which is the real problem to shippers. In 2012 shipping lines made a number of major changes to their schedules and ports of call in order to restructure capacity. This left many manufacturers and retailers around the world, who had built their distribution strategies on reliable and consistent service levels, complaining that they had been severely let down by shipping lines.

Capacity problems on an industry-wide basis are not something that air freight shippers have had to worry too much about in recent years. Since the economic recession of 2008–09, capacity on many routes has been plentiful, not just because of weak volumes. Many airlines have renewed their fleet with wide-bodied aircraft in order to more economically carry increasing numbers of passengers. Air freight volumes have not risen nearly so fast, but as the majority of freight is moved on passenger airlines, the additional capacity that wide-bodied airplanes provides has suppressed rates.

This was not the case in the mid-1990s, when a surging global economy meant that capacity could be hard to come by, especially out of China. This situation was exploited by giant high-tech manufacturer, Apple, which at an early stage realized it could achieve a competitive advantage by booking up air cargo capacity and denying space to its competitors. More recently, as airlines have cut back on freighter-only capacity, forwarders have struggled to service regular customers on specific routes at times of big product launches by the major high-tech manufacturers, including not only Apple but also Samsung and Sony.

## Oil price volatility

The fluctuations in the oil market are impossible to forecast, injecting uncertainty into the transport market. In turn, the disproportionate growth of transport as a part of the world's economy has amplified the demand for oil.

Oil prices have also been volatile in the past three years, albeit not at the same level as shipping rates. From $70 a barrel in mid-2010, the price climbed to $120 in the second quarter of the following year, spurred on by concerns over the security situation in the Strait of Hormuz. With manufacturers planning their production strategies on much longer timescales than just a matter of months, this volatility has obvious implications on costs.

Oil prices are now at a level much lower than at the peak of the economic cycle in 2008, when they reached $130 a barrel ($50 per barrel March 2017). At the high point, manufacturers started to reassess their production and distribution strategies in order to mitigate risks of fuel costs should they continue to spiral. With centralization of production a key trend in the industry for two decades or more, this presented executives with a seismic shift in strategic thinking. With the emergence of developing economies, the market environment has become confused, presenting companies with the challenge of finding the best way to efficiently supply these markets.

Initiatives to reduce oil costs sometimes run contrary to efficient supply chain management. For instance, at the peak of the market in 2008, global FMCG manufacturer Unilever was prompted to start discussions with customers with the goal of reducing frequency of deliveries and increasing size of shipment; in other words, rolling back JIT best practice. IKEA is also known for its distribution strategy, which prioritizes the efficiency of its transport assets over inventory reduction/customer service.

The market for fuel is also changing in other key areas. Most notably, both aircraft and container ships are becoming much more fuel-efficient. Newer aircraft such as the Airbus A380 and Boeing 787 utilize both size and design to deliver lower fuel consumption per ton carried, possibly as much as a 20 per cent improvement. However, the sector is still vulnerable to oil prices, with the cost of fuel as a proportion of overall aircraft operational costs somewhere between a third and a half.

The situation in container shipping is more dramatic. Here, the fall in consumption of fuel per container/kilometre has been substantial, largely as a result of economies of scale. Shipping consultant Drewry estimates that the Maersk E-class vessels burn 35 per cent less fuel per TEU than the previous class of Post-Panamax ships. In turn, these vessels consumed 20 per cent less than the 9,000 TEU vessels that they had replaced. Essentially, fuel consumption per TEU has halved since the introduction of Post-Panamax ships in the 1990s (Ship and Bunker, 2013).

The successful attempts to control fuel consumption in the air and sea sectors must be seen as important progress towards a more stable and viable transport sector worldwide, making the role of transport more predictable in increasing the productivity of shipping goods. The big exception to this is road freight. If this industry ever sees comparable management of fuel consumption and energy efficiency, the market will be completely transformed.

There are other reasons why the chances of another 'oil shock' (as seen in the 1970s) are diminishing. The oil and gas production boom taking place in North America (through fracking technology) will influence the economic landscape for many years, keeping oil prices more stable than they have been historically. It has yet to be seen what impact a security crisis in the Middle East would have on oil prices in this new environment, although it is certain that its effects would be lessened.

## Trade restrictions

Trade restrictions are often a major impediment to the efficient flow of goods throughout supply chains. However, trade restrictions on their own do not create a threat to supply chains, as shippers and forwarders are often adept at working around the regulations. Of more concern is the breakdown of relations between trading nations, trade wars and the sudden imposition of tariffs and non-tariff barriers (NTBs), including quotas and bans. The World Trade Organization was set up in a post-war environment to try to prevent such tensions as well as to successfully reduce tariff and non-tariff barriers. However, the stalling of the Doha round of negotiations increases the probability of disputes running out of hand, especially between major trade partners such as China and the United States.

Under any circumstances trade wars have enormous implications for the logistics sector. One of the primary engines of growth for the sector over the past decade or more has been the expansion of trade with China. Shipping and air freight are dominated by this trade and any disruption or change in its nature will gravely affect these sectors. Yet the rise of China as a world superpower, at least in industrial terms, has created many tensions with its trading partners. Countries with waning manufacturing industries often complain (with varying levels of justification) that the Chinese government unfairly supports its exporters, allowing them to 'dump' product on international markets at below-market prices.

The phenomenon of global supply chains, driven as previously discussed by the unbundling and outsourcing of production processes on an international basis, has increased the importance of stable trade relations to consistency of supply. Complicating the issue, rather, has been the proliferation of suppliers across a range of emerging markets, where governance in trade issues is not yet mature.

There are also trade disputes that stem from geo-political relations. For example, sanctions that were placed on Iran by the United States and the EU considerably increased risks for importers and exporters in the region. Before they were partially lifted in 2015, the sanctions placed Iran on the US Specially Designated Nationals List (SDN List) of the Office of Foreign Assets Control (OFAC), which makes many dealings between companies (including logistics operators) and Iranian nationals illegal. Because of the complexity of global supply chains, it is highly challenging for even the most scrupulous of companies to ensure that their supply chain is free of contact from countries that have sanctions such as these placed upon them, most latterly, of course, Russia.

One example of a prosecution involved a shipper who was found to have used an Iranian ship within its logistics operations. Even though it had re-flagged as a Liberian vessel, the fact that its registration number had remained the same meant that the US authorities had cause to levy a fine on the company.

The implementation of sanctions on Syria is also a problem for the industry because of its historic position as a transit country. Shippers must also beware that although they might not be contravening legislation in one country, if they have a corporate presence in the United States they could still be held liable for breaches of US law.

## Russian customs dispute illustrates familiar problem

In 2013, the Russian authorities announced that they would end the Transports Internationaux Routiers (TIR) agreement that has for many years facilitated the flow of international transport across its borders.

The agreement underwrites customs duties for goods passing through, but not destined for, a particular state. This agreement enables trucks to avoid having their load inspected at every border they pass through as well as simplifying the application of customs duties.

It was unclear why Russia had chosen to do this and how the new rules would be applied. However, European truck operators became concerned that the consequence would be the collapse of traffic between Russia and its European neighbours. After intense negotiations between the EU and Russian customs, it was announced that the plan to end the TIR agreement had been suspended until the beginning of December.

It remains unclear why Russia sought to end what is a fairly basic international trade agreement. Previously working effectively, the Russian authorities had already begun to inspect loads in transit moving out of Lithuania. It has been speculated that the Russian government had an ulterior motive connected to tax revenues, or alternatively in-fighting within the Russian bureaucracy; however, substantiating these suggestions is very difficult.

Road traffic between Poland, Belarus, Lithuania and Russia has often been problematic, with delays often triggered by underlying political issues. Logistics service providers are forced to build flexibility into their planning, with movement out of the Finnish ports augmenting traffic out of the Baltic States. However, these sorts of issues also illustrate that politics and bureaucracy in Russia is still a significant obstacle to the smooth operation of supply chains into and out of the country.

# Industrial unrest

Despite the focus of the transport and logistics industry in recent years on assets and technology, the sector is still highly labour-intensive. Whether as truck drivers or warehouse staff, millions of workers around the world are employed by logistics companies, airlines, shipping lines, ports, airports and of course manufacturers and retailers.

This dependency on the intensive use of labour is also a major vulner-ability. Many people who find themselves employed in the industry are low-skilled, low-paid workers and this has meant that in many parts of the world it has become highly unionized.

In fact, labour is one of the fundamental reasons why the outsourcing trend has become so prevalent. Many manufacturers and retailers have taken advantage of the lower labour costs in the logistics sector and shifted large proportions of their higher-earning workforce to outsourced companies. Although in the developed world existing employees are protected to a certain degree (for example in the UK by the Transfer of Undertakings Protection of Employees (TUPE) legislation), new employees are not. This means that in some cases, some employees working alongside each other doing a similar job could be on different pay and conditions. In fact in some cases, outsourced and non-outsourced employees may work alongside each other, and this can create considerable tensions in the workforce.

This has certainly been the case at Jaguar Land Rover, which in the UK outsources its logistics to DHL. In 2013 members of the Unite trade union voted in favour of strikes at all three Jaguar Land Rover (JLR) assembly plants in the UK.

The dispute at the assembly plants in the Midlands revolved around the differences in pay between staff employed by JLR and those by DHL Supply Chain and goes to the heart of the outsourcing project. The logistics operations at JLR are one of DHL Supply Chain's most ambitious contracts, with the company operating a lead-logistics supply/single-sourcing arrangement that encompasses almost all logistics processes into and around three assembly plants.

This means that DHL Supply Chain staff are working alongside JLR employees, often doing very similar work. Yet, the DHL workforce earns less and has less job security. Indeed, one of the objectives of such an outsourcing operation is to focus resources on operations directly concerned with assembly rather than the feed of components, the latter being in the hands of suppliers, such as DHL Supply Chain, who have a lower cost base.

The issue of different pay and conditions for employees of vehicle manufacturers and suppliers is a familiar problem in the automotive sector. Indeed, it is really about the need to control the wage costs of assembly line workers employed by the vehicle manufacturers. However, it is a significant problem for the more sophisticated logistics service providers who aspire to a more central role in automotive assembly.

A similar situation has arisen in Germany – this time in the retail sector – where Amazon has experienced industrial disputes related to the status of its warehousing staff. Essentially, the staff and the company are arguing over the definition of their jobs. The workforce is looking for parity with retail workers who, in Germany, have higher agreed wage levels than logistics workers, Amazon's definition of its staff. There also appears to be a wish for better job security for employees at the Bad Hersfeld and Leipzig hubs, many of whom are temporary staff.

It is interesting that the union concerned, Ver.di, describes the dispute as being driven by arguments over the definition of what Amazon actually does. In essence, a large part of the retail sector is being shifted to a business model characterized by much lower costs. One element of this change is the more efficient use of land and inventory, but also includes the opportunity to decrease employee unit labour costs as workers in fulfilment centres can be controlled and worked much harder than staff in traditional shops.

Disputes over the status of workers are not just limited to the in-house/outsourced debate. It is also apparent within the transport industry itself. Trade unions are particularly upset by the strategy of many logistics companies to expand the function of self-employed/owner-operator, small business or 'informal' work. Unions see this as a means of undermining their role by fragmenting workforces. This is of particular importance given the growth of the courier industry on the back of e-commerce deliveries. Many companies employ subcontractors to make their deliveries as they are cheaper, fall outside employee law, run their own vehicles and can be used flexibly to meet peaks in demand. Unions in the United States and France are challenging this business model in the courts as they believe the strategy is being used to deliberately circumvent employee protection legislation.

While the industrial dispute process in the Western world is highly regulated, giving employers time to make contingency plans and mitigate many of the supply chain consequences, of more damage is direct action undertaken by a combination of companies and unions. The fuel 'strikes' of the 2000s were an example of this.

One example of this was a catastrophic strike by the Italian road transport industry in 2007, which paralysed the economy. The 'strike', which lasted for four days, was prompted by rising fuel prices, which Italian truckers saw as threatening their livelihoods. Seven unions were involved in the action, with strikes being coordinated by an umbrella group, Conftrasporto. A spokesman for the group said that there was almost 100 per cent support for the action from Italy's estimated 100,000 haulage companies and their drivers. Unions were demanding compensation for the rise in diesel prices.

Action was taken across the country and 2,000 Italian trucks blocked the French border. In addition to food shortages, petrol ran out at filling stations. Auto manufacturer FIAT was forced to shut down all its plants in the country because of the disruption of the supply of parts. The cost to the company ran into millions of euros.

These types of blockade occur throughout the world. In 2011 truck drivers blockaded the Port of Shanghai, affecting traffic using the terminals at

Waigaoqiao and Yangshan. Alongside complaints about fuel price increases, the owner-drivers serving the Shanghai container terminals also appeared to be protesting at the fees imposed by freight forwarders and container yard operators at the port.

North America is not immune to this problem and disputes in the rail and ports sectors in particular are commonplace. There are signs that US shippers have become more prepared for this type of disruption, learning a valuable lesson from the crippling US West Coast port dispute in the early 2000s, which had a negative impact of over $1 billion on the US economy. As a result, many shippers spread their shipments across several ports so as not to be so exposed again. If there is indeed another strike or slowdown among the East and Gulf Coast ports, while it will have a negative impact particularly to local and state economies, freight will more than likely be shifted to West Coast ports, as well as to Canadian and Mexican ports, which are linked to the US heartland via a growing rail and intermodal system.

Work stoppages or slowdowns are among the most important risks with supply chains that companies need to account for and manage accordingly. However, with the growing economic uncertainty throughout the world, this will prove difficult as labour unions fight to maintain existing jobs in ports and other transportation points. This is likely to create a vicious cycle as strikes, as seen in the past, can easily cripple an economy – thus further exacerbating an already difficult situation.

## Summary

'Virtual' and global supply chains are at risk from economic volatility. The 'Great Recession' in 2008 revealed that global manufacturers reliant on outsourced supplier networks were severely impacted by company failures, which created production bottlenecks. In addition, 'supply shocks' resulting from high and sharp increases in shipping rates, a shortage of capacity or a hike in fuel prices can compromise companies' ability to serve their customers. Trade relations are also important. Protectionist regulations, especially sanctions affecting the transit of goods cross-border, can significantly add costs to distribution operations. Industrial unrest should not be ignored. The transport and logistics industry is highly unionized and labour organizations are mindful that outsourcing of some production processes to logistics providers can lead to wage reduction.

## Key points

- Outsourced supply chains are more vulnerable to economic shocks because of the risk of supplier failure.

- Globalization and the emphasis this places on international transport means that international supply chains are at risk from increases in rates, oil prices and, on occasion, lack of capacity.

- 'Slow steaming' strategies introduced by shipping lines had a major and unexpected impact on inventory levels.

- Trade restrictions and, worse, trade wars are particularly disruptive to the efficient functioning of supply chains.

- Changing manufacturing and retailing patterns, including the outsourcing and e-commerce trends, are placing additional emphasis on industrial relations and increasing risk.

# Societal risks to 07 supply chains

**OBJECTIVES**

This chapter will familiarize the reader with:

- the impact that the Fair Labour campaign has had on global supply chains;
- the problems highlighted by the Rana Plaza disaster and responses by Western retailers and manufacturers;
- societal issues in the fashion, consumer electronics, and fresh fruit and vegetable sectors;
- how major manufacturers are dealing with regulations governing the use of resources extracted from 'failed' countries such as the Democratic Republic of Congo;
- the problem of water usage and pollution in certain parts of the world;
- the illegal trade in e-waste;
- food shortages and post-harvest food losses.

Perhaps one of the defining features of the next decade in terms of supply chain strategies of global retailers and manufacturers will be the pressure that they will come under to justify their sourcing decisions from a corporate social responsibility (CSR) perspective.

There has been growing pressure on companies to demonstrate that they implement ethical policies when it comes to the conditions in which their suppliers' employees work, not least their wages and their environmental practices. No longer is it morally acceptable for manufacturers to outsource production or for retailers to purchase goods from suppliers without having full visibility of these issues.

The CSR dimension is critical to the supply chain. With globalization of industry predicated on the trade-off between cheap labour, production and transport costs on one hand, and more expensive inventory holdings on the other, a shift in the cost dynamics of any one of these factors is highly important.

# Fair labour

One of the most prominent campaigns in recent years has been the Fair Labour initiative, which has sought to highlight working conditions in developing countries, with particular reference to the global manufacturers and retailers who source from these countries.

China has seen the most publicity, not least because of the massive labour forces employed by consumer electronics companies, such as Foxconn, supplying major Western brands. However, companies right across the industry spectrum are involved in this practice, with fashion being one of the biggest sectors. Asda-Walmart, for example, is the largest buyer of clothing from Bangladesh, with labour costs in that country half of what they are in China.

Working conditions refer to basic labour principles and standards in the manufacturing of goods and services. They include such issues as:

- child labour;
- wages and benefits;
- working hours;
- forced labour;
- freedom of association;
- health and safety;
- harassment and discrimination.

## Fashion supply chains

Fashion supply chains attracted a large amount of bad publicity because of the Rana Plaza factory incident in Bangladesh (see box on page 141). The trend towards 'fast fashion' in the major Western consumer markets has reinforced retailers' requirements for sources of cheap and, from the consumers' perspective, disposable fashion items. In the UK, the fast-fashion industry is led by specialist stores Primark, Matalan, TK Maxx and ASOS and by supermarket retailers Tesco and Asda. Marks & Spencer has also been forced to focus its products around the offering of its rivals to avoid being outcompeted.

These demand trends have influenced the sourcing strategies of the major fashion retailers, leading them to seek out ever cheaper sources of production delivering to tighter and tighter schedules. As labour costs are an important cost element, markets with large and cheap workforces have become popular. This has resulted in what some labour rights activists have called a 'race to the bottom', and they insist that legislation is required to provide for a 'living wage'.

However, it is not just the cost of labour that has upset activists. The just-in-time nature of 'fast fashion' has resulted in a move from long product runs to shorter production schedules, manufacturing much smaller quantities of goods. The consequence of this is that whereas previously the workforce would be able to rely on longer-term employment, terms are now much more temporary. This favours the employment of informal workers, even on daily terms. The short lead times also result in increased overtime requirements, often leading to night shifts, weekend working and a greater level of flexibility in order to fulfil the contract.

The unpredictable nature and 'short-termism' of a contract award has also led to an increased probability of an outsourced supplier subcontracting to a third party. The Western manufacturer or retailer has even less visibility of the conditions and terms and conditions under which its products are being made and temporary labour is likely to be used to fulfil these ad hoc contracts. In Bangladesh and Guangdong, China, one campaign group claims that less than half of workers have a permanent contract.

The hyper-competition of high streets in the developed consumer economies has resulted in much lower prices. This has obviously had major benefits for hard-pressed customers, but this fall in prices has only been made possible by retailers driving down costs, with predictable consequences to the labour force in emerging markets.

In order to compete effectively, retailers such as Primark have hundreds of suppliers around the world. Their buying power makes it possible to force down costs, but also to switch supplier quickly to remain responsive to the needs of the market. Retailers also like to exert a large degree of power over suppliers, preferring those that do not work for competitors.

## Bangladesh factory disaster

The fire that took place at a factory in Bangladesh demonstrated the reputational risks to Western manufacturers and retailers of sourcing from suppliers in the region. In April 2013, a clothing factory in Rana Plaza, Dhaka, collapsed, killing 1,129 workers. The disaster was blamed on poor construction practices, with the owner directly responsible. It transpired that UK retailers Primark, Matalan and Bonmarché were amongst a number of Western stores sourcing goods from the factory and their reputation took a severe knock. Critics suggested that their cut-price clothing business model was based on sourcing unsustainably from low-cost suppliers who would exploit workers in terms of pay and, in the case of the Rana Plaza factory, the structural integrity of its buildings.

As a result of the disaster, a range of retailers (including Marks & Spencer and H&M) have signed up to a new compact, which will mean rigorous factory inspections and the introduction of fire measures. Of course, these will come at a cost.

Although non-governmental organizations have been quick to criticize the conditions of many workers in Bangladesh, they perhaps recognize the problems that are faced by the country. If costs are driven up, either by minimum wages or by regulatory burdens, retailers and manufacturers may leave the market completely, heading for lower-cost countries. Whereas Primark claims that it has done more than most for the workers of Rana Plaza, compensating families for example, there are many other companies that sourced products from the factory that have not come forward. It is these, which make up the majority of the market, who would be happy to source goods first and worry about the conditions in which they were manufactured later.

Following the fire at Rana Plaza, a multi-stakeholder Accord on Fire and Building Safety was developed in conjunction with retailers, unions and the United Nations. Tesco, although it did not source any goods from the Rana Plaza factory, has gone further, and has conducted structural surveys at all its suppliers' locations (it does not source from shared-use factories).

The importance of an ethical sourcing policy to reputation has not been lost on retailers. In its CSR report, Tesco highlighted that in May 2012 it launched a pilot project in Bangladesh that:

- increased pay for suppliers' workers by 19 per cent;
- reduced working hours by 16 per cent;
- decreased staff turnover by 45 per cent and absenteeism by 25 per cent;
- increased efficiency by 20 per cent.

The company rolled out this programme to 100 factories, positively affecting over 250,000 fashion and textile workers (Tesco, 2012).

Tesco is committed to the Bangladesh market and says that, while some commentators are calling for retailers to pull out, especially in the light of the Rana Plaza disaster, it should remain. Western companies have the opportunity to provide a positive influence on working conditions. For instance, Tesco presently employs 54 people in Dhaka whose roles involve improving the standards at its 100 suppliers' factories. In order to address the issue of temporary contracts, which has proved so problematic in terms of taking on and laying off staff, it offers the suppliers that meet its standards a two-year permanent contract. It has also published a list of its suppliers in order to improve visibility.

## Consumer electronics

The consumer electronics industry has been the focus of attention for groups campaigning to improve the working conditions in factories throughout the world. Assembling electronic goods is a highly labour-intensive activity, which is one of the reasons why manufacturers have located this function in regions where labour is plentiful and low-cost – such as China. The ease of access to global markets through ports and airports has facilitated this trend.

The electronics sector has also been at the forefront of the 'unbundling and outsourcing' phenomenon that has resulted in the creation of virtual manufacturing networks. This has meant that brands, such as Cisco, Dell and a vast array of other household names, have focused their attention on design and marketing, leaving the production of goods to electronic component manufacturers (ECMs) such as Flextronics or Foxconn. It is estimated that three-quarters of manufacturing is outsourced.

One of the risks of this approach, however, is that brands become tarnished if the outsourced providers do not live up to the expectations of consumers by failing to adhere to stringent working practices usual in the West.

Pay is obviously at the forefront of concerns, not just the level but also the structure. Wages are designed to be flexible enough to meet production demands. This often equates to a low basic wage, augmented by:

- overtime – typically 150 per cent, 200 per cent or 300 per cent depending on weekday, weekend or statutory holiday working requirements;

- food subsidies;

- skills bonuses depending on grades;

- attendance bonus.

While Foxconn has in place minimum wage protection in the season of low production, many others do not. Some companies do not allow their staff to resign in peak season in order to maintain production levels; those that do sacrifice back wages.

Shifts range from eight hours a day in low season to 12 hours in peak season. During periods of high demand, workers can be expected to put in 60–100 hours' overtime and work through the night if necessary.

The consumer electronics sector is characterized by heavy use of temporary labour. It is estimated that around 60 per cent of all employees are contracted on a temporary basis, and in Mexico some companies utilize up to 90 per cent. Although temporary workers have rights written into European law, in many countries (especially in the developing world) the same level of protection does not exist.

The benefits of employing a temporary workforce, as in the fashion industry, are self-evident. Consumer electronics products have very short lifecycles and hence delivery schedules to support product release are very tight. This means that companies such as Apple or Samsung need their suppliers to have access to a large pool of labour that can be brought in quickly to fulfil a contract. Flexibility is essential to be able to ramp production up and down as required. For this reason, employees are also asked to work overtime to meet demand.

The concerns are not just about pay and conditions. Examples have been cited that include health and safety issues: for example, exposure to toxic chemicals and lack of ventilation causing respiratory problems and skin allergies. Other health issues include:

- back problems from standing for long periods of time;

- noise pollution;

- stress;

- eye irritation (for example due to inspecting circuit boards).

Also a common complaint is the level of discipline regarding quality control – an issue that has been given very high priority because of supply chain management strategies that aim to keep inventory to a minimum. Getting things wrong can result in a deduction from wages.

## Apple in China

Although Apple's supply chain has been much celebrated for its efficiency, it has also come in for a lot of criticism from an ethical perspective. Both Apple and Foxconn, its major contract manufacturer, have been under media scrutiny following a series of events that raised questions about the working conditions at the factories in China. A *New York Times* article described poor working conditions within Foxconn facilities, which prompted Apple CEO Tim Cook to state, 'We care about every worker in our worldwide supply chain. Any suggestion that we don't care is patently false and offensive to us' (Duhigg and Barboza, 2012).

As a result, Apple entered into a partnership with the Fair Labor Association (FLA), the first technology company to join the association as a participating company. In doing so, the company agreed to uphold the FLA's workplace code of conduct throughout their entire supply chain. The FLA spent 3,000 staff hours investigating three of Apple's factories and surveying more than 35,000 workers. Apple and its supplier Foxconn agreed to its recommendations, and the FLA plans to verify progress and report publicly. Three Foxconn factories were scrutinized by the FLA: Guanlan, Longua and Chengdu (the factory at the centre of the *New York Times* exposé).

While Apple is at the centre of the controversy, the changes at Foxconn will be made across the board. This will mean that the improved working conditions will also affect factories that manufacture electronics for companies such as Microsoft, Amazon and Dell. Apple and its main supplier Foxconn have agreed to share the cost of improvements to be made at the factories that manufacture iPads and iPhones.

## International retail supply chains in fruit and vegetables

Retailers are now more able than ever before to provide a wide range of exotic products to their customers, often sourced from emerging markets with much lower standards of production procedures and working practices than in the developed world. This includes the fresh fruit, vegetables (FFV) and fish sectors.

This has meant that there is considerable reputational risk to international retailers if they are shown to be sourcing goods from farms where workers are being exploited. Some of these pitfalls are listed next:

- One of the major problems for FFV supply chains is seasonality. Products may be harvested over a short timescale – perhaps weeks – which means that a high volume of labour is required to work intensively through-out this period. The work is often temporary, providing for an unstable labour force.

- Child labour is often employed in many parts of the world. Although it may be characteristic of many markets, and often an important source of family income, it is unacceptable for Western retailers to be seen as exploiting this form of labour.

- Illegal workers – migrant workers, some illegal, are often employed on farms and, because of their lack of legal status, can be exploited by employers.

- Wages – because of the manual nature of the work, wages are low, often below the legal minimum wage.

- Exposure to chemicals – in undeveloped markets good practice in the application of chemical fertilizers is often not adhered to. This can result in health and safety issues for the workforce.

The fact that these problems exist in the markets from which international retailers source their goods is not the fault of the retailer, of course. They bring welcome foreign exchange and the market they provide to farmers creates employment, with all the associated trickle-down benefits to the local economy. However, this does not mean that they do not have a duty of care to the workers of the farms from which they source – a fact that the majority recognize.

In 2011, a report by the Centre for Research on Multinational Corporations (CRMC) (Vander Stichele *et al*, 2011), an organization part-funded by the European Union, highlighted the Peruvian mango supply chain as being of particular concern and named Dutch supermarket giant Ahold as being implicated.

Peru exports about 300,000 tonnes of mangos a year, most of which are fresh. Most workers are hired for just three to five months a year because of the seasonal nature of the product. The mangos are then shipped by sea to export markets. In the case of Ahold's mangos, they were exported by a large Peruvian agri-business, Camposol, to Rotterdam, and bought on behalf of Ahold by Bakker Barendrecht, the retailer's exclusive fresh fruit and vegetable trading company.

Research by CRMC found that wages paid by Camposol were below the legal minimum and working hours were excessive, often 11 hours a day for six to seven days a week. Sanitary conditions were poor and drinking water was lacking. Health and safety conditions were sub-standard.

This was despite both companies, Ahold and Camposol, being signed up to the UN Global Compact, which seeks to protect workers' rights, and the fact that Camposol had signed Ahold's Business Social Compliance Initiative (BSCI). In fact, Ahold has in the past been commended for its commitment to improving the conditions of suppliers' workers. However, in this instance its due diligence processes were found to be wanting, with the resultant bad publicity and impact on its brand equity.

In response to the allegations, Ahold made the following statement:

> In January [2011], Ahold representatives visited Camposol to review the situation. During this visit, several meetings took place with both top and middle management in charge of the fields, as well as with HR representatives. The Ahold representatives found Camposol to be willing to take responsibility for their business and for treating their employees fairly and respectfully. Camposol had already been informed that the BSCI process is now a requirement to do business with Ahold and they have started the process which begins with a self-assessment. An independent audit will be scheduled, and will lead to the identification of any areas for improvement. Because of the findings of our visit and Camposol's willingness to commit to the BSCI process we have not suspended them as a supplier, which would be likely to have an adverse impact on their workers and have instead chosen to support them in the social compliance process.

This example highlights a number of key points:

- Retailers have accepted that they have a moral responsibility to the workers who help in the production of goods supplied to their stores.
- Consumers have a level of trust in retailers that the products they buy have been produced ethically.
- Campaign groups can have an immediate impact on the working conditions at international retailers' suppliers.
- Even major retailers with a generally good track record of social commitment are susceptible to bad publicity, if their CSR processes are not comprehensive.
- It is generally recognized that retailers are a source of good in terms of the influence they can have on conditions of employment in developing markets.

## Labour costs and their impact on supply chains

With rising labour costs already evident, low-cost manufacturing in China will increasingly become unsustainable. Policymakers in China have recognized this and have consequently seen the necessity to refocus their economic development policy around technological innovation. This will eventually see labour costs become less important.

This is obviously a pragmatic response by the Chinese government and follows the well-trodden path of many other formerly developing nations. It is also part of China's new assertiveness on the world stage as it moves from component supplier to original equipment manufacturer in its own right.

Rising labour costs in China will not necessarily deter foreign direct investment. One piece of research for the World Bank concluded that a 1 per cent increase in the ratio of skilled workers in the labour force resulted in a 2.66 per cent increase in the likelihood that a foreign company would choose Guangdong, a province in southern China. To many Western companies, access to highly skilled staff in China is more important than the cheapness of the labour. This would seem to suggest that China's overall strategy to increase the value of its output is in line with the requirements of many multinational manufacturers.

Labour costs in Asia shift much faster than may be thought, and manufacturers are very responsive to these costs. Japanese companies have moved production from their developed and high-cost home market to other locations in the Asia Pacific region. For example, for more than 10 years, Nikon has been developing assembly operations in the Thai city of Ayutthaya, outside Bangkok. This was part of a significant investment in the country by the electronics sector from the 1990s onwards, with Sony and Canon also having substantial manufacturing operations in Thailand. These facilities are generally used to assemble finished products using components produced in Japan.

However, subsequently Nikon opened a new assembly plant in Laos in Savannakhet Province, which is located on the border between Thailand and Laos. This move is indicative that the strong growth in Thailand has pushed wages upwards, with the labour market now quite tight and the country increasingly tapping into migrant labour from Laos, Cambodia and Burma. Thailand has also recently introduced a minimum wage of approximately 300 baht (US$10) a day.

Therefore, the opportunity to access the lower-cost labour force in a country such as Laos, and benefit from the development of its infrastructure, must surely be an attractive next step for many of the businesses that have already established a presence in Thailand. There had been rumours that Nikon was looking to expand its presence in China; however, Laotian wage rates are markedly below those of the cities of the Chinese eastern seaboard.

In one respect, of course, this will bring major benefits to the Laotian economy, and help bring increased prosperity to an impoverished country. However, it also provides ammunition for those who would claim that it is exploiting workers to increase profits, the so-called 'race to the bottom'.

# 'Conflict-free' minerals

The interest that regulators and administrators are paying to manufacturers' supply chains does not end with labour practices and environmental behaviour. Increasingly companies are being asked to verify that materials used in the production of finished goods are ethically sourced in other ways. This is most apparent in the mining of minerals in parts of Africa, which has been tainted by corruption in regions of armed conflict and human rights abuses.

For example, in West Africa cassiterite, wolframite, coltan, as well as tantalum, tin, tungsten and gold (3TG) – all used extensively in high-tech manufacturing – are extracted (sometimes illegally) and then pass through multiple intermediaries (both legitimate and criminal) before entering the supply chains of global electronics manufacturers.

In some cases the profits from these minerals directly fund armed groups that are involved in waging civil wars in countries throughout the region, especially in the Democratic Republic of Congo (DRC).

In 2010, the issue was addressed in a piece of US legislation, which has prompted many manufacturers to take an active interest in the upstream provenance of their materials. The issue was included in the Dodd-Frank Wall Street Reform and Consumer Protection Act, which decreed that all publicly listed companies reporting to the Securities and Exchange Commission (SEC) must disclose any exposure they have to conflict minerals in this region. Materials should be described as 'DRC Conflict Free', 'Not DRC Conflict Free' or 'DRC Conflict Free Undeterminable'. Conflict-free is defined as those minerals that do not finance or benefit armed groups in the DRC or adjoining countries.

One unforeseen consequence of regulation and legislation, however, is the possibility that it could drive manufacturers away from the region entirely – a de facto embargo – causing widespread hardship to local populations.

Hewlett-Packard, along with Apple, Motorola and Intel, have been at the forefront of developing an alternative solution to this problem, which will provide conflict-free minerals while ensuring that investment in the region continues. As with other forms of supply chain risk, increasing visibility to tier 2/3 suppliers is at the heart of their efforts.

However, the auditing and tracing comes at a cost. The SEC estimated that the cost of compliance would be $3–4 billion to start up, with annual costs of $206–609 million. For the aerospace industry alone it could cost anywhere from $100 million to $2 billion.

The Enough Project – an organization campaigning against the use of conflict minerals – measures manufacturers on three key metrics:

- **Tracing** – most consumer electronics manufacturers, starting with Apple, have undertaken mapping of their supply chains to identify the smelters that they source goods from.

- **Auditing** – following on from identifying where their goods are sourced from, the next stage is to audit the smelters for use of non-conflict minerals – the so-called Conflict-Free Smelters (CFS) programme. In 2010, the Electronics Industry Citizenship Coalition (EICC) and Global e-Sustainability Initiative (GeSI) Extractives Work Group launched the first Conflict-Free Smelter (CFS) programme. This programme independently audits smelters and refiners to determine if they are sourcing DRC conflict-free minerals. There is the hope that consumer electronics manufacturers will instruct their suppliers to only use materials sourced from these smelters.

- **Certification** – in the DRC and surrounding areas, a certification system has been set up with the aid of the US government, NGOs and consumer electronics companies called the Public Private Alliance for Responsible Minerals Trade (PPA). Mines certified as 'clean' by a regional government body can provide minerals to smelters involved in the CFS programme. Manufacturers such as Intel, Motorola and HP were behind this initiative.

Whereas in the past, Congolese tin may have been smuggled across the border and passed off as Rwandan, with new controls in place this is proving much harder to achieve for the armed groups involved. This has led, by one estimate, to armed groups' revenues from conflict minerals dropping by 65 per cent in two years.

## Hewlett-Packard's approach to conflict-free minerals

In understanding its supply chain, Hewlett-Packard scrutinizes both its first-tier suppliers and the smelters identified by those suppliers that process mineral ores into metals. HP requires its first-tier suppliers to provide information about the smelters they use, adopt a DRC conflict mineral-free policy, and set the same requirements for their own suppliers.

HP has also been working to mitigate an embargo of minerals from the DRC and is committed to using metals produced from 'closed pipe' projects if they are available. These metals, which directly benefit local communities, are available through programmes such as the Solutions for Hope Project and the Conflict-Free Tin Initiative. To establish a complete conflict mineral-free supply chain, a mineral must be certified at the source and during the chain-of-custody process in the DRC. Creating a validated supply of minerals to smelters from the mines poses significant challenges. Because there is no way to distinguish minerals from different mines, a form of secure traceability at all stages from mine to smelter is needed.

In addition to the operational work outlined above:

- HP publishes the identity of its 195 3TG smelters and refiners that it has confirmed to be in their supply chain.

- HP has been a member of the CFS Programme Audit Review Committee since its inception. HP also helped to develop the Conflict Minerals Reporting Template to facilitate the common exchange of information between suppliers and the smelters used in their supply chains.

HP believes that the deep-rooted problems in the DRC require coordinated action by the business, government and NGO community. HP has committed resources to education, administration, and the development of tools to validate mineral sources.

The key to achieving its goals is growing the number of CFS-compliant smelters. When a critical mass of CFS-compliant smelters is attained, HP plans to require its suppliers to source only from those smelters. However, HP states that the journey towards conflict-free minerals for HP and all companies sourcing these minerals will take time.

**SOURCE** Hewlett-Packard

The minerals have a wide variety of uses. They are sourced extensively for the consumer electronics, automotive, industrial machinery, mining and jewellery sectors. The Enough Project hopes that in the coming years all smelters will be audited (Dranginis, 2016). Many of the costs of auditing are covered by companies such as HP in their efforts to make all minerals used in their supply chains traceable. However, it will take efforts by companies in other sectors that presently are not displaying the same level of concern to encourage smelters to participate in such programmes.

In the automotive and engineering sectors, Ford and GE have signed up to the PPA initiative, and in the aerospace sector, Boeing, Northrop Grumman, United Technologies, and Lockheed Martin have started pilot projects.

The OECD has been at the forefront of the campaign against the use of conflict minerals and has developed a due diligence process framework that companies such as Ford (see Table 7.1) have followed (OECD, 2015):

> Ford will be required to report annually to the SEC whether our products that contain conflict minerals are 'conflict free.' All suppliers globally that provide parts contained in Ford vehicles, service parts, or other parts sold by Ford are required to support this effort. Specifically, suppliers will be required to respond to an annual survey to identify whether products they manufacture or contract to manufacture for Ford contain any Conflict Minerals necessary to the functionality or production of their products. If any Conflict Minerals are contained in the affected product supplied to Ford, the supplier will be required to determine the country of origin of these materials and whether the Conflict Minerals can be identified as 'conflict free', and to report this information to Ford (Ford, 2014).

Preliminary results of Ford's research show that about a third of its suppliers use conflict minerals in its products, involving thousands of parts (Ford, 2014). Tracing these parts back to their countries of origin and deciding on whether they are conflict-free or not is an immense task and will take several years (plus a large degree of expense).

If a part is determined to be non-conflict-free, Ford has committed to work with the supplier to find alternative sources that do not involve raw material processors who support, directly or indirectly, armed conflict. The company is also looking at developing certified conflict-free smelter capacity, and eventually, when enough exists, to insist that its suppliers use these resources.

As part of its efforts, Ford (as well as other automotive manufacturers) is looking at extending the International Material Data System (IMDS) to include conflict minerals. The IMDS was established in 1997 by a number of the world's largest manufacturers to establish the content of all the

**Table 7.1**   OECD five-step process

| Step 1 | OECD recommendation | Establish strong corporate management systems |
|---|---|---|
| | Ford action | Assigned accountability and cross-functional team; revised policy and supplier guides to address conflict mineral issues |
| Step 2 | OECD recommendation | Identify and assess risk in the supply chain |
| | Ford action | Requiring supplier material content reporting and assigning prioritization of suppliers based on declared content |
| Step 3 | OECD recommendation | Design and implement a strategy to respond to identified risks |
| | Ford action | Balanced strategy of Ford and industry action to ensure robust sourcing policies, practices and reporting |
| Step 4 | OECD recommendation | Third-party audit of smelters'/refiners' due diligence practices |
| | Ford action | Participation in the conflict-free sourcing programme through the Automotive Industry Action Group |
| Step 5 | OECD recommendation | Report annually on supply chain due diligence and outcomes |
| | Ford action | Public disclosure in the Sustainability Report and planned SEC filing for 2013 calendar year |

components used in vehicles. This was brought about because of legislation by various authorities on end-of-life disposal of vehicles, creating the need to be able to identify and trace substances and materials of concern (such as chemicals) before they are scrapped. Although the database identifies all the materials involved in the production of a car, it does not identify the countries where they are extracted or processed. This is a key element of the extension of the IMDS.

Ford also uses its Global Material Integration and Reporting portal, which enables it to communicate with its suppliers and holds information such as suppliers' certification status. In 2012 it carried out a survey through

**Figure 7.1** Ford programme – covered countries for conflict minerals

this portal to identify which of its suppliers were affected by the conflict minerals legislation and then assist with compliance.

Although compliance is costly, some commentators believe that it will provide benefits to the companies involved in the long run. For the first time it will allow them to map out their supply chains, giving them deep visibility. This will provide them with all sorts of advantages in terms of risk mitigation strategies, far beyond the conflict-free dimension.

An example of this is Intel. In order to achieve its goal of making its microprocessors totally conflict-free (they are at present conflict-free of tantalum), it has already mapped 90 per cent of its supply chain.

# Environmental practices of supply chain partners

Manufacturers and retailers are coming under increasing pressure to ensure that the way their products are sourced, made and then disposed of is sustainable from an environmental perspective. This 'whole life' approach has placed additional burdens on the supply chain, but as is the case with conflict minerals, it also provides the opportunity to achieve far higher levels of supply chain visibility.

When looking at supply chains such as those in the consumer electronics industry, it is possible to identify three distinct sectors:

- mining and extraction of raw materials (upstream);
- manufacturing and assembly (downstream);
- recycling and disposal (reverse logistics).

Upstream, many of the materials used in consumer electronics products start life being mined in Latin America, Africa or Asia. Just as companies have recently been required to take responsibility for sourcing non-conflict minerals (see above), many environmental lobby groups are campaigning for OEMs to ensure that materials used in their products are sourced in a sustainable manner.

For instance, mining has the potential to result in a devastating impact on the surrounding environment, not only because of the physical disruption but also because of the chemicals utilized in processing raw materials. The influx of immigrant workers can also have a negative impact on indigenous peoples and destabilize local communities.

In the downstream supply chain, processing of materials and assembly can employ the use of hazardous chemicals. For instance, a cathode ray tube contains 2–4 kilograms of lead, barium and phosphorus, and flat screens contain mercury. Lead solder is usually used to connect semi-conductors to mother boards and integrated chip units. Not only does this have potential detrimental impact on the health of workers, but waste product needs to be disposed of in a responsible fashion.

This is not always straightforward. Although many technology manufacturers in the developing world may use licensed waste treatment companies to remove their toxic waste, some unscrupulous companies have been found to subcontract the movement to illegal operators, who then dump it indiscriminately.

Large amounts of water can be used in the manufacturing process itself (creating a water management issue) and waste water emissions are also a problem. They can contain organic solvents, heavy metals, acid/alkalines and volatile organic compounds. In Taiwan, in order to increase water supply to the industry, a river has been dammed and water diverted from agricultural use. The production process can also result in air pollution and soil contamination.

UK retailer Tesco has recognized that it has a responsibility for the environmental impact of the factories from which it sources fashion items, not least in the effect that it has on water supplies and waste water (Tesco, 2016). Textile washing, dyeing and finishing use large amounts of water, energy and chemicals in the manufacturing process, and consequently polluted waste water is also a problem. A pilot that the company ran in Bangladesh at 18 fabric mills resulted in a saving of 300 million litres of water as well as 19,000 tonnes of greenhouse gas (GHG) emissions. There were also economic benefits, with a saving of £520,000 being achieved.

Tesco has worked with Cranfield University in the past to identify ways in which its supply chain water usage could be made more resilient. The company says that 30 times more water is used in its supply chain to grow, process and manufacture the products it sells than it uses in the operation of its retail outlets.

Of course, pollution can be a problem in all manufacturing sectors, not just those that have adopted outsourcing, such as fashion and consumer electronics. However, the difference is that outsourcing reduces control and visibility, meaning that OEMs have to work harder to identify breaches of environmental compliance. If they do not proactively undertake environmental audits, for instance, they can be held responsible by lobby groups (and hence consumers) for washing their hands of their environmental obligations.

Manufacturing waste is tracked by the major manufacturers. For instance, Intel states that it is able to recycle 75 per cent of its waste, most of which comes from the construction of its production facilities. It also recycles 75 per cent of its chemical waste. They have goals to reduce waste over a period of time and to eventually achieve zero per cent landfill.

The end-of-life supply chain is problematic for manufacturers and governments alike. Whereas once the disposal of goods, such as electronics equipment and cars, was seen as the responsibility solely of the consumer, legislation in Europe and North America has trended towards pushing this responsibility onto the producer.

Many manufacturers were already involved in recovering product, not least because it is financially beneficial to be able to refurbish or repair faulty products and reintroduce them back into the supply chain. However, the legislation has gone further, enshrining in law the moral responsibility of the producer to ensure the safe disposal of the product at the end of its life.

In Europe the main legislation covering the electrical sector is the EU Directive on Waste Electrical and Electronic Equipment (WEEE). Any equipment that connects to the normal electrical power supply or normal industry standard of a three-phase supply is covered by the regulations. These include:

- large household appliances;
- small household appliances;
- IT and telecommunications equipment;
- consumer equipment;
- lighting equipment (with the exception of household luminaries and filament light bulbs);
- electrical and electronic tools (with the exception of large-scale stationary industrial tools);
- toys, leisure and sports equipment;
- medical devices (with the exception of all implanted and infected products);
- monitoring and control instruments;
- automatic dispensers.

The regulations apply to importers, manufacturers who make goods under their own name as well as those who brand goods from suppliers under their own name. They must either arrange for the collection, treatment, recycling and environmentally sound disposal of WEEE, or pay a producer compliance scheme (PCS) to do this on their behalf.

The law has been tightened further following a vote in the European Parliament in 2011. From 2016, member states of the EU have been expected to collect 85 per cent of e-waste that has been produced, with a 50–75 per cent recycling target.

The legislation has meant that, by law, manufacturers have had to extend their supply chain to include reverse logistics, whether or not there was a commercial imperative for doing so. This issue is now seen as an essential part of their CSR policies.

## Illegal trade in e-waste

Where there is regulation that carries a cost burden, grey or black markets will develop. This has been the case in the disposal of end-of-life product. It is estimated that 12 million tonnes of e-waste is generated in the EU, and presently two-thirds of this is unaccounted for, despite the WEEE regulations. It is believed that this waste either ends up in landfill, is treated at sub-standard facilities or exported illegally.

The illegal export of waste from developed countries to the emerging world is now a major industry that, despite efforts by authorities, only seems to be getting worse. The UK is the biggest exporter in Europe for second-hand electronic equipment, followed by France and Germany. However, Germany and Belgium are the most important in terms of the export of second-hand cars. Italy is important in the export of refrigerators.

As more regulations are imposed on the disposal of products in the Western world (for instance, landfill tax), the incentives to export the problem to countries with lower standards of regulation become ever greater.

The problem was addressed in 1989 by an international treaty to which over 150 countries signed up – the Basel Convention. Many campaigners thought that this agreement did not go far enough, and in fact legitimized the dumping of hazardous waste exports. It was amended in 1995 to cover all forms of hazardous waste that are exported from the OECD group of countries to the rest of the world.

However, it is clear that this law is being flouted, although this is unrecognized both in many countries of export and also those of import. For instance, India has no record of any illegal import of waste as it doesn't track this problem as a crime. China banned the import of e-waste in 2000 but there is evidence that it is still going on, especially in Guangdong Province, the centre of waste recycling in the country.

One report by the Basel Action Network and Silicon Valley Toxics Coalition estimated that 50–58 per cent of e-waste that was collected for recycling in the United States found its way illegally to Asia. Recycling and processing facilities in Asia, Africa and elsewhere are often unregulated, putting at risk the workers, local communities as well as the wider environment (BAN, 2002).

For example, computers and electronic equipment can contain lead and mercury, and the uncontrolled burning of cabling can result in the emission of dioxins that can travel long distances and find their way into the food chain.

In Kenya alone it is estimated that the amount of waste annually includes:

- 11,400 tonnes of refrigerators;
- 2,800 tonnes of televisions;
- 2,500 tonnes of personal computers;
- 500 tonnes of printers;
- 150 tonnes of mobile phones.

The UK's Environment Agency says that it takes illegal export of e-waste very seriously, working in conjunction with the INTERPOL Global e-waste Crime Group. One problem that the regulator faces is that companies are allowed to export functional items that can be reused in developing markets. However, it is sometimes difficult to assess what is working and what is not (for example, second-hand television monitors would have to be plugged in to be tested) and the vast volume of exports makes it impractical for authorities to regulate effectively.

In one investigation covered by the *Independent* (London) – 'Dumped in Africa: Britain's toxic waste' (18 February 2009) – GPS tracking devices were placed in TV monitors that had been disabled. From a UK recycling centre, the monitors were then tracked to a recycling facility in Ghana. According to Greenpeace, inspections at European seaports in 2005 found that almost half of all waste was being exported illegally. Criminal gangs see this as a relatively low-risk method of making large sums of money, as illegal waste export does not attract the same levels of attention from police authorities or of penalties from judicial authorities. The Belgian customs authorities believe that 90 per cent of illegal waste is exported by co-loading into used cars that are being moved legally.

The problem is deeply intractable, as to ban the export of second-hand equipment would impact severely on many economies in the developing world, especially markets in Africa. The trade supplies low- and middle-income families with information and communications technology equipment that they would never otherwise be able to afford. This access provides them with significant opportunities for economic advancement, which authorities should be encouraging.

There is evidence that manufacturers are more accepting of the need to take responsibility for the disposal of their products – especially those in the consumer electronics sector. A forum in 2012 brought together a range of private sector companies, including Dell, HP, Nokia and Philips, with government and intergovernmental organizations under the auspices of the United Nations Environment Programme (UNEP) and the Secretariat of the Basel Convention to discuss the issue of increasing e-waste in Africa (see box opposite).

## The African e-waste initiative

The African e-waste initiative is a partnership between four OEMs – HP, Dell, Nokia and Philips –and a specialist recycling company, Reclaimed Appliances Ltd, and the United Nations Industrial Development Organization (UNIDO).

Developed to address the fast growing e-waste crisis in Africa, the initiative seeks to build on some of the strengths of the recycling industry. For instance, a compelling business model has meant that collection of waste in Africa can be highly effective. In Ghana, 95 per cent of waste is collected as 'refurbishers' and scrap metal businesses are willing to pay a good price for obsolete equipment. The price that scrap metal can fetch on the international market supports this model.

The vision of the e-waste initiative is that all waste can be collected and properly treated to international standards as part of a profitable business model, and as a result protect health and the environment.

At present, the companies work together in four countries: Ghana, Nigeria, Kenya and South Africa. In Kenya the project was initially set up by HP, which was the second recycler working to international standards. It has since developed as a hub for the entire region, with 20 per cent of materials coming from the informal sector. Its goal is to become self-sustaining. The centre's customers include the International Committee of the Red Cross, who chose it because it offered, 'a formal, accessible channel for the safe, environmentally responsible dismantling and recycling of e-waste, allowing us to meet our environmental credentials in the region'.

The initiative depends on viewing e-waste as a resource, and consequently an opportunity. It believes that the work that has been undertaken will act as an encouragement to major global recyclers to come to the continent. Although additional investment will be required to scale up operations, if governments and other stakeholders can be involved, there is no reason why regional solutions cannot be developed. Although producers accept responsibility for their part of the market, the extensive second-hand and counterfeit element means that they do not have full control. Therefore government will have an important role in the development of recycling projects, not least with the enforcement of recycling legislation.

Instead of looking at e-waste as solely a problem, it is now being seen as a potential opportunity. One tonne of obsolete mobile phones contains more gold than one tonne of ore, and the same can be said for other precious substances. Recycling of this equipment will provide manufacturers with a much cheaper source of the 'rare earth minerals' essential to their production, and at the same time provide business for African economies. It will also reduce the pressure on exploiting natural resources as well as carbon dioxide emissions.

It has been suggested that manufacturers of original equipment adopt the same extended producer responsibility (EPR) for their end-of-life supply chains that is undertaken in developed countries. This would only work, however, if more flexibility is given to manufacturers over how they wish to deal with obsolete equipment, combined with the introduction of world-class recycling centres in various emerging markets. Governments have a role to play in this, as well as ensuring that administrative processes are fast, efficient and corruption-free.

One example of an early recycling initiative is Nokia's partnership in Kenya with Safaricom, which involves a network of collection points for mobile phones. This is likely to be just the start, with EPR proposals likely to be formally adopted in legislation across the region. Projects are likely to include:

- the establishment of collection centres;
- the establishment of take-back schemes by producers and producer responsibility organizations (PROs);
- treatment facilities;
- disposal mechanisms.

However, it will be less than straightforward to implement these schemes in the developing world. One of the reasons for this is the large amount of counterfeit products in the market, which nobody wants to take responsibility for.

Second, in many markets there is already a large amount of second-hand equipment in circulation, imported from the developed world. It is not clear whether EPR commitments would cover this equipment if it has already been refurbished by a third-party operator once before. Given that much of this equipment only has a short life span, this only adds to the problem.

Third, government commitment to this problem is not as robust as it could be, with the subject being generally low on priority and inadequate facilities available to deal with the waste.

It is, however, significant that there have been calls to relax the control of e-waste exports to certain locations in the developing world. Some markets are now becoming expert in the processing of waste, and see the opportunities that building a strong recycling competence can create. For instance, one market in East Africa is looking at creating a 'virtual mines' model from recovering the precision metals in imported e-waste.

## Pollution havens – real or imaginary?

Considerable research has been undertaken into whether multinational companies have been guilty of using some emerging markets as 'pollution havens' when deciding on the best location for investment in new production locations.

There is no doubt that the stringency in environmental regulation varies substantially from the developed world to the developing, and even within markets. Where countries devolve a large amount of responsibility to states, provinces or municipalities, such as in the United States or China, there can be a high degree of variance in costs associated with compliance to environmental regulations. In Europe this is perhaps evident in the difference in environmental standards applied in Central and Eastern Europe in comparison with members of the European Union.

At a superficial level it would seem reasonable that some companies would be attracted to locate production in markets where costs of environmental compliance were lower. Although the United States is regarded as a high standard country and receives a high level of foreign direct investment, these inflows come largely from other industrialized markets with similar standards. Hence, investment decisions are likely to be based on other factors, and not just the level of regulatory stringency.

One piece of research, part-funded by the World Bank, looked at whether investors were attracted to provinces in China with lower levies on polluted wastewater discharge (Shang-Jin Wei and Smarzynska, 1999). The research found that there was no evidence that this influenced foreign investors' production location behaviour. Instead, the researchers concluded that location decision was driven by:

- agglomeration of foreign direct investment in a region;
- size and growth of local markets;
- abundance of skilled workers;
- large numbers of skilled suppliers;

- infrastructure links (transport and ICT);
- special incentives.

In fact, foreign investors seem to be attracted to 'cleaner' provinces in China (for example in the coastal regions), where levies are higher on pollution. This is a positive sign of economic and political development. In these regions, it is more likely that the ecosystem of factors highlighted above exists.

However, there was an indication that lower environmental stringency was a factor for investors from Taiwan and Hong Kong, especially when involved in high-polluting industries. This latter point is of considerable importance, especially to modern global supply chains where large amounts of Western production is unbundled and outsourced to Asian manufacturers.

The results of the research may not give Western investors a clean bill of health; instead, they may just be outsourcing their environmental responsibilities to Hong Kong or Taiwanese companies that do not have to answer to lobbying from campaign groups and consumers or adhere to as tight regulation in their home markets.

High-tech manufacturer Apple is a case in point. Apart from the ethical dimension of whether its products are built on the back of low labour costs and poor conditions, it has also faced criticism for allegedly turning a blind eye to unsustainable environmental practices undertaken by its major Taiwanese supplier Foxconn in China. According to campaigners, the standards adhered to by its supplier fall well short of those that it would have to comply with if it manufactured its products in the United States. As with labour, it is likely that the Chinese authorities will increase the regulatory pressure it brings to bear on environmental practices, and this will again force a rise in costs.

If this happens, manufacturers and retailers have three options:

- Absorb the additional costs and keep manufacturing locations where they are.
- Repatriate (near-source) production to higher-cost home markets, where although costs are higher, transport costs are lower and there are time-in-transit savings.
- Seek out lower-cost locations where administrators are not so concerned with poor labour/environmental practices.

The third option would seem less attractive, given the increased attention that Western media is paying to ethical supply chains.

## Mitigating risk through 'compliance'

Retailers and manufacturers have started to address the concerns raised by pressure groups over environmental and labour-related issues in a range of different ways. One of the key ways in which they have attempted to show their commitment to sustainability is through the publication of 'codes of conduct', which are then audited by external compliance consultancies. Auditing often involves site visits by these consultancies, who approach the exercise using a tick-box methodology.

However, these compliance efforts are not always effective (see Bangladesh fire above). According to one charity, suppliers can be informed in advance of a visit and can cover up illegal practices or brief employees on what they should be saying. Suppliers often feel that they have no option but to try to conceal actual working practices – they are squeezed between increasing cost pressures, including the cost of compliance, and the low prices that they are being offered by their customers.

One common complaint, relating specifically to the supply chain strategies employed by the major retailers, is the effect of short lead times on overtime. Excessive overtime has been proscribed by many companies who have adopted codes of conduct. However, in order to deliver against the delivery schedules, companies often are forced to adopt practices that break the regulations to which they have committed.

**CASE STUDY**   Intel – mitigating supply chain risk through CSR

Intel, the world's largest manufacturer of microprocessors, recognizes that the operations of the suppliers in its supply chain are also its responsibility (Intel, 2012). In a CSR report, the company stated that:

> We hold the many suppliers with whom we do business accountable for operating with the same high standards that we expect of ourselves. We communicate our expectations clearly, work to identify and address issues at the system level, and share our findings and best practices across the industry. Through accountability and transparency, we are raising the social and environmental performance bar for companies around the globe and building the supply chain of the future.

Intel's position with the supply chain is highly important. Admittedly it manufactures a larger proportion of its products in its own factories than other companies in the electronics sector. However, it still does business with 16,000 suppliers in over 100 countries, and of course its own products are used extensively in the assembly operations of many OEMs. Its suppliers include Flextronics and Foxconn. Inevitably the number of its tier 2 and tier 3 suppliers will run into tens of thousands and therefore allocating responsibility for supplier ethics is critical to ensuring the integrity of Intel's supply chain.

Intel was a founder of the Electronic Industry Citizenship Coalition (EICC), and in 2004 adopted the Electronic Industry Code of Conduct, which it expects all its suppliers to comply with. In order to help with compliance, Intel offers its suppliers training and runs education programmes across all the key ethics categories. These include:

- child labour;
- forced labour and human trafficking;
- freedom of association and collective bargaining;
- diversity and non-discrimination;
- working hours and minimum wages;
- ethical practices; and
- worker health and safety.

Intel's approach to supplier selection embodies its CSR policy. Request-for-proposal documents, the first stage in the tendering process, include corporate responsibility metrics and questions. Its supplier audits take place on a quarterly basis, and if a CSR issue is not, in its opinion, properly addressed, steps are taken to 'exit' a supplier. As part of its Supplier Continuous Quality Improvement (SCQI) programme, Intel tracks the performance of its suppliers against a range of CSR metrics. The company stated that 82 per cent of its suppliers met these standards.

It is perhaps of significance that it highlights its relations with Taiwanese electronics supplier, Foxconn. The company, also known as Hon Hai, has attracted a considerable amount of bad publicity over previous years, mostly related to working and environmental practices in factories manufacturing goods for Apple. Intel is keen to highlight how it audited Foxconn's operations and identified significant CSR issues. The following year, it re-audited Foxconn's locations and found that there were still outstanding issues related to working hours, labour conditions, safety and management systems.

As a result, Intel loaned two members of senior management to help address the problems and share best practice. According to Intel, this resulted in Foxconn's practices and processes improving to an acceptable level.

# Food shortages in developing countries

In October 2011, the United Nations estimated that the world's population had reached 7 billion. This landmark event was accompanied by many warnings regarding the impact of overpopulation. Wars, hunger, water shortages and disease have been forecast by many commentators should the number of people in the world continue to grow at its present rate. It is forecast that the world's population will rise to 9.1 billion by 2050 and that food production will have to rise by 70 per cent if it is to keep pace with people's needs.

Developments in farming and technology have so far allowed food production to keep pace with the growth in the number of hungry mouths. However, if the world is to keep feeding its ever-burgeoning population, more will have to be done. Population growth is occurring in developing regions with the most fragile economies, societies and inefficient infrastructure. This means that an increasingly large proportion of the world's population will be located in high-risk areas, where a poor harvest or conflict can result in disaster.

Consequently, an improvement in food production, although important, is unlikely to be sufficient on its own. There must be improvements in all sections of the food supply chain and this includes fundamentally how products are moved to market – that is, the role of logistics and transportation. A cursory look at the processes involved show the enormous inefficiencies that presently exist in the movement and storage of food stuffs. This, as we shall see, results in a large proportion of product perishing en route to market.

A survey undertaken by researchers at Loughborough University very clearly shows that inappropriate warehouses and transportation have a high impact on the level of food losses (Despoudi, Papaioannou and Dani, 2012). As well as being a major problem for developing countries and their populations, it also offers a major opportunity. After all, if the logistics can be successfully addressed, a vast amount of additional food can be brought to market with no increase in production output.

## The extent of the problem

Although empirical evidence is scarce, it is estimated that in the developing world, between a third and a half of food is lost post-harvest, between farmer and consumer. This occurs through poor handling or bio-deterioration by micro-organisms, insects, rodents or birds. Livestock products, fish, fruit and vegetables are most at risk because of poor standards of refrigeration. Most fresh produce is transported in an unpackaged form and is often sold at markets, where handling dramatically reduces its shelf life.

**Figure 7.2**    To what extent do you think the following process-related factors influence the level of food losses of your products?

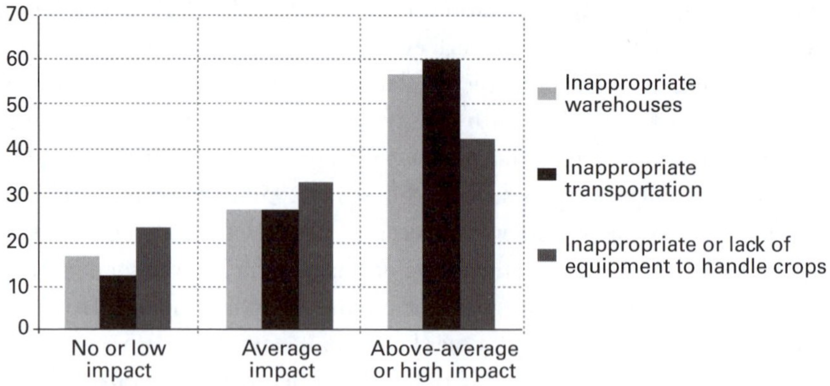

One of the core reasons behind the wastage is the extreme level of fragmentation involved in production and indeed food supply chains as a whole. The industry in developing markets is dominated by micro-farmers who own less than one hectare. They have access to very limited resources in terms of temperature control and, for that matter, very little understanding of how to sympathetically handle produce. Marketing channels are disorganized and complex involving traders, middlemen and wholesalers, which leads to enormous inefficiencies. On top of this, transport systems and operations are expensive and undeveloped.

The larger commercial farmers have much more efficient supply chains, but in many cases they produce for the export markets. They supply products to a high specification for international retail chains, but are untypical of the market as a whole. Poorer farmers producing for a domestic market are unable to invest in their facilities to anything like the same degree.

However, the success of export-led farmers in markets such as Kenya can be used as an example for wider agriculture. The demands of Western retailers for consistent production levels and standards of quality have increased cooperation amongst farmers. This has increased their resources and allowed them to take more control of the supply chain, initiating the introduction of cold chain systems, for example, alongside their marketing channels.

## Improving logistics to reduce risk

Upgrading transport infrastructure, superior trucks, better packaging and enhancing the reliability of power supplies (allowing for more refrigerated storage) as well as improving training would have immediate supply chain benefits. Much can be done to encourage private and government support for these highly achievable aims. The points below summarize some of the problems and solutions to mitigating post-harvest food losses.

## Better transport infrastructure

A robust road network is an essential element in getting product to market, but one that in many parts of Africa is sorely lacking. This is one of the primary reasons why cost of transport can be five times more expensive in Africa than in some parts of Asia.

One of the key ways to address this problem is to stimulate investment from the private sector. Some of the biggest investors, however, in Asia, Africa and Latin America are Chinese state-owned enterprises, who have been encouraged to invest by the Chinese government. The reason for this is obvious – improved road infrastructure is necessary to efficiently move raw materials from inland locations to ports, and Chinese companies are some of the biggest players in the exploitation of natural resources. However, the improved infrastructure will also help food supply chains and further investment from organizations such as the FAO, EU, USAID, UNDP and the Asian Development Bank has been encouraged.

Governments in developing countries have also been encouraged to take a more holistic view of transport. Cost–benefit studies can show that returns on transportation projects far outweigh the investment. These benefits are not only economic, but also society-wide.

## Improved road transport services

Distribution of produce in Africa and many countries in Asia is characterized by transportation in open-sided trucks, which are used to move goods up to 850 kilometres. As well as the obvious problem of decay in hot conditions, poor handling, overloading of goods without separation, rutted roads and a lack of ventilation all play a role in the degradation of produce.

Obviously, investment in better trucks would improve the condition of the product at the end of the journey. Improvement of vehicle stock will be a natural consequence of increased GDP and value-creation.

One of the most important steps is training. At a management level, some very basic steps can be taken to ensure that transportation professionals optimize transport planning. At an operational level, the way in which goods are loaded and unloaded can also be addressed. Training seminars and the dissemination of information materials can play a role in this.

Improving the availability and quality of specialized transport assets is also important. Although refrigerated containers are in use in many developing countries, they are certainly not universally available. For instance, they are still fairly rare in India, having only been introduced latterly.

## Better packaging

There is an acute lack of packaging technology in developing countries, and this includes labelling. Packaging is important not only to protect the products in transit, but also once they have been purchased by the consumer. In many countries, such as India, most vegetables are transported loose.

The problem is most acute in the perishable fruit and vegetable sector. Considerable research has been undertaken showing that use of (very cheap) low-density polyethylene film, combined with temperature-controlled storage (13–14 degrees Celsius), can extend the shelf life of bananas, for example, from 5–7 days up to 45 days. Even at a very basic level, the use of corrugated fibre board (CFB) and moulded trays or partitions, instead of timber, significantly reduces bruising.

The use of CFB boxes would be a first step towards unitization of shipments on pallets, and the introduction of forklift trucks would be a major step in reducing product damage.

In terms of labelling, there is a lack of regulatory systems that provide supply chain partners and consumers with essential data about the product. This can be addressed by governmental initiatives and regional coordination.

## Improved storage facilities

Warehousing and storage facilities throughout the food supply chain in developing countries are often weak or non-existent. This includes at the farm premises themselves and at each supply chain node as far as the market or port. Temperature-controlled facilities are often in short supply and sanitation is poor. In addition, there is also a lack of training and awareness related to temperature requirements and on ethylene restrictions for mixed loading. For example, ripening climacteric fruit (bananas, avocados, tomatoes, for instance) should not be transported with leafy or succulent vegetables, which will be harmed by ethylene emissions.

This latter point can be addressed by improved training as well as research and dissemination of best practice.

As regards the provision of staging/storing facilities, it has been suggested that individual government support for clustering of warehouses could bring significant benefits. This could be incentives or tax breaks for warehousing zones, which would then lead to investment, the development of support services, a trained workforce and shared expertise.

Refrigerated warehousing is hugely problematic. The process is energy-intensive and relies on a continuity of energy supply, which in developing countries can never be relied upon. However, the impact on the food chain is considerable. Shelf life of produce properly cooled can be extended from three days at room temperature to 90 days.

## Better cooperation

One area in which there could be immediate improvements for little investment is in cooperation between supply chain partners. Better coordination among supply chain partners was cited as being a key factor in the reduction of post-harvest food losses, along with better infrastructure and better skills, training and information-sharing. However, while supply chains remain so fragmented and complex, this in practice will prove difficult to achieve.

## *Conclusion*

The priority given to increasing farming productivity, while ignoring the inefficiency of the overall supply chain, has clear parallels with the now discredited industrial production strategies of the 1970s. What manufacturer these days would be happy with half its products being unusable by the time they arrived at the customer?

By focusing on reducing waste in the supply chain, rather than purely on production efficiencies, more food will arrive where it is most needed and at a lower cost to the consumer. This will not only increase farmer income, but also alleviate poverty and hunger. As Dr M.L. Choudhury, former Horticulture Commissioner in the Indian Ministry of Agriculture, commented, 'It is unfortunate that in India, policy makers and planners set targets for increased production without making any effort to reduce post-harvest losses.'

It is clear that while there is no doubt that advances in food technology and farm productivity will help mitigate the effects of the world's rising population, these gains will be negated unless more is done to improve the efficiency of supply chains.

Improving food logistics in developing countries does not just have humanitarian implications. It would decrease the need for additional areas to be cultivated, which would reduce the environmental impact of agriculture. It would also reduce the level of farming intensity, meaning fewer pesticides and chemical fertilizers are required.

Production levels are already sufficient to feed the world's population for many years to come. The real challenge is getting these products from farm to table with the minimum of waste.

## Summary

Global supply chains have brought many opportunities to developing countries in terms of economic development. However, they have also brought many challenges in terms of the conditions in which workers are employed, a situation highlighted by the Rana Plaza disaster in which many people died because of the inadequate state of the factory building. This has consequences for global manufacturers and retailers, as Western consumers are increasingly concerned that the products they buy, whether electronic goods, fashion items or fresh vegetables, are sourced ethically. Likewise, the impact that suppliers' factories have upon the environment is an increasingly important issue.

## Key points

- Manufacturers and retailers are increasingly concerned about the damage that poor ethical and environmental practices of their suppliers can have upon their brand.
- This was highlighted by the Rana Plaza disaster in Bangladesh, in which many workers employed making goods for global brands were killed.
- In many cases Western manufacturers and retailers have the leverage over their suppliers to enforce higher levels of working conditions, but first they need higher levels of visibility.
- In some cases profits made from mining important elements used in consumer electronics can go to insurgent groups. Manufacturers now have the legal responsibility to ensure that this doesn't happen.
- At the other end of the supply chain, e-waste is an increasing problem, with health implications in developing regions where end-of-life tech products are dumped.

# Corruption in the logistics industry

08

**OBJECTIVES**

This chapter will familiarize the reader with:

- the reasons why the logistics industry is so vulnerable to corruption;
- recent legislation that has had a profound impact on the logistics industry in developing countries;
- the most corrupt markets around the world;
- the types of corruption that can take place;
- why customs corruption is such a major problem and how to deal with it;
- corruption in the freight forwarding and air cargo industries;
- defence logistics corruption in Afghanistan;
- organized crime in transport operations.

## Why is the logistics industry so prone to corruption?

One of the defining trends of the past three decades has been the phenomenon of globalization. In order to take advantage of low-cost labour in emerging economies, companies have unbundled production processes and outsourced manufacturing to remote markets. As economies, such as China, move from 'emerging' to 'emerged' status, manufacturers seek new, even more remote markets to take advantage of lower rates of pay. Such countries may be unstable, have a fragile security situation and weak legislative and judicial systems, factors that have allowed corruption to become endemic in society and government.

One of the little-understood implications of this trend has been the exposure to corrupt practices that companies establishing operations in emerging markets face. This not only applies to manufacturers but also to the logistics companies they employ.

Although corruption is not a subject that many companies are willing to discuss, there is no doubting its importance. Corruption has been identified as the leading barrier to conducting business in 22 out of 144 economies, according to the World Economic Forum's (WEF) Global Competitiveness Report (WEF, 2013b). In fact, the WEF describes corruption – the widespread and deep-rooted abuse of entrusted power for private gain – as the single greatest obstacle to economic and social development around the world. This includes fraud, bribery and kick-backs, but can also include, in other contexts, non-financial forms of corruption, such as preferential treatment in the assistance or hiring processes of family members or friends, or even the intimidation of staff to turn a blind eye to illegal acts.

Part of the problem is cultural. In many parts of the world kinships and affinity to social networks is highly important and therefore it seems perfectly legitimate to provide job opportunities or kick-backs to friends and family. Even in the EU this can be a problem, especially on the eastern border of the region. For instance, the Russian ethnic community on both sides of the Russian/Latvian border has been identified as being complicit in organized smuggling networks, and the border officials are also drawn from the local community. Bribery is often not needed to ensure that a customs officer turns a blind eye, as a culture of exchange of favours already exists.

# Anti-bribery, anti-corruption legislation

In recent years, there has been a push by many administrations to clamp down on corruption in a range of 'anti-bribery, anti-corruption' legislation. The United States and the United Kingdom have been at the forefront of these moves, initiating far-reaching legislation.

The UK's Bribery Act 2010 makes companies accountable for the actions of third parties working on their behalf. It also applies to any British citizen either making or taking a bribe anywhere in the world. This is perhaps one of the main reasons why British expats working for forwarders are now very wary of becoming involved in import/export transactions in many developing countries.

A bribe doesn't necessarily need to be a direct payment under the terms of the Act. It could cover, for instance, a payment to an official's nominated charity if it was viewed as an inducement.

A controversial part of the Act is that a company can be held liable for an act of an employee or third party even if it had no knowledge of it, unless it can show that it had implemented a robust compliance process. This could involve, for example, the appointment of a compliance officer and the development of policy documents related to proper behaviour.

In the United States, sanctions against bribery are contained within the Foreign Corrupt Practices Act (FCPA). The UK's Bribery Act is viewed as being more severe than the FCPA, which creates an exemption for facilitation payments; the Bribery Act makes no such exception.

The UK Ministry of Justice guidelines on 'facilitation payments' are as follows:

- Companies should have a clear and issued policy.
- Companies should have written guidance available to employees as to the procedures they must follow where a facilitation payment is requested or expected.
- It must be demonstrated that such procedures are being followed (monitoring).
- There must be evidence that gifts are being recorded at the company.
- Proper action, collective or otherwise, must be taken to inform the appropriate authorities in countries when a breach of the policy occurs.
- The company must take practical steps to curtail such payments.

A survey was undertaken in August 2012 by the UK-based Good Corporation looking at the publicly available anti-corruption policies of 30 leading freight forwarding companies (Good Corporation, 2012). The research organization found that, of these, a third had no stated policy on corruption. This was all the more surprising given that the UK's Ministry of Justice (MoJ) guidelines state that management commitment to bribery prevention includes communication of an organization's anti-corruption stance.

Overall, Good Corporation said that it was extremely worrying that freight forwarders had not taken a more proactive stance on bribery and added that this would make them far more at risk from prosecution.

One of the reasons for this is that forwarding networks often rely on third-party agents. In many cases, little due diligence is undertaken to assess agents' policies and practices on bribery.

## Most corrupt markets

According to research by Transparency International, a consultancy involved in highlighting corruption on a global basis, emerging markets score particularly badly in terms of perceived levels of public sector corruption (Transparency International, 2016).

Countries highlighted by the organization for the high levels of corruption include Somalia, North Korea, Syria, Yemen and South Sudan – the bottom five in the ranking of 176 countries. This is perhaps not surprising given that these countries could all be classified as failed or on the verge of failing.

However, it is perhaps more interesting to look at the performance of the major emerging countries – for example, those included in the BRIC group. On the list, Brazil, China and India were in joint 79th with Russia lagging behind in 131st. Given the importance of these countries to the logistics sector, it is not surprising that international freight forwarders have run into trouble when attempting to do business in them. Nigeria, a country with massive potential for economic growth, appears at 136th in the list.

Of the members of the European Union, the worst countries in terms of corruption were countries in Southern and South East Europe. This includes Romania (57th), Italy (60th), Greece (69th) and Bulgaria (75th). That four European economies should be so poor in terms of corruption is shocking, especially Italy.

At the other end of the spectrum, there are countries in emerging regions that have exceptional records in suppressing corruption. The two that stand out the most are Singapore (7th) and Hong Kong (15th), both of which have high regulatory standards and governance. In the Middle East, the United Arab Emirates also performs well (24th). It is no coincidence that these three countries have very successfully transformed themselves into global logistics hubs, with efficient administration and customs processes that are largely untroubled by corrupt practices.

## Freight forwarding and customs corruption

One of the reasons why the logistics industry – and freight forwarding in particular – is so vulnerable to corruption is its close engagement with customs officials. In the developing world, government employees are often poorly paid, and there is an understanding that they will make their wages up from 'facilitation' payments made by forwarding and express companies to ensure fast clearance of goods. In many countries, particularly in

Africa (but certainly not restricted to the continent), corruption is so deeply engrained within the system that it is simply seen as an operational cost to be absorbed within the cost of moving goods.

In any case, customs corruption is very much a two-directional problem. Not only do customs officers attempt to solicit bribes, but they are also the targets of bribes from organized crime attempting to smuggle goods across borders, and in some cases private sector companies; the involvement of the latter organizations is by far the most frequent, as companies attempt to expedite slow and bureaucratic processes.

## *Corruption and bribery can take many forms*

### Customs officers as 'racketeers'

- Importers can be asked for money to speed up clearance, even if all their documents are in order.
- Officers mis-declare the value of a product and retain the duty that would have been paid on the full value.
- Officers can incorrectly categorize a high dutiable product (such as cigarettes) as a lower one and retain the difference.
- Officers register a different weight for the product and retain the difference in duty.

### Customs officers as targets

- Bribes are paid to officers by organized crime gangs to turn a blind eye to shipments of illegal contraband. This could involve frontline officers or shift managers who can orchestrate a network of corrupt officers.
- Officers receive bribes to prevent investigations or warn criminals of potential investigations.
- Officers provide false documentation for illegal shipments.

In parts of the world customs corruption goes right to the very top and includes politicians and big business as well as, of course, organized crime. For example, in Greece, the head of customs and a range of other management positions, including heads of border posts, are seen as political appointments. Revenues from smuggled goods can be diverted to political fundraising, and this explains why in some major anti-corruption drives even town mayors have been implicated.

An investigation by the Indian authorities found that the numbers of people involved in bribery schemes goes a long way beyond just the logistics companies and customs officers. In one instance, it was estimated that 100 people at Nhava Sheva Port, Mumbai, were involved, including middle men and couriers collecting bribes and delivering them to the officers. Couriers may even take the money direct to the officers' home towns or villages to give directly to their families.

## Oil and gas logistics corruption in Nigeria

In 2010, Swiss freight forwarding company Panalpina was forced to pay a fine of $85 million to the US authorities in order to resolve a long-running corruption case. Since 2007 the Swiss forwarder and a number of its clients in the oil and gas sector had been under investigation for contravening the American 'Foreign Corrupt Practices Act'. Panalpina's customers included Shell, Nabors Industries, Schlumberger, Transocean and Noble Corp.

The core of the allegations concerned the bribing of Nigerian customs officials in order to expedite the movement of oil rig engineering equipment through customs. There were also accusations that Panalpina staff bribed customs officials in Saudi Arabia, Algeria and Kazakhstan.

These allegations did substantial harm to Panalpina. Not only did the provisions for fines damage the company's balance sheet, but the company was forced to withdraw from servicing the Nigerian oil fields, losing some of its most lucrative business. The apparent vulnerability of the company to accusations of bribery also raised questions over Panalpina's business ethics and, as a result, the company put in place a compliance strategy. This issue added to the company's woes as it had also just paid $12 million in fines under the US 'Sherman Antitrust Act' and faced investigations in a number of countries, alongside other freight forwarders, over allegations of price-fixing.

Corruption in the Nigerian Customs Service is still ongoing. In 2012, the US Securities and Exchange Commission (SEC) charged three oil services executives with violating the Foreign Corrupt Practices Act (FCPA) by participating in a bribery scheme to obtain illicit permits for oil rigs in Nigeria in order to retain business under lucrative drilling contracts. Rigs are able to operate in Nigeria on the basis of temporary import permits granted by the Nigeria Customs Service (NCS).

The SEC alleged that former Noble Corporation executives bribed customs officials to process false paperwork purporting to show the export and re-import of oil rigs, when in fact the rigs never moved. The scheme was designed to save Noble Corporation from losing business and incurring significant costs associated with exporting rigs from Nigeria and then re-importing them under new permits. Bribes were paid through a customs agent.

Corruption is a worldwide phenomenon, as demonstrated by a selection of recent cases below:

- In 2016, UK forwarder FH Bertling and seven of its employees were charged by the Serious Fraud Office (SFO) with making corrupt payments to an agent of the Angolan state oil company, Sonangol, in order, allegedly, to further its business interests.

- In 2013, Ralph Lauren Corp was fined $882,000 for violating the US Foreign Corrupt Practices Act by bribing customs officials in Argentina. This activity occurred between 2004 and 2009, enabling its merchandise to clear customs without delay and often avoid inspections altogether.

- In 2013, 17 people were arrested in the northern port of Rijeka, Croatia, including 10 customs officers, heads of shipping companies and importers, suspected of being part of a bribery ring worth €1 million. Merchandise included shoes and fashion items.

- In 2013, India's Central Bureau of Investigation arrested three customs officers at Nhava Sheva Port for allegedly demanding a bribe of Rs50,000.

- In 2012, 30 Bulgarian customs officers at the Kapitan Andreevo border crossing to Turkey were detained in the act of distributing bribes at the end of a shift. Bribes collected during the shift added up to around €7,000. The bribes were taken to turn a blind eye to contraband smuggled across the border.

- In 2011, 34 customs officials were arrested in Turkey, including the Chief Director of the Istanbul Customs Regional Directorate. It appears that bribes were collected on a weekly basis and then distributed to officers on the basis of rank. In this instance, the government was also being defrauded as duties were diverted into the bribe pool. It was estimated that the ring was worth at least $128 million.

# Customs corruption in the EU

As mentioned earlier, corrupt customs officials are not reserved for emerging countries; the problem is also evident in the EU. However, in this respect there is a considerable dichotomy between newer members and the established economies in Western Europe. In surveys of customs administrations and public opinion, only 25 per cent of those people asked in the original EU15 countries thought that corruption was endemic, compared with 46 per cent in the 12 new member states (CSD, 2010). Looking deeper, 60 per cent of respondents in countries such as Bulgaria, Greece, Romania, Cyprus and Latvia considered their customs organizations corrupt. The problem is considered to be particularly acute on the eastern land border of the EU – in Bulgaria, on average 20–30 officers a year are dismissed on charges of corruption. On its own, this figure is more than the rest of the EU15 countries in total.

Customs corruption in many countries in Europe is inextricably linked with organized crime, which is a particular worry for authorities. Again there seems to be a split between the original member states and new members, once more with the notable exception of Greece. The problem is particularly evident in Greece, Romania, Estonia, Latvia, Slovakia, Bulgaria, Lithuania and Poland.

The lack of corruption in the EU15 region (as compared with new member states) is not wholly about better law enforcement, better pay or cultural issues. It can be partly put down to the fact that within mainland Europe, there are few border crossings as goods can circulate freely as a result of the Schengen Agreement. Customs are mainly based at ports and airports and here the chances of smuggling goods through are so high (because of the high volumes) that organized crime sees the challenge of bribing corrupt customs officials as an unnecessary risk and expense. In the early 1990s, corruption was said to be widespread before the removal of customs checkpoints at road border crossings.

It has also been pointed out that, in terms of drug smuggling, which is an important causal factor of customs' corruption, many gangs involved in organized crime will bring in shipments by fast boat along Europe's long coastline.

In fact, the high-risk nature of drug-smuggling and its priority on many law enforcement agencies' agendas means that few customs officers are implicated. Instead, excise-tax products are far more likely to be involved, with alcohol, cigarettes and oil amongst the most popular. However, the illegal import of some consumer goods and electronics is also a problem, especially from China.

# Dealing with corrupt customs officials: WEF best practice

The World Economic Forum (WEF) has developed best practice guidelines to be used in situations when an attempt is being made to extort a bribe. The following is an excerpt from 'RESIST' – Resisting Extortion and Solicitation in International Transactions: a company tool for employee training compiled by the International Chamber of Commerce, Transparency International, United Nations Global Compact and the World Economic Forum:

**Scenario: Long-awaited essential equipment is stuck in customs for clearance and only the payment of a 'special' fee can secure its prompt release**

**Description:** You are the local manager of your company's operation in a foreign country. For weeks, the shipment of critical technical equipment has been delayed by red tape at headquarters. When the equipment finally arrives in the country, your personnel are told by a customs officer that the paperwork is 'incomplete'. This will prevent the release of the equipment until the problem has been solved. The customs official indicates that a resolution could take several weeks. He adds, however, that the problem can be solved quickly through an expeditor's fee or cash payment of $200, which would ensure customs clearance of the equipment in one business day.

**1 Demand prevention:** How to reduce the probability of the demand being made?

Communicate to employees the company's anti-corruption policy that includes extortion and facilitation payments and provide training on how to avoid and deal with demands, especially the employees who may be more exposed to such situations.

Establish and implement systems available to employees to report and seek advice for demands for small payments.

Order goods early – avoid time pressures on delivery.

Have an adequate supply of parts and consumables that must be imported. Perform due diligence on customs procedures at various points of entry to the country (ie seaports, roads, airports), determine which ones pose the highest and the lowest corruption risks, and find out the time required to clear goods; set out primary and alternative import routes accordingly.

Switch to an alternative import route and point of entry if obstructions are experienced at the primary point of entry.

Research official customs procedures and familiarize necessary personnel with the procedures; clarify unclear parts of the procedures with the central customs authorities.

Take steps to make the official customs procedures widely available in the country to counteract ignorance and opaqueness, e.g. with the help of business associations, in cooperation with customs authorities or other government departments.

**2 Response to a bribery demand:** How to react if the demand is made?

Quality-check your customs clearance paperwork to ensure full compliance with procedures.

Verify whether customs procedures provide for any official expedited services.

If so, verify size of fees for such services – never pay for any such services without an invoice and/or receipt.

Ensure that any payment made is recorded in the company's accounting system in the correct amount, together with the invoice/receipt and an explanation of the purpose of the payment.

If the customs procedures do not provide for expedited services or are not clear on the size of fees for such services and an invoice or a receipt is not provided:

- Make it clear to the customs officer that payment to public officials for a service to which one is already entitled is against company policy and is illegal.
- Refuse to pay facilitation payments to expedite customs clearance of goods.
- Demand reasons why the goods are stuck and do so on a daily basis.
- Demand that measures be taken to mitigate such reasons.
- Make it clear that normal customs procedures shall be followed.
- Do not reveal that you are under time pressure.
- Ask for the name and position of the customs officer and request to meet his/her superior.

If the customs clearance delays have impacts on the company's business relationships, inform business partners of the situation and of the potential consequences. Explore if and how to approach the customs authority jointly.

Request a meeting with the central customs authority or relevant ministry to request that actions be taken.

Explore whether other companies face similar problems and jointly address the customs authority.

Report the incident internally in the company; analyse the case, develop a plan to reduce the risk of reoccurrence and design responses for future demands (ICC, 2011).

# Smuggling and customs corruption

In Africa, customs corruption affects local traders and international shippers alike. Cross-border activity in parts of West Africa is characterized by the endemic payment of bribes and harassment. A common catchphrase of customs officials is 'sans argent, on ne passe pas.' In one instance a trader had to make a payment to 30 different officials as he made his way to Goma in the Democratic Republic of Congo.

One of the problems that has been pointed out about trade with Nigeria has been the length of the restricted goods list, which prohibits or limits the importation of goods from neighbouring countries. This means that smuggling of these goods is rife, and consequently the payment of money to customs officers by organized crime.

Another problem is the extent of bureaucracy and delays. An African Development Bank report found that the average customs transaction involves 30–40 different parties, 40 documents, 200 individual pieces of data (30 of which are repeated at least 30 times) and the re-keying of 60–70 per cent of data at least once (Ben Barka, 2012). This is not only an issue on the importing side of the border – there are controls to go through on the exporting side too, doubling the bureaucracy. Waiting time for a truck at a border crossing can be anything up to three days. It has been estimated that customs clearance adds about $185 for each day delayed to the cost of a consignment. It is for this reason that many shippers prefer to bribe customs officials in order to short-cut the process. Of course there has to be a willingness on both sides of this transaction.

It is not just customs that is a problem. At a border post there are multiple government agencies present, including immigration, police, internal revenue, ministry of agriculture, public health, and so on. This provides each of these agencies and their officials the opportunity to delay a shipment and also to take their portion of facilitation payments en route.

One of the ways in which corruption could be overcome is through the greater use of technology, automating the customs process. This not only cuts down on the time taken to clear goods, but by doing so, reduces the need for facilitation payments. Also, by limiting the opportunity for customs officials to manually mis-declare goods, customs revenues actually increase. In Angola, the introduction of a new IT system brought about a 150 per cent increase in tax revenue.

**CASE STUDY**  Importing goods into Russia

Many companies have found it expedient to short-cut Russian customs procedures to avoid both delays and paying full duty. There remain stories of 'black' channels and 'white' channels and between these a 'grey' channel, which has become institutionalized.

'Grey' customs clearance started in the early 1990s. Faced with a shortage of commodities, the Customs Committee of Russia, in an effort to encourage import trade and simplify customs procedures, allowed customs clearance companies to provide one-stop services that covered both transportation and clearance procedures.

These companies, with close relations with Russian customs and backed up by influential figures in Russia, enjoy many privileges, most notably that they pay customs duties on only a small portion of the imported commodities, bribing the officers to let the rest pass. However, they normally do not supply customs clearance manifests, resulting in importers who use their services often being suspected of smuggling.

Russian police have then been known to make raids on retail outlets checking for legal customs clearance documents. The position is made more complex by the presence in the Russian retail market of counterfeit goods made both inside and outside Russia. Recent attempts to improve the position appear to have had little effect. There are importers who have developed the expertise to get their goods cleared expeditiously, but there remain many importers with limited expertise in customs clearance who face the dilemma of using 'white' channels and incurring delays and possibly uncompetitive tariffs, or using grey or black channels with the risk of police raids as described above.

Multinational companies have distanced themselves from this procedure by entering contracts with Russian distributors of their products to deliver the goods to a warehouse close to the border and leave it to the distributor to clear customs and deliver goods to the retail chain in Russia.

Russia's progress to WTO membership and other pressures have led to a number of initiatives to reform customs procedures. Many of the respondents also report that these initiatives have resulted in greater contact with officials and the Russian customs body and there appears to be a clear intention to 'regularize' Russian customs practices. There have been clear signals of a change in attitude, notably in clearance through the Moscow airports.

It is clear from reports that delays still occur, particularly at the road borders through the Baltic States. Many people in the industry think that eventually the new attitudes will reach the outlying customs administrations, but it is uncertain how long it will take.

It was reported by one respondent to a survey undertaken by research organization Transport Intelligence that the authorities were seeking to maintain the integrity of the new white customs procedures by checking retail prices of goods in shops against the official price list and investigating those sold at lower prices.

Under the new arrangements that the authorities seem to wish to encourage, international companies will establish legal trading entities within Russia and be subject to Russian corporate taxation and be required to apply Russian VAT. Some respondents identified new sets of problems in relation to transfer pricing and similar matters. The different Russian tax and revenue departments act independently and often have differing objectives in relation to matters such as transfer pricing. It may well be that, as customs problems diminish, a new range of problems with Russian bureaucracy may arise.

There are seven regional customs directorates in Russia and 141 customs offices that process goods and vehicles. Although customs procedures are based on the same legislation, regulation and instruction, interpretation and implementation of these instruments vary widely, depending on customs officers throughout the territory. The opportunities for discretionary behaviour give rise to corruption, which is a serious problem. For example, at the border crossing points to Russia from Yerevan, it has been reported that truck drivers are asked for $1,800–2,000 for the '02 guardservice' provided by the Ministry of National Security. If they refuse, drivers meet difficulties with police or organized local gangs.

A report by the European Commission found that an anti-trafficking unit of a local law enforcement agency was also implicated in such security scams. If a trucking company refused to pay a bribe, it became subject to excessive checks by police (CSD, 2010).

## VAT fraud schemes

There are a variety of illegal schemes that have succeeded in swindling governments out of taxation revenues. In recent years the biggest such fraud was estimated to be worth £2–3 billion and affected the UK.

A simple fraudulent scheme is known as 'acquisition' or 'missing trader' fraud. A trader imports a product into the UK VAT-free and then sells it on, this time charging VAT (at 20 per cent). However, the trader then goes missing, failing to pay the VAT to the tax authorities.

'Carousel' fraud is a more complicated version of this. Products are imported VAT-free into the UK and then sold on through a number of other co-conspiring companies, each time attracting VAT. The product is finally then exported (sometimes back to its initial seller – hence the term 'carousel') and the VAT is claimed back before the first and last seller go missing.

In both types of fraud, the goods need never be physically moved from the port to which they have been imported and can often be used multiple times in different 'carousels'. It has been very difficult for the tax-collecting authorities to prove that there has been any wrongdoing and refuse to refund the VAT to the exporter. The opacity of the 'supply chain' means that vast sums of money have been made by criminals, adding an extra layer of complexity by using offshore bank accounts.

Overcoming this type of fraud without wholesale reform of the taxation system in Europe is near-impossible. However, there has been talk of changing the tax process so that VAT is only payable on the final sale to the end-user, preventing the VAT refunds further down the chain being stolen. Alternatively, tax could just be levied on the manufacturer when the initial sale is made. However, as yet, authorities have focused their attention on investigation and enforcement of the law as it stands. Unfortunately for many legitimate traders caught up in a carousel racket, this has meant that they have been left out of pocket, with the tax authorities refusing to refund tax paid.

# Cracking down on customs corruption

Authorities have initiated several processes to reduce the instances of corruption in customs:

- strong investigative powers of customs officers by other law enforcement agencies – including visibility of bank accounts;
- ensuring that officers do not stay in the same role for too long, to prevent them developing long-term and potentially compromising relations with shippers;
- rotating officers within their job so that they do not work in the same shift or to predictable patterns – this reduces their ability to facilitate movements of illegal goods. In the UK, software is used to randomly select which officer will inspect a specific truck;

- using random checks by mobile units, who themselves are not aware of what or who they will be checking;
- maintaining robust technology systems that are able to track individual customs officers' use of databases and the information that was accessed;
- a structure in place to encourage anonymous tip-offs and whistleblowing;
- payment of higher salaries to customs officials – this reduces the temptation to augment the wage with bribes;
- severe legal penalties are a further way to prevent customs officers being drawn into criminal behaviour by making the risks of corrupt activity outweigh the potential rewards.

# Freight forwarding, airlines and cartels

In the past decade, freight forwarders have found themselves being investigated in a range of different geographies for anti-competitive behaviour. This has resulted in fines of hundreds of millions of dollars across the industry.

The case of the anti-cartel fines levied by the European Union (EU) on a string of freight forwarders in 2012 is a useful insight for any shipper looking to understand how they are charged by forwarders and how forwarders manage their margins. No less than four different processes were deemed anti-competitive by the EU Competition Commissioners. The first 'cartel' was that relating to British Customs' 'new export system' introduced in 2003. Here, forwarders were found to have illegally agreed to establish a surcharge on customers for operating this customs reporting service and to fix its amount according to the size of the customer's consignment.

The next issue concerned the US's 'advanced manifest system'. A group of forwarders agreed a common surcharge for the transmission of data to US Customs and decided amongst themselves not to use the charge as a 'tool for competition'.

The third 'cartel' concerned the 'currency adjustment factor', where forwarders paid for Chinese transport services in renminbi yet were billed in US dollars. In order to cope with the rising value of the renminbi, forwarders agreed amongst themselves to charge a 'currency adjustment factor' surcharge or changed billing into renminbi.

The last illegal practice related to the 'peak season surcharge'. Here, the forwarders held 'breakfast meetings' in Hong Kong on the introduction and timing of a surcharge and its level on services before Christmas.

A total fine of €169 million was levied by the European Commission on 14 different forwarders, of which the largest were levied on Panalpina and Kuehne + Nagel for the 'peak season surcharge' abuse, with the two companies paying €19.6 million and €11.2 million respectively. The two Swiss-based companies also paid fines related to some of the other cases as did companies such as UPS Supply Chain Solutions (as economic successor of Menlo Worldwide Forwarding), Hellmann Worldwide Logistics, Schenker (as economic successor of BAX Global), Expeditors and UTi. DHL Global Forwarding and to a lesser extent CEVA paid reduced fines as they cooperated with the Commission in the investigation of the cartels.

Unsurprisingly, Kuehne + Nagel was not happy about the case. Karl Gernandt, Chairman of Kuehne + Nagel, commented in a statement that: 'We are of the opinion that the Commission has not correctly investigated the facts and the participation of Kuehne + Nagel and has drawn significantly incorrect factual and legal conclusions.'

However, the EU found that the forwarders involved had taken specific measures to conceal their anti-competitive conduct. This included the use of private e-mail accounts and the use of code words (such as the 'Gardening Club').

In another unrelated case, the Swiss Competition Commission fined four freight forwarders for fixing prices on air freight passing through Switzerland. The authorities imposed a fine of CHF6.2 million on four air freight forwarders for fixing fees. The commission, or COMCO, handed the biggest fine of CHF3.12 million to Panalpina, while another Swiss company, Kuehne + Nagel, was fined CHF1.17 million. DB Schenker received a CHF1.02 million fine, while the Kuwait-headquartered Agility was fined CHF907,349. DP DHL had also taken part in the cartel, but since it turned itself in and alerted the authorities to the illegal practices, it was offered immunity.

It was not only freight forwarders that were affected by anti-cartel operations: investigations were undertaken into the role of airlines in fixing surcharges by a range of authorities, including those in the United States and the EU. The main thrust of these investigations was related to fuel surcharges and security costs. The airlines stood accused of using the events of 9/11 as an excuse to impose additional costs on customers. According to some shippers' organizations, such as the UK's Freight Transport Association, these 'temporary' surcharges became permanent. One spokesman for an airline commented that it was not surprising that airlines put up their charges at the same time as they were all responding to the same global events. However, in no way did this indicate 'collusion'.

However, after a four-year investigation, the EU found differently. In 2010 it fined 10 airlines a combined €800 million for their role in a global cartel that colluded to fix rates. Air France-KLM was handed the largest fine of €310.1 million, while British Airways had to pay €104 million and Singapore Airlines €76.4 million. In addition, the EU also fined Air Canada, Cathay Pacific, Cargolux, Japan Airlines, LAN Chile, Scandinavian Airlines Systems, Qantas and Martinair for their involvement. Lufthansa was also found guilty of price fixing; however, the company received immunity because it had alerted the Commission to the existence of the cartel and cooperated in the Commission's investigations.

# Unofficial tolls and crossing controls

## *India*

Corruption in the Indian road freight market is endemic and is blamed for a highly negative impact on the local economic growth prospects. A research project by Transparency International India claims that truck drivers pay between Rs211 and Rs266 per day (£2.11–2.66) as bribe money (TII, 2007). It estimates that the total value of corrupt payments, mostly made at road checkpoints or en route stoppages, amounts to Rs22,000 crore a year (£2.2 billion). Their survey of truck drivers found that 95 per cent reported paying bribes.

The problem is made worse in India by the number of checkpoints at state borders. India, in this respect, is not a single market as it does not allow for the free flow of goods and people throughout the country. Large amounts of documentation are needed, and because contact with the authorities is high (police, internal revenue, transport authorities, local authorities, forestry department, weights and measures, plus many more), there is considerable scope for abuse of power. The bribery has become so institutionalized that truck drivers can even be issued unofficial permits to allow them to move freely once the bribe has been paid.

Stops at border crossings can be long – up to 11 hours – creating enormous amounts of inefficiency in supply chains. In one example, it was estimated that a truck journey from Delhi to Mumbai could be reduced from five to six days to just three days.

Ways to overcome this level of corruption have been suggested. These include:

- rationalizing the number of agency inspection squads to just one, which issues comprehensive permits – the lower contact with bureaucracy will reduce the opportunities for corrupt officials to extort bribes;

- standardizing regulations across the entire country, which will simplify movement documents.

- trucking organizations should be encouraged to stand up to corruption by raising instances of it at a high level;
- building more expressways that bypass local towns and villages, thereby providing local authority officials with fewer opportunities to elicit bribes;
- higher priority of the prosecution of corrupt officials.

Corrupt practices have also allowed the continuance of a major safety scandal in the Indian truck industry. Legislative attempts have been made to clamp down on the overloading of lorries, which in New Delhi alone is said to result in the deaths of over 1,000 people a year. However, despite the good intentions, the result of this legislation was to create another opportunity for corrupt police and officials to extort money from drivers. The problem of overloading has not improved – although the amounts paid in bribes to turn a blind eye to the overloading have soared.

Unofficial tolls and checkpoints are not the only examples of corruption in the Indian transport industry. Multiple stages of bureaucracy exist, from initial registration of a vehicle to issuance of permits for national or interstate movement, and at each stage a bribe has to be paid by operators. This is usually done through middlemen who have the relationship in place with the required official.

An operator's cost structure is very different in India from that in Europe or North America. Some large fleet owners pay as much as 20 per cent of their revenues on a monthly basis to officials to avoid disruption.

## *Africa*

The African market is plagued by numerous issues that make importing goods, and the subsequent distribution, extremely problematic. Bureaucracy, corruption, local conflicts, civil unrest, poor roads, lack of rail infrastructure, weak bridges, and so on, all hinder the efficient movement of goods.

Considerable research has been undertaken into the impact of checkpoints in West Africa and the opportunities that these provide in terms of bribery. In this region there can be two to three checkpoints per 100 kilometres of road, and it has been estimated that bribes range from $3–23 per 100 kilometres. The research, by the Improved Road Transport Governance Initiative (IRTG), identifies the Abidjan–Bamako corridor as having the highest number of checkpoints, and hence the highest incidence of bribery. Vehicles can be delayed by up to 30 minutes per 100 kilometres, adding up to seven hours in total per average trip (IRTG, 2011).

One example, highlighted in the research, was of a lorry moving millet/sorghum between Mali and Senegal on the Koutiala–Dakar corridor. It passed through 100 checkpoints and border posts, with the driver paying $437 along the way. For more perishable goods, the delays can be disastrous, and this has very severe implications for food security.

Levels of corruption are worse in failed or failing states. For example, the descent of Ivory Coast into civil war in 2010–11 resulted in a surge of informal checkpoints and bribes. Many of these were run by the rebel 'Forces Nouvelles' operating in the northern part of the country.

However, there is progress being made in reducing bureaucracy. A number of regional groupings have understood that if they were to streamline processes and reduce the time taken to clear customs, there would be several benefits. These include:

- stimulation of local economies;
- increase in duty raised as less informal trade/smuggling;
- lower levels of corruption.

The Southern Africa Development Community (including countries such as South Africa, Zimbabwe, Tanzania, Zambia) has concluded agreements to set up One Stop Customs Inspection, designed to eventually eliminate duplicate controls. This has been augmented by bilateral agreements, such as the one between South Africa and Mozambique and the establishment of the Chirundu One Stop Border Post, a jointly developed project by Zambia and Zimbabwe.

The latter development has been a considerable success story, reducing delays for trucks from two to three days to just a few hours. The reduced costs have stimulated trade and volumes have actually increased. While before it was notorious for corruption, there are now far fewer opportunities for customs officers. This has resulted in higher duty and tax revenues for both countries.

# Allegations of corruption in government contract negotiations

When vast sums of money are at stake, there is obvious temptation for individuals to seek to take advantage of opportunities to defraud customers. This is even more the case when government contracts are involved, due to a perception, often accurate, that civil servants have a poor grasp on commercial realities. In fact, whether a subcontractor has taken advantage of commercial naïveté or in fact has indulged in sharp practice is a moot point, and one that has been tested in the court. The cases below are good examples of when logistics providers have been vindicated and when they are guilty of overstepping the mark.

## Contract dispute or criminal activity?

In 2007, Agility won a series of multi-billion-dollar contracts from the US Defense Logistics Agency to supply US troops in Iraq with food and related items. This was to provide Agility with a foundation for a highly successful defence logistics business. At its peak, the company provided 1 million meals per day (four meals/person for 150,000+ troops and 100,000+ contractors).

The first sign of a problem arose when the US Department of Justice began an investigation into allegations of fraudulent activity around aspects of these contracts. Originally starting as an investigation into a single businessman, the inquiry rapidly expanded to cover a number of large US food companies, including Sara Lee and ConAgra Foods. The US authorities examined suggestions that food sold to Agility for the US armed forces contract was overpriced.

Originally it appeared that Agility was not under suspicion. However, in November 2009 the company was placed under an indictment by a grand jury, effectively accusing the company of overcharging the government by $60 million on contracts worth $8.5 billion. New business with the US Department of Defense was suspended, hitting the company's revenues and profits.

However, in 2007 a magistrate in Atlanta recommended that fraud charges against Agility be struck down. His objection was that the US prosecuting authorities had improperly served the charges. The Department of Justice subsequently asked the court to drop the charges against one of Agility's subsidiaries.

Agility's management strongly made the case that the US government had attempted to criminalize a contractual dispute. According to the company, prices, suppliers and business practices were disclosed to, approved and routinely reviewed by its US government customer.

From one perspective, it might be concluded that in some instances the balance of risk lies with the supplier in doing business with governments, whether in the developing or developed world, rather than the other way round. Governments are prone to being influenced by political factors. It might be surmised that a view took hold in the US government that it was being defrauded by subcontractors and that prosecutors were encouraged to 'deliver some heads'. The lack of progress that it made through the courts with Agility showed that in this instance it was erroneous in its judgement. Notwithstanding this, Agility has paid a high price. It was not able to bid for new work with the US government, and consequently restructured its entire company. In order to recover some of this money, Agility filed a claim seeking about $225 million from the Department of Defense for breaching contract terms.

## Kick-backs and false claims

### Eagle Global Logistics

Another forwarder that ran into conflict with the US authorities was Eagle Global Logistics (EGL), later taken over by CEVA. The company paid $750,000 to settle allegations that, in violation of the False Claims Act and the Anti-Kickback Act, the company paid gratuities to employees of KBR, the prime contractor for the US Army's LOGCAP III contract for logistical support of military operations overseas.

The DoJ said EGL, a Houston-based company, had a subcontract with KBR to facilitate shipments of military cargo to Iraq and Kuwait. From March 2003 to March 2005, EGL had provided various meals, sporting event tickets and other gifts to KBR employees responsible for administering the subcontract.

Previously EGL had paid $4 million to settle False Claims Act allegations that the company had inflated invoices for military cargo shipments to Iraq. EGL had also paid the government $300,000 to settle allegations that the company's local agent in Kuwait had overcharged the military for rental charges on shipping containers to Iraq for the period from January to June 2006.

The suit against EGL had been filed under the qui tam ('whistleblower') provisions of the False Claims Act. Under that act, private persons might bring a suit on behalf of the United States alleging the submission of false claims to the government and might receive a portion of the proceeds of any recovery.

### APL

Shipping line APL Limited agreed to pay the US government $26.3 million to resolve allegations that it submitted false and inflated cost claims in connection with contracts to transport containerized cargo to support US troops in Iraq and Afghanistan.

The US government alleged that APL, a wholly-owned US subsidiary of Singapore-based Neptune Orient Lines Limited (NOL), had 'knowingly overcharged and double-billed the (US) Department of Defense to transport thousands of containers from ports to inland delivery destinations in Iraq and Afghanistan'.

The government alleged that APL inflated its invoices in several ways. For example, APL billed in excess of the rate it paid to plug refrigerated containers holding perishable cargo into a source of electricity at a port in Karachi, Pakistan; billed in excess of the contractual rate to maintain the operation of refrigerated containers at a port in Karachi and at US military bases in Afghanistan; and billed for various non-reimbursable services performed by APL's subcontractor at a Kuwaiti port.

# Major defence logistics corruption in Afghanistan

A report published by the US Congress laid bare the corruption and racketeering that accompanied the physical distribution of goods to the US troops stationed in Afghanistan (US House of Representatives Subcommittee on National Security and Foreign Affairs Committee on Oversight and Government Reform, 2010).

The report, entitled *Warlord, Inc.*, detailed the reality for logistics providers in the region, and warned that money paid to trucking companies by the US Department of Defense (DoD) was ending up in the hands of the Taliban.

The controversy related to the so-called 'host nation trucking' (HNT) contracts, worth around $2.16 billion, and split between eight Afghan, US and Middle Eastern companies. The contract provided trucking for 70 per cent of the total goods and materiel distributed to the US troops in the theatre, and involved around 6,000 to 8,000 truck missions a month.

The amount of materiel moved to US and NATO forces in Afghanistan was immense. In 2009, at the height of operations, they required 1.1 million gallons of fuel per day, and military and contractor planes delivered 187,394 tons of cargo. However, this was dwarfed by the extent of the overland operation, which involved nearly 10 times that amount, accounting for about 80 per cent of all goods moved.

The challenges were equally huge. The major lines of supply linked the military bases with Pakistan in the south and Central Asia in the north, including Kyrgyzstan. The southern supply routes were exposed to attacks from insurgents, while the northern alternatives, although less dangerous, involved the transiting of politically unstable administrations.

Supplying the theatre by air was the fastest route, but costly, and with serious limitations to non-military aircraft (only four airports were open to contractor-operated cargo planes).

When in Afghanistan, all materiel was hubbed from two distribution locations: Bagram Airfield in the north and Kandahar Airfield in the south. Although some helicopter movements were possible, conditions, weight limits and costs usually compelled movement by road. This in turn left the supply columns vulnerable to attack.

Added to this was the lack of processing capacity at the distribution hubs. In some cases, the inquiry found, trucks waited for several weeks outside Kandahar Airfield before being able to unload their cargoes. These factors led one official to describe Afghanistan as 'the harshest logistics environment on earth'.

This was the background to the investigation into the workings of the $2 billion spend by the United States on supplying troops. The subcommittee at the outset recognized that the operation was hugely challenging but believed that this in no way excused the reality of the contract.

The subcommittee's report found that the very nature of the contract with the trucking companies made the likelihood of corruption in such an environment unavoidable. One crucial component of the terms of the agreement required that each contractor must provide the security for the cargo that they carried. This was usually provided by local Afghan security providers, which undertook armed protection of the convoys. The report cites the example of a convoy of 300 supply trucks needing 400 to 500 guards carrying heavy machine guns and rocket-propelled grenades. One leading convoy security commander estimated that he spent $1.5 million on ammunition per month protecting trucks.

However, this is just part of the story. The inquiry found that security subcontractors working on the HNT contract included local warlords and militia leaders, who compete with the Afghan central government for influence. They operated what to all intents and purposes was a protection racket, with the trucking companies that refused to pay up most likely to come under attack. In practice almost everyone paid up. The report also suggested that these warlords in turn made protection payments to the Taliban for safe passage, although the inquiry has not been able to find hard evidence of this.

These are not the only implications of the lack of control that the United States had over the large sums of money that were paid to the HNT contractors. It is also believed that the payments fuelled corruption amongst Afghan government officials. One contractor said that they had to pay sums of between $1,000 and $10,000 to every governor, police chief and military unit through whose territory his vehicles passed.

The report also found that there was a serious lack of oversight of the private security guards being used in operations. Certainly no US military personnel had knowledge of what happened between origin and destination. This meant that there could be no control over the weapons and behaviour of security guards and that incidents of death could not be investigated. The Department of Defense, it found, was 'grossly out of compliance' with applicable regulations.

While the Committee acknowledged that the HNT contracts had in many respects been a success, in as much as they had allowed the US forces to concentrate on waging war against the Taliban rather than protecting supply chains, it recommended a number of urgent changes to the set-up.

These measures included taking on the responsibility for overseeing the security of subcontractors, a role that it was evident that the trucking companies were totally unable to conduct with any degree of capability.

It also recommended that the DoD conduct a comprehensive review of the 'unintended consequences' of the HNT contracts, including their effect on corruption, Afghan power politics and economic impact.

The increased level of visibility that this report called for would require more of a 'hands-on' approach to the management of the operation. Overall the report gave the impression that there was little concern about what happens 'outside the wire' – in other words, beyond the confines of army bases, a state of mind that was counterproductive and ultimately deleterious to NATO's war aims.

# Humanitarian aid logistics corruption

Corruption is a critical factor even in humanitarian logistics. The problems faced by NGOs and aid agencies are exacerbated as they often work in regions where the rule of law has completely broken down. As a paper by the Humanitarian Policy Group points out, aid is often delivered in countries where powerful figures have a disproportionate control over resources. Large sums of money are often at stake and, where armed conflict takes place, there is considerable opportunity for certain parties, including governments, to divert these resources (Savage *et al*, 2007).

However, the problem is by no means reserved for developing countries. It has been estimated that contracts in the order of $8.75 billion placed in the wake of the Hurricane Katrina disaster in the United States were affected by waste, fraud, abuse and mismanagement.

As in the case of corruption related to business logistics, there is little appetite to talk about corruption by aid agencies because of the fear of negative publicity and the impact that this could have on donations.

However, the problem is very real. It is felt most acutely at the outset of a humanitarian crisis, when the movement of relief supplies to an affected area is most acute. Here aid agencies may feel that the pressing need to deliver the goods is more important than a principled stand against corruption. This leads to the payment of unofficial fees in order to expedite shipments through ports or across checkpoints.

An examination of a humanitarian crisis in Liberia in the mid-2000s found that the logistics process was highly vulnerable to government corruption. Although charging for processing various licences, vehicle registration, customs clearance and import duties is evident in all countries, in Liberia there was evidence that officials in the various ministries concerned were making large sums of money from the aid agencies, who felt that they had no option but to comply with regulations.

As with business logistics, the smaller the agency, the worse affected they were. Larger NGOs with a global presence that faced requests for informal, unauthorized payments were able to take these up with government officials directly. Experience in Liberia showed that they could even ignore some requests with relative impunity, and saw no impact on the transit times of their shipments. This was most evident in the import of goods through ports in Liberia. Larger shippers said they were able to resist extortion by exerting influence at the highest levels of government. They could take up individual cases and clear the way for a container to be processed. However, smaller agencies did not have this option.

By 2006 the Liberian government had taken steps to address the problem of corruption, both at the ports and Roberts International Airport. One way in which it overcame the problem of officials overcharging shippers for their services was to publish a set of official fees. However, an unintended consequence of this was that processing times actually increased, as the officials stuck rigidly to bureaucratic processes. 'Facilitation' payments had, it seemed, been just that – a one-off cash payment to speed goods through the system.

Ironic as this example may be, it should not be viewed as a case of 'swings and roundabouts'. By stamping down on corruption, the Liberian government took a step towards establishing a more robust and normalized (by Western standards) trading process. Although bureaucracy has replaced corruption as a supply chain cost, it is far easier to address this problem than the informal and immeasurable problem of bribes and kick-backs.

Food aid and drugs are two of the most highly prized commodities and are vulnerable to being diverted during transportation or storage to non-deserving recipients. This can happen in a number of ways, either directly or through the manipulation of registrations and assessments of need. For example, locals in North Uganda would charge people for inclusion of their names on the lists that were then provided to aid agencies. Other examples cited include wholesale pilfering from 'aid packs', where various consignments were broken into and relief items were removed. Packaging was replaced so that it appeared that nothing had been taken. Drugs could be diverted to be sold in private pharmacies outside of the refugee camp.

Goods that go undistributed and are being transported back to the warehouse are also vulnerable. Not only does this situation foster ill-feeling (communities often feel that these goods are rightly theirs and will take steps to recover them), but they are vulnerable to sale in transit by the lorry driver.

The fair distribution of aid is not the only major challenge. The fuel used in the vehicles undertaking the relief movements is highly valuable and is vulnerable either to theft, or to diversion by those third parties managing or working in the distribution process. This process of 'skimming off', as it is called, can be mitigated by controls implemented by an agency. For example, best practice would suggest that managers should know the average fuel consumption of all its vehicles on a monthly basis. It should therefore be possible to flag up potential instances when 'skimming off' is taking place.

Part of the problem is the lack of visibility that aid agencies have when distributing relief supplies. For example, in camps for displaced people, distribution structures are established to disperse supplies fairly. Camps are often organized by blocks, and each block will have a leader responsible for distributing aid. These block leaders will report to the camp leader. The problem is that the power vested in these figures is liable to abuse. Family links and even sexual favours can influence the amount of goods that a certain block will receive. Often aid agencies have no knowledge of what is going on at these levels and in some cases local partners can be part of the problem.

Logistics controls are essential to mitigating the problem of 'shrinkage' of goods and materials. As in business logistics, ensuring the right volume of goods arrives at the right time is an important part of the process, and reduces opportunities for product to be diverted. However, this is not helpful

**Table 8.1**  Corruption risk examples in humanitarian logistics

| High-risk areas | Corruption risk examples |
| --- | --- |
| **Assistance process** | |
| Assessment | Incorrect information provided to direct assistance to certain households, groups or regions, or to inflate needs |
| Registration | Names added to beneficiary lists in exchange for payment or sexual favours; bribes demanded, multiple registrations |
| Targeting | Leaders/staff/committees provide false information about which households meet targeting criteria |
| Distribution | Distributors modify ration amounts or composition, or knowingly distribute commodities to 'ghost' or non-beneficiaries |
| **Sector** | |
| Food aid | Manipulation or bribery in assessments, registration and targeting; diversion and sale during transport or storage; skimming rations |
| High-value items (eg medicines) | Manipulation or bribery in assessments, registration and targeting; diversion during transport or storage, substandard goods |
| Construction | Intentional use of substandard materials, manipulation of land titles |
| **Programme support** | |
| Procurement | Collusion, kick-backs, multiple submissions of same invoices, conflicts of interest |
| Human resources | 'Ghost' staff, nepotism |
| Finance | Falsified or inflated invoices or receipts, manipulation of exchange rates, abuse of bank accounts, embezzlement |
| Fleet management | Unauthorized private use of vehicles, siphoning off fuel, collusion with fuel/service providers, falsified records |
| Logistics | Falsification of warehouse documents, diversion during transport |

**SOURCE** Humanitarian Policy Group

if too many goods, for example at a construction site, have been ordered in the first place with the express intention of selling the surplus on the black market. This sort of supply chain corruption can only be overcome by the employment of experienced staff who are able to minutely manage projects and processes.

One of the key issues that has been pointed out is that there is a major gap between the policies and commitments that are developed at the head offices of aid agencies and the practice 'on the ground'. Part of the problem is that local partners and staff sometimes have loyalties that lie elsewhere other than to the relief organization for which they work.

Governmental 'institutionalized corruption' can also be a key factor in hindering relief operations, including the Indonesian tsunami aid effort in 2006. In Indonesia, which has many internal security disputes, the distribution of relief supplies from Banda Aceh's Sultan Iskandar Muda Airport was originally undertaken from a military-run warehouse. It was alleged that the military was highly selective in choosing which areas should receive these goods. Some of the most needy, just miles from the airport, were still lacking supplies days after relief flights started arriving. A civilian organization was put in charge of the distribution following complaints from some of the largest international charities. However, in some regions where the local civilian administration was wiped out by the tsunami, the military was the only alternative.

# Organized crime in transport operations

## Ports and shipping

The transport, warehousing and shipping industries are very labour-intensive, and in many countries unions play a very important role in the organization of the workforce. At certain times, unions have been vulnerable to infiltration by organized crime, not least because of the large sums of money unions have access to through contributions from their members and the political influence that these unions can exert.

Right the way through the latter half of the twentieth century, such a situation existed in the United States, where a powerful transport union, the International Brotherhood of Teamsters (IBT), became inextricably linked with organized crime. The leader of the IBT, Jimmy Hoffa, became infamous during his lifetime for being connected not only to gangland, but also for his connections at the very top of US politics, including US President Richard Nixon.

However, it was not just the IBT that was involved. The International Longshoreman's Association (ILA) was made famous for its racketeering practices through the novel *On the Waterfront* by Budd Schulberg. Even in the 1970s senior members of the union reported directly to mafia bosses.

The power of the unions allowed them to extract money from the companies for whom their members worked in order to maintain good industrial relations. In the case of the ILA, the companies making these payments were often shipping lines.

Members of the union/gang were often placed in positions of significant power within the shipping line. They would award contracts to stevedores, container repair and other service companies that were 'approved'. These companies would either have on their payroll other members of the gang or members of the mafia family, would pay the union/gang for the privilege of being awarded the contract, or would be actually owned by the crime syndicate itself.

Shipping lines would know that using suppliers unauthorized by the union/gang would result in delays and disruption. Suppliers would know that they had no chance of winning business without complying with the demands of the union/gang.

Other scams employed by the union/gang included 'sweetheart' deals. One such would allow a company to use non-union labour. This would dramatically reduce costs and allow the company to outbid unionized rivals. In return, union leaders would be paid a considerable bribe by management, and this money finds its way back to the organized crime syndicate.

In the case of the IBT, the organization was characterized by corruption from grassroots up to national level, and its senior hierarchy was made up of organized crime figures.

It made its money in various ways:

- embezzlement of union and pension funds;
- kick-backs to allow transportation companies to use non-union labour;
- extortion to prevent labour unrest;
- placing of gang members on transportation companies' payroll.

The links between organized crime and the transport industry are still very much in evidence, and are not constrained to gangland United States.

## Criminality and corruption in the express sector

Evidence that emerged from a criminal investigation in 2006 showed that there were flaws in the security processes put in place to prevent terrorist attacks on the air cargo system. The trial, which was related to criminal acts rather than terrorism, raised concerns over the 'known shipper system' used by express parcel carriers to expedite packages from identified customers through customs.

The system works by the parcel carrier – working with the customs authorities of a number of countries in Europe and the United States – identifying packages originating from shippers who send large quantities of packages across international borders. These key customers are given identifying numbers, which are printed on the package by the client, acting both as a billing system and as a means of speeding up customs operations. The logic of the system is that these 'known' customers are cleared for security purposes and their packages deemed to be free of any illegal materials or contraband. This enables the parcel company to avoid customs scans on these packages.

Research revealed, however, that 'known shipper system' numbers had been sold by the employees of international express parcels company FedEx to criminal gangs engaged in drug smuggling.

The investigation cited a case involving the prosecution of a Nigerian drug smuggler operating in the UK. He was able to buy the 'known shipper' numbers from a FedEx employee at a London depot. The court was told that the practice appeared to not be unusual. This enabled the criminals to smuggle drugs in from the United States using parcels marked with the 'known shipper' numbers, safe in the knowledge that the packages would not be scanned or searched.

During the trial, FedEx's head of security in the UK admitted that it would be quite possible to smuggle bombs as well as narcotics onto aircraft by abusing this system. He also admitted that freight originating from the United States and destined for the UK was not x-rayed or scanned at all.

This case showed up flaws in the risk-based system of air cargo security, and provides ammunition to those policymakers who assert that there should still be moves towards 'comprehensive' x-raying of consignments.

## Summary

The supply chain and logistics industry is highly vulnerable to corruption, not least because of its reach into developing markets where governance is weak and government officials lowly paid, making them easy targets for bribery. Legislation passed in the UK and US has attempted to reduce corrupt practices by making Western companies responsible for the actions of suppliers as well as employees. However, corruption also occurs in the EU, especially amongst the newer members, where it is part of business culture. Further afield, Russia has an extremely bad reputation, making the import of goods into the market very hazardous for Western traders. In parts of the world, such as India and Africa, freight carriers often have to pay 'unofficial' tolls on roads, which proves time-consuming and expensive. Corruption can also occur in other large-scale logistics operations, such as in Afghanistan or in regions where large amounts of humanitarian aid is provided.

## Key points

- Lowly paid customs officials are easy targets for bribery and can also have the opportunity to be organizers of illicit activities.

- Large shippers are often better placed to resist demands for bribes because of their influence at higher government level – smaller traders are often more vulnerable.

- Legislation passed by the UK and US has increased risk for large importers and exporters by making them responsible for the actions of their employees and third-party suppliers.

- Corruption is high in developing markets, where there is little governance, but also in parts of the EU, where cultural factors play an important role.

- Unofficial tolls are a daily part of life for many road freight carriers in India and Africa.

- Wherever there are large logistics operations in the developing world, there is the risk of major corruption because of the sums of money involved – such as defence or humanitarian logistics.

# Cargo crime and piracy

09

**OBJECTIVES**

This chapter will familiarize the reader with:

- the reasons why cargo is so vulnerable to theft;
- how some simple precautions can reduce the risk;
- the cargo crime hotspots around the world;
- the challenges in protecting air cargo from theft;
- threats to supply chains from cyber-attacks;
- how the threat from pirates was countered in Somalia while it grows unhindered in Nigeria.

## What is cargo crime?

The FBI has defined cargo crime as:

> the criminal taking of any cargo including, but not limited to, goods, chattels, money, or baggage that constitutes, in whole or in part, a commercial shipment of freight moving in commerce, from any pipeline system, railroad car, motortruck, or other vehicle, or from any tank or storage facility, station house, platform, or depot, or from any vessel or wharf, or from any aircraft, air terminal, airport, aircraft terminal or air navigation facility, or from any intermodal container, intermodal chassis, trailer, container freight station, warehouse, freight distribution facility, or freight consolidation facility.

However, one of the issues with reporting cargo crime is that it is not an offence in its own right. It is often classified as property theft (burglary or robbery), extortion, fraud, bribery, motor vehicle theft and, in some cases, assault or murder. This means that law enforcement agencies rarely allocate or train officers to address its specific needs.

Another reason why cargo crime is often regarded by authorities around the world as a low priority in terms of policing resource allocation is because of its perception by many as 'victimless'. However, this is anything but the case. Not only are drivers and other logistics staff often caught up in the crime and may suffer violence and intimidation – in some cases even death – but there are many economic consequences.

The billions of dollars' worth of goods that are stolen each year transfer legitimate business revenue to the black market. This has an impact on corporate health and also taxation revenue. For instance, cigarettes are often targeted and then sold on using illegal channels. The duty and tax on the revenue from the sale is lost to the tax authorities.

Cargo crime is also not necessarily an end in its own right. Because of the prevalence of organized crime in this sector, the sales of the stolen goods often go to fund the drugs trade. For this reason, the crime is often described as a 'gateway' crime.

There is also a link with terrorism. Breaches in supply chain security are highly worrying considering the importance that authorities place on the integrity of security around ports and airports. Trucking is often the first and last part of the transport chain.

At the point that a consignment leaves the factory or distribution centre, it becomes highly vulnerable to theft or some other type of intervention, perhaps substitution or tampering. This is largely outside of the control of the shipper, especially if they are relying on a third-party logistics company to undertake the movement.

Even inside the distribution centre, security is a problem. In fact, 'shrinkage' is one of the reasons why reduction of inventory is so important these days to manufacturers and other shippers – the less stock that is held, the less that can be lost. 'Shrinkage' is not just the result of pilfering of goods by employees. It can also involve much larger instances of criminality – for example, if an employee provides inside information to organized gangs about shipments, security codes or other sensitive information.

Cargo theft is often difficult for the authorities to pursue, as many crimes are not reported until several days after they have occurred. It may take this long, for example, for a consignment on board a vehicle to be missed, or it may be considered most likely to have been lost rather than stolen.

Being a 'mobile crime' also makes it difficult for the authorities to investigate. Criminal networks cut across traditional police force lines of demarcation and the ability to move stolen vehicles and their loads quickly across state lines or international borders can outmanoeuvre police efforts. In the United States, while bank robbery is classed as a federal crime, investigated by the FBI, cargo crime is not. Therefore it is only pursued by local forces, which in many cases do not have the resources, jurisdiction or political will to effectively take on the criminals concerned.

In terms of commodities, food and drink is one of the most popular targets, along with electronics and pharmaceuticals due to their high value.

The latter sector is of particular concern. Many drugs have to be kept in appropriate conditions – for example, a particular temperature band. If a truck is stolen, there is no guarantee that the thieves will maintain these conditions, although they will still seek to introduce the drugs into the supply chain. This may mean that they become ineffective and potentially life-threatening.

If a pharmaceutical consignment is stolen, this may lead to a wholesale product recall, with considerable economic consequences for the businesses concerned. One example of this was an incident in the United States that involved the theft of a trailer-load of pharmaceuticals worth $10 million. The vehicle contained a shipment of immunosuppressives, sensitive to humidity and temperature. As a result, the manufacturer was forced to contact all of its supply chain partners, warning that the drugs may be reintroduced into the supply chain by the criminals. In the end it was forced to recall all of this particular type of drug, costing the company $47 million and reducing its revenues that quarter by 10 per cent.

# Theft from trucks and warehouses

Crime involving theft from freight vehicles is on the rise around the world. As freight travels longer distances, and becomes more cross-border in character, there are more opportunities for criminals to exploit this particularly vulnerable stage of the supply chain. A report for the International Road Transport Union (2008) has found that, over a five-year period, around a fifth of drivers were attacked, with 30 per cent of drivers attacked more than once. Forty-two per cent of the attacks took place in parking areas, indicating that breaks and overnight stops are a particularly dangerous time for drivers.

In Europe, it has been found that the most likely countries for cargo-related crime on trucks are Romania, Hungary and Poland.

A Europol (2009) report into cargo theft defined several different types of cargo crime:

- **Hijacking** – this is an aggravated crime in which the driver is physically intimidated and their vehicle stolen, along with the load. In many cases this is undertaken by criminals posing as police officers and using blue flashing lights to pull them over, or by staging an accident.

- **Lorry theft** – this involves the stealing of an unattended vehicle.

- **Load theft** – stealing of a load or part of a load from a stationary vehicle. One of the most popular ways of committing cargo crime is the simple 'curtain slash'. The 'curtain' is the tarpaulin that covers the side of many trucks and can be pulled back to facilitate loading/off-loading of the vehicle. Unfortunately this also reduces security significantly and makes loads vulnerable to a simple cut with a knife.

- **Deception/diversion** – this involves cases where a business or their driver is duped into delivering a load to the wrong destination. For instance, fraudulent documents can be used by a criminal purporting to be the real driver or to effect the unauthorized release of a shipment from a distribution centre.

- **Bogus transport companies** – these can be set up to tender for contracts or loads. The shipments are then diverted and the company disappears.

- **Warehouse crime** – theft of goods being stored in a warehouse (see below).

It is unsurprising that the most frequent instances of cargo crime occur on the major arterial road networks, especially at various economic nodes. In the UK, Kent – the gateway to the country for many foreign drivers – is a particular hotspot. The West and East Midlands – hubs of manufacturing – are also problem areas. In France, the main areas of crime radiate around Paris to about 150 kilometres.

With theft of pharmaceuticals on the rise, it is not surprising that one of the biggest manufacturers, Novartis, takes the issue very seriously. In the United States, the company has adopted the following provisions:

- trips are predetermined, and obvious high-risk areas are avoided;

- drivers are told not to stop in certain areas, and if there is an unscheduled stop, calls are made by the transport management team to inquire why;

- trucks are monitored by GPS locators;

- outsourced trucking companies are vetted and need to comply with a list of requirements.

Shipments of metal have been very popular targets for some time because of the high prices that can be achieved for scrap and recycling. In one case, a number of French recycling firms were implicated in the theft of four loads of metal (nickel and copper) totalling over 100 tonnes. The robberies were conducted by a highly organized gang posing as armed police officers and stopping the trucks at a fake police checkpoint.

Transported Asset Protection Association EMEA has highlighted several cases showing the breadth of cargo crime across Europe in terms of the range of modus operandi employed:

- Six drivers in the province of Emilia-Romagna, Italy, were arrested for stealing parts of the shipments they were carrying. Police recovered goods worth €1.5 million.

- Police in Italy also arrested a gang of truck hijackers in the Naples area whose method involved blocking the road with a car, and forcing the vehicle to stop before the driver was assaulted and the truck stolen.

- A driver in Austria was arrested for stealing high-value goods over a period of 12 months. He was able to break seals on the cargo and repair them with glue.

- A French police operation involving 400 officers led to the arrest of 41 Romanian criminals who had stolen about €2 million worth of copper from vehicles.

- A British gang were jailed for staging a fake heist that led to the theft of over €1 million of gold and silver in Belgium. The driver, it transpired, had been involved in the plot.

# Combating vehicle-based cargo crime

One of the simplest ways of cutting vehicle-related cargo crime is to improve overnight parking areas for vehicles, for instance in secure compounds. It is often very difficult for companies wishing to develop lorry parking areas to get planning permission because of local opposition. However, the result is that drivers often make do with lay-bys near inter-junctions with the motorway. This means that not only are they vulnerable in isolated areas, but the criminals have an easy getaway and can distribute stolen goods very quickly.

Other recommendations include:

- Vet driving staff to ensure no criminal history. This should also extend to subcontractors.

- If a consignment to be hauled is of high value or is termed 'highly fenceable' (that is, easy to be sold on the black market), a special set of processes should be followed, making sure that the driver is trustworthy and experienced.

- Stops en route should be limited – steps such as filling up a vehicle with fuel before it sets off should be taken. Many thieves will follow a truck once it has left a depot and, if it stops to fill up with fuel at a local gas station, it will be targeted. One recommendation is that the truck should not stop for at least 200 miles once it sets off.

- For exceptionally high-value loads, the carrier and shipper should consider a two-man driving team. This will mean that rest time and overnight stops are limited to the minimum.

- Drivers' hours should also be taken into account when loading a vehicle. Shippers should, for example, avoid loading a truck if the driver is coming to the end of their allotted hours. The alternative would increase the risk to the shipment with the truck stationary while the driver takes their rest period.

- Increase security in the freight yard – this can involve what has been termed as a 'layered' approach: ensuring that perimeter fencing is secure; there is CCTV; good lighting; security guards; identification and documentation checks. If possible, vehicles should be scheduled to arrive when the yard is open, so they are not left waiting overnight in a vulnerable state.

- Install GPS tracking devices – many vehicles are now fitted with devices that allow them to be tracked, either in the normal course of their business or should they be stolen. Thieves are more adept at disabling these devices and technology security companies are continually trying to make them more effective. In one instance in Italy, a specialist gang jammed GPS signals after stealing the vehicle.

- Seals – sealing trucks is an effective way of checking to see whether a vehicle has been entered illegally. RFID is now being employed to track individual shipments.

- Use branded vehicles. White, generic trucks are difficult for the authorities to track once stolen. It also gives the shipper confidence that the consignment is being handed over to a bona fide carrier.

- Make sure that locks on the tractor and trailer unit are fitted, for instance, a 'king pin' lock on the container, and a lock that disables the air brakes.

- Ensure that the driver does not have to wait around – or overnight – at the point of delivery.

As the problem has moved up the political agenda, it is evident that police are starting to take the issue more seriously. One technique to catch criminals is to leave a loaded 'unattended' trailer as bait for criminals to catch them in the act.

However, the problem is not just a localized one. The integration of economies across the EU means that a strategic approach to law enforcement is needed, especially considering that it is likely the stolen goods are 'fenced' throughout the whole market, in some instances using pricing differentials (cigarettes for example). When a load of high-tech, high-value equipment could be valued at perhaps €2 million, the vulnerability of the vehicle and driver to criminal action is obvious.

One indirect consequence for the industry, but one nevertheless of major importance, is that the fear engendered by endemic levels of crime is a major factor in putting women (in particular) off applying for driving jobs. In a period of driver shortages this has a considerable cost implication for employers, as well as creating issues in diversity.

## Cargo crime in North America

In Canada, the Canadian Trucking Alliance estimates that cargo crime is a $5 billion problem (CTA, 2015). Southern Ontario is regarded as the main location for this type of crime, and police estimate that $500,000 of goods go missing every day in the Greater Toronto Area. Despite this, only a handful of police officers are dedicated to the problem.

Part of the challenge in Canada is to coordinate an integrated response from provincial and national police forces. Cargo crime there, as in many other parts of the world, falls through the cracks: although car theft, traffic and organized crime divisions exist, there is no agency dedicated to cargo crime and no legislation that specifically deals with the problem.

In the United States, cargo crime is put at around the $30 billion a year mark (Washington, 2016), although, since up until recently the crime was not dealt with separately under the FBI's Uniform Crime Reporting System, there has been little visibility of the extent of the problem. The US Patriot Improvement and Re-authorization Act of 2005 changed this, as it was recognized that cargo theft was having a major impact on the US economy.

One particular hotspot for crime is in New Jersey, which has two large port areas: Port Elizabeth and Port Newark. The high levels of distribution facilities and trucking activities mean that it is a major attraction for criminality.

Cargo crime has been shown to have a strong correlation with retail sales. The reasons for this are fairly obvious, as the more goods that are being imported and shipped to stores, the greater the opportunity for criminals. As well as being cyclical, cargo crime is also seasonal. In the United States, thefts have been shown to peak at around the holiday period (November and December). They then fall off and correlate with retail sales activity for the rest of the year.

In terms of volume, food is the single largest category of goods stolen, followed by electronics. Base metals are also important, not least because of the rising cost of scrap metal on the international market. However, in terms of value, electronics make up almost half of the value of all goods stolen.

The geographical location of cargo crime in the United States is distributed closely to the country's major hubs. From the map in Figure 9.1, it is possible to see clusters of crime in California (major port gateway from the Far East); Miami (gateway from Latin America); Texas (major crossing point for goods moving from Mexico); New York (transatlantic volumes); Atlanta, Georgia (a rail, road and air hub); as well as Chicago (rail, road and air hub). This reinforces the point that goods are at risk when they are at rest, rather than moving along an interstate, on a ship, train or in the air.

**Figure 9.1**  Map of cargo crime hotspots in the United States

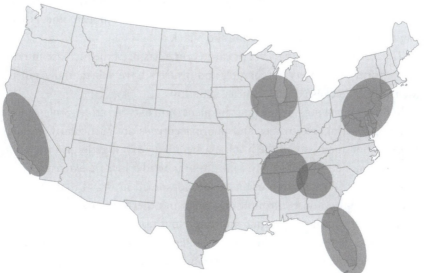

# Cargo crime in emerging markets

If cargo crime is widespread in Europe and North America, it is out of control in many emerging markets. In Mexico, attacks on vehicles have become so frequent that some transport companies have started to group their vehicles together in convoys.

Because of the general lawlessness in parts of Mexico, not least as a result of the drug cartels, cargo carriers are extremely vulnerable to attack. Mexico City is generally regarded as the major crime hub, with most attacks taking place when the vehicles are parked at the roadside. Although the attacks are opportunistic, the targeting is far more planned, with corruption and/or intimidation of drivers widespread. Employee or driver collusion is a major factor.

There is anecdotal evidence that criminals are becoming more aggressive, with raids on carriers' yards increasing, resulting in the theft of full truckloads. Other major crime blackspots include cities in the states of Chihuahua, Tamaulipas and Coahuila.

Of particular significance in recent years has been the increase in theft of auto parts. The increased use of Mexico as a near-sourcing location by US and Japanese vehicle manufacturers to supply the US market has led to a surge in the level of automotive-related parts being shipped northwards across the border. In addition, car transporters have been targeted.

The level of violence in cargo crime in Mexico is of particular concern. According to CANACAR, the association representing Mexican truckers, and the Mexican Insurers Association, up to two-thirds of thefts are carried out at gunpoint. Many of these are undertaken by fake police officers who flag down vehicles before effecting the hijack.

The direct result of the level of cargo crime has been the increase in rates in the form of a 'safety surcharge', and insurers have substantially put up their premia because of the security situation.

In Brazil, hijackings are the most frequent form of cargo crime. Stolen goods – food and drink, electronics and pharmaceuticals are particularly popular targets – find their way to the black market because of high levels of tax and duty on products traded legally. Links to organized crime are extensive.

It is reported that cargo crime is so widespread in Brazil that incidents tend to be more non-confrontational than in other parts of the continent. Drivers see the crime as routine and rarely put up resistance. In an attempt to address the problem, the use of security escorts and convoys have become more widespread. Organized crime gangs also employ sophisticated distribution networks for stolen goods. One report says that these often rival legal supply chain networks in terms of complexity and efficiency.

# Theft from airports

Fifty million tonnes of cargo are transported by air each year. This translates to $5.3 trillion of business and accounts for about 35 per cent of the value of goods traded internationally. It is not surprising, then, that air cargo security is such an important topic for industry and regulators.

Airports are the focus of attention for criminal gangs, as the goods carried by air cargo are usually high-value, comprising, for example, high-tech, pharmaceuticals and even cash or gold. Once these goods are offloaded into transit sheds, they become vulnerable to a range of criminal activities. It is perhaps surprising that although airports have been subject to a high increase in security since the 9/11 terrorist acts, the amount of thefts from airports has continued undiminished.

The two issues – terrorism and crime – are closely linked. If the air cargo chain is not secure enough to prevent freight from being illicitly removed, regulators would consider it highly vulnerable for material – such as a bomb – to be introduced into the system.

The worry is that with gangs seemingly able to infiltrate cargo workers, corrupt customs officers and even (see below) penetrate airport security to hold up aircraft while on the apron, air cargo supply chains have little protection.

Below are some examples of major air cargo 'heists' from around the world.

In February 2013, a heavily armed gang wearing police uniforms and driving two police cars forced their way into Brussels airport. They made directly for a Zurich-bound aircraft onto which was being loaded a consignment of diamonds. They offloaded the diamonds, which were conservatively estimated to be worth $50 million, and made off. There was obviously a large degree of inside knowledge related to this particular operation. First, the gang would have been alerted to the shipment and, second, they would also have had to have known the precise time at which the consignment was being offloaded from the armoured van onto the aircraft. Since then many arrests have been made, as the gang was less efficient in the way it tried to offload the diamonds onto the gem market.

In November 2012, $1.5 million of iPad minis were stolen from JFK Airport, New York. Criminals were able to access the cargo terminal and removed two pallets of the product before fleeing the location when challenged. Police suspected that the thieves had the help of an insider who would have had knowledge of the shipment and its location, and arrested an airport worker. The 3,600 iPads had recently arrived from China.

Around $1.4 million in consumer electronics were stolen from Miami International Airport in February 2012. The cargo was loaded onto a vehicle that was left unattended while the driver entered the facility to complete his paperwork. This was the fourth incident at Miami International in a month, all targeting the same high-tech sector.

## Combating air cargo theft

### 'Chain of custody'

Best practice in air cargo security suggests that there should be clearly defined handover points, where responsibility for a consignment is transferred. This is referred to as a 'chain of custody'.

### CCTV

A total of 650 CCTV cameras were installed at Chhatrapati Shivaji International Airport after a series of cargo thefts between 2007 and 2009. The cameras are used to monitor staff, such as loaders, warehouse operatives and scanners, who, according to the authorities at the airport, have a history of being involved in criminal gangs. Even cleaners can be used to move stolen goods out of the airport by concealing them in rubbish bags.

### Staff screening

Air cargo handling staff screening is essential. With some estimates suggesting that 85 per cent of air cargo crime is undertaken solely by, or with the help of, an insider, making sure that appropriate staff are hired in the first place is critical. Employers typically screen staff for criminal records but they should also be searched on entering and leaving facilities.

### Vetting suppliers

In some cases, such as the movement of drugs, it is a legal requirement for importers to screen their business partners. In terms of logistics, the importer must know the quantity of the product being shipped, its packaging, the conditions it is being kept in and even the airline that is being used to carry the consignment. This requires personal visits from the importer to their suppliers, during which facilities and security must be assessed. An essential part of this is looking at the arrangements in place for shipping goods to the airport and even the security arrangements at the airport itself.

## Technology

Hong Kong Air Cargo Terminals Limited (Hactl) deploys handheld computers, increasing cargo and terminal security integrity for its airline customers. With these it is possible to perform on-site checking of vehicles, cargoes, unit load devices (ULDs) and permits during daily terminal surveillance. With this wireless technology, Hactl security staff get instant access to Hactl's online logistics management systems – the Community System for Air Cargo (COSAC) – to remotely update and retrieve related security information. This access enhances close monitoring of truck and human movement in and out of the terminal, strengthening overall cargo and terminal security.

## Conclusion

One of the major problems the industry has in tackling cargo crime is the low priority given to it both by police and by the judicial system. Whereas drug smuggling, for instance, is likely to incur a custodial sentence, stealing high-tech equipment may not. Cargo theft is not regarded any differently than other property theft, and the role that organized crime plays is often overlooked. This is partly because of a low political profile, as it does not impact directly on the general public.

Another problem that has been pointed out is that many crimes go unreported. This is due in some cases to a delay in finding out that a consignment has been stolen, or in fact not knowing for sure if it is missing because of theft or whether it has just been misplaced. Given the high volumes of many carriers, the latter is often the case.

However, non-reporting is also often due to the carriers affected not wanting to tarnish their reputation – in many cases it is regarded as better to sweep the affair under the carpet. This culture of cover-up means that it is difficult to build up a statistical body of evidence that could then be used to lobby governments.

# Cyber-threats to supply chains

## The rising threat of cyber-attacks to logistics networks

Criminals, terrorists, security agencies and political activists are increasingly targeting the information and communications technology systems of large corporations and government agencies. The logistics and supply chain industry is finding itself increasingly in the firing line.

For many decades, logistics companies have invested most of their time and money into ensuring the integrity of their physical infrastructure and assets. Airlines and express operators have, for instance, been very mindful of the risks to their business of a terrorist infiltration of a bomb on board an aircraft or into a shipping container. Physical screening of consignments and the validation of shippers is commonplace. The major logistics companies also have huge security operations in place to prevent theft of shipments from their warehouses, the substitution of counterfeit goods or the use of their networks to move illegal drugs or firearms around the world.

However, less attention has been paid to the possibility of an attack on their IT systems, which, depending on the source of the threat, could have consequences ranging from inconvenient to catastrophic.

Supply chains dependent on sea freight are perhaps uniquely exposed to cyber-attacks because of the way in which shipping has become increasingly channelled through the ever-decreasing number of ports capable of loading and offloading the largest container ships. For example, a successful cyber-attack on a port community system (a system responsible for the coordination of all port activities) of one of the big 'gateway' hubs, such as Rotterdam or Los Angeles, would have a substantial region-wide economic impact because of the lack of options available for re-routing of ships. Shipping is increasingly reliant on information technology, from navigation to propulsion, from freight management to traffic control. With the development and deployment of e-freight or e-maritime systems, the risk is only going to get worse.

The airline and air cargo sectors are also at risk. Future aircraft designs developed to deliver efficiency gains will be based on network connectivity and electronic data exchange. This will make the industry ever-more reliant on the transfer of real-time automated data from ground to aircraft. If the systems were compromised, there could be disastrous consequences for the safety of the crew, passengers and cargo. The same goes for air traffic control systems. Ensuring that this data is transferred between the ground and aircraft securely is the challenge that all stakeholders in the civil aviation sector must address.

The logistics industry also faces threats, not so much to the control of transport assets, but to the goods themselves that are being moved or stored. In terms of data, supply chain networks could be described as being inherently insecure, with parties encouraged to share information with their suppliers and their customers. The availability of data heightens the risk that the integrity or confidentiality of that shared information could be compromised. Supply chain management systems facilitate the dissemination of shipment-level information, which, while enabling the efficient movement of goods, is also invaluable to criminals. The widespread use of handheld devices and GPS technology in the field can increase the risks. Companies understand and manage this risk internally but have difficulty identifying and managing it across a large supplier base.

Regulators are slowly waking up to the fact that transport and logistics IT systems are vulnerable to attack, as well as to the severe consequences for society and commerce should air, sea, road or rail transport networks be disrupted. Although its inquiries are at a very early stage, the EU may require that transport operators have backup systems in place for computer systems that will allow swift recovery of core activities, especially relating to the safety of transport, should a cyber-attack occur.

Perhaps the changing attitude to cyber-threats can be summarized by one transport security expert, who commented that while five years ago he was spending most of his time on the physical aspects of security, now the majority of his time is dedicated to technology and data exchange issues. It is clear that from now on the focus for the transport and logistics sector as a whole must be as much on the integrity of its data streams as it is on the physical aspects of its systems.

## CASE STUDY   Port of Antwerp security breached

The cyber-threats to supply chains are not just theoretical. In October 2013 it was revealed that organized criminals had employed hackers to launch a cyber-raid on port systems at the Port of Antwerp, pinpointing the locations of containers concealing smuggled drugs and releasing them to bogus drivers.

Hackers had been employed to break into the port technology systems of two companies in the port. They were then able to identify the location of certain containers in which consignments of drugs had been concealed. The containers were from bona fide shippers, but before the customers were able to collect their goods, the gang had sent in their own drivers. The breach of the technology system not only told the driver where to find the container, but also provided the necessary security codes, which enabled the container to be released from the port.

The cyber-breach occurred in two different ways. To begin with, targeted employees were sent 'malware' by the hackers, which allowed them to gain access to secure databases. When a firewall was installed to prevent this, the criminals broke into offices and physically installed devices on computers that could detect keystrokes, consequently providing them with passwords.

In one instance, when the criminals were not able to get to a container before it was removed by the rightful customer, they tracked it out of the port and then hijacked it in Limburg in an armed raid.

Police conducted a number of operations themselves, and this resulted in cocaine and heroin being seized with a street value of several hundred million dollars. They say that the case was an example of organized crime utilizing the services of internet hackers, who were advertising their services on the 'dark web'.

The success of the cyber-attack on companies operating in the Port of Antwerp and the subsequent success of the organized gang in subverting container supply chains sends out a very clear message to the industry – cargo crime is moving to a new level of sophistication. If criminals are able to identify and steal containers in which drugs are concealed, there is no reason why they couldn't use the same method to hijack consignments of high-value goods such as electronics and pharmaceuticals. The implications of these revelations for supply chain integrity are enormous.

# Piracy

In recent years, piracy on the world's shipping lanes has become a major issue for shipping lines, shippers, insurance companies and governments. Piracy off the coast of Somalia achieved the height of its media profile in 2011, even prompting a Hollywood film, *Captain Phillips*, although the problem has diminished since that time, for reasons that will be discussed later in this chapter.

However, piracy is not just an issue affecting the east coast of Africa. The problem is endemic in the waters off Nigeria and it is a constant factor in and around the Strait of Malacca in Indonesia, through which a vast proportion of the world's shipping passes.

The response from the global community to begin with was very slow, but eventually naval resources were deployed, which have had some effect on the problem. This was not before the private sector, including insurance companies, were forced to take matters into their own hands. Private convoy systems were established, and armed guards employed by security companies on board ships became the norm. This raised concerns – ethical and otherwise – about unregulated and possibly untrained operatives being given the right to deploy armed and possibly deadly force in a hijacking situation. There have also been issues about the flood of illegal weaponry that has entered the Horn of Africa as a result of the number of security companies being used.

Despite the recent reduction in the number of piracy incidents being reported, the problem is still a factor in the risk to supply chains. Shippers, directly or indirectly, have to pay for the cost of insurance, and time is lost on transits because of redirection of shipping.

## Piracy hotspots

Despite a fall in the number of piracy attacks on merchant ships, significant threats still remain, particularly off the coasts of East and West Africa. The overall reduction has been attributed to a significant reduction in Somali piracy; however, the seas off East and West Africa remain highly volatile.

The overall reduction in attacks was attributed to the presence of naval forces disrupting pirate operations, the implementation of self-protection methods on board vessels, and increased awareness of where potential threats are located.

The continuing threat has been highlighted by an escalation in attacks off the coast of West Africa. In Nigerian waters, attacks increased from 14 in 2015 to 36 in 2016 (ICC International Maritime Bureau, 2016). In this particular region, there is no UK, EUNAVFOR or US naval presence and, as such, the UN Security Council has recognized it as a specific threat to international security. The increasing number of attacks in West Africa emphasizes the necessity for further anti-piracy measures and better support for ship operators to eliminate the threat of piracy in the long term.

Incidences of actual and attempted attacks, according to the International Maritime Bureau, are detailed in Table 9.1.

Table 9.1 shows that the phenomenon of piracy is not just a Horn of Africa problem, with Nigeria and South East Asia of growing importance. These areas will be examined in more detail below.

**Table 9.1**  Incidences of actual and attempted piracy attacks, 2015

| | |
|---|---|
| South East Asia | 75 |
| Far East | 16 |
| Indian subcontinent | 17 |
| South America | 27 |
| Africa | 67 |

**SOURCE** International Maritime Bureau (2016)

## Somali piracy

The failed state of Somalia has, for two decades, spawned high levels of criminality, both within the country itself and in the waters off its coasts. Locals, usually former fishermen, turned to piracy as a way of augmenting their meagre incomes and, many would say, as a result of the extreme poverty that exists in this part of the world. However, this characterization oversimplifies the situation, as many of the groups involved in piracy have links with criminal and Islamic fundamentalist terrorist organizations, such as Al-Shabaab, which controls parts of the country. Despite the success of stemming the number of attacks, these links still exist.

Piracy was a hugely profitable activity for the local community because of the complex 'supply chains' that have, themselves, built up around the industry. The World Bank estimates that 70–86 per cent of the revenues generated from ransoms go to the suppliers of goods and food to the pirates guarding the hostages, as well as in bribes and payments to local politicians and administrators (World Bank, 2013).

The fast growth in Somali piracy was perhaps fundamental to catching the international community and shipping industry off-guard. Global supply chains were severely affected by this development because of the important shipping lanes that pass in close proximity.

**Figure 9.2**   Map of trade lanes passing Somalia and high-risk areas

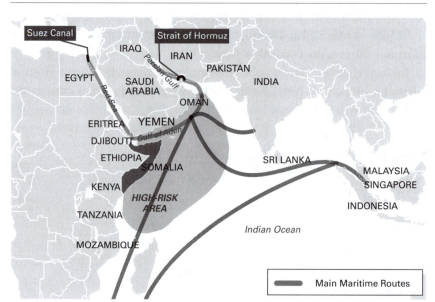

The modus operandi of Somali pirates evolved over the years from simple inshore forays to board passing shipping, to the use of mother ships that allowed them to extend their reach far out to sea. In 2007, the farthest ship from the Somali mainland to be attacked was 800 kilometres from the pirate hub of Eyl. In 2010 this had extended to 3,655 kilometres. This is highly unusual behaviour, as in most other parts of the world most crime occurs in inshore waters, usually at anchorage or in ports themselves.

Once hijacked, the pirates guarding the taken ship were usually supplied for several months (the average kidnap period for seamen was five months – although some hostages were held for the best part of three years). This supply was undertaken from onshore command centres, which also dealt with the hostage negotiations and the arrangement for the ransom delivery.

The existence of these command centres was predicated on the lack of rule of law, the ability of criminal (and terrorist) organizations to come to an agreement with local communities (either through bribes, financial incentives or physical coercion) and the ability to evade attempts by the international community to shut down their operations.

The cost of Somali piracy has fallen substantially but is still significant. It was put at over $6 billion in 2012, whereas in 2015 it was estimated to be $1.3 billion. Of this, ransoms and recovery are only a small part of the overall costs. The Oceans Beyond Piracy project estimates that the total cost is broken down as shown in Table 9.2 (One Earth Future Foundation, 2015).

**Table 9.2**  Breakdown of the costs of piracy (%)

| | |
|---|---|
| Security equipment and guards | 29% |
| Re-routing | 5% |
| Increased speeds | 27% |
| Labour | 8% |
| Prosecutions and imprisonment | <1% |
| Military operations | 19% |
| Counter-piracy organizations | <1% |
| Ransoms and recovery | 1% |
| Insurance | 10% |

**SOURCE** Oceans Beyond Piracy (2015)

## Naval operations

There is a range of government-led military initiatives in the region involving navies from around the world. Efforts and assets are coordinated mainly through NATO (Operation Ocean Shield) and the EU (Operation Atalanta/ EU NAVFOR).

The European Union Naval Force (EU NAVFOR) Somalia – 'Operation Atalanta' – was launched in December 2008 in accordance with United Nations Security Council's resolutions. The operation has the following objectives:

- the protection of World Food Programme (WFP) vessels delivering aid to displaced persons in Somalia and the protection of African Union Mission in Somalia (AMISOM) shipping;
- the deterrence, prevention and repression of acts of piracy and armed robbery at sea off the Somali coast;
- the protection of vulnerable shipping off the Somali coast on a case-by-case basis.

In addition, the EU NAVFOR also contributes to the monitoring of fishing activities off the coast of Somalia.

EU NAVFOR operates in an area covering the Southern Red Sea, the Gulf of Aden and a significant part of the Indian Ocean, including the Seychelles.

The campaign against Somali pirates entered a new stage in 2011 when a combined European naval force undertook operations against targets on land. A helicopter fired upon the boats of Somali pirates, destroying up to five that had been pulled up on the beach. Naval vessels from France, Germany, Italy, Spain, the Netherlands and Portugal were involved. This was the first time that operations had been undertaken against pirates on the shore and followed a mandate by the EU that allows for more robust action to be taken.

One of the problems with operations has been that captured pirates have been difficult to imprison or get to trial because of the lack of countries willing to take them. This has led many to be repatriated after a brief spell on a European warship.

NATO Operation Ocean Shield, NATO's contribution to international efforts to combat piracy off the Horn of Africa, commenced in August 2009 and ended in 2016.

The operation is regarded as being highly successful, with hijacks, attacks and disruptions falling significantly from 2012 onwards.

NATO, the United States and the EU were not the only forces to be deployed in the region. Others include:

- China;
- Japan;
- India;
- Russia.

NATO and Russia have identified piracy in Somalia as a common security challenge and have committed to joint information-sharing as well as other mutual support, such as shared medical aid and refuelling.

## 'Typhon' – the private sector response

The only other counter-measure available to ship operators, aside from naval protection, was the use of armed guards, known as vessel protection detachments (VPDs). This protection model provides armed personnel to live on board the client ship for the duration of transit. Although this method contributed to the overall decline in attacks, it had limited appeal to the ship operators as vessels still had to detour at great expense to avoid the most volatile areas and remained vulnerable to attack.

At the height of the piracy attacks, private sector maritime protection agency, Typhon, launched a convoy escort service that enabled ship operators to transit the Gulf of Aden, Arabian Sea and Indian Ocean with naval-grade protection. Typhon's 'Integrated Protection Model' incorporated three levels of protection: detecting piracy by sea (using radar), by air (using satellite) and by land (through an onshore operations centre in the UAE).

The concept, mirroring naval protection services, also included close protection vessels that shadowed the client vessel in an 'umbrella' formation to identify threats of piracy and create a 'protection zone' around the vessel should an attack occur.

## *Piracy in the rest of the world*

### Piracy in South East Asia

Piracy in South East Asia is very different in modus operandi from that experienced in Somalia and the Gulf of Aden. While the latter invariably involves attempts to hijack vessels while they are moving, in Indonesia attacks are more likely to occur while they are at anchorage. However, they can involve hostage-taking.

In the region there are several areas of particular concern:

- Strait of Malacca;
- Singapore Strait;
- Indonesia.

Over the past few years the number of incidents has been rising, but their location has changed. While in the mid-2000s the Strait of Malacca (which carries 40 per cent of the world's trade) was seen as a particular hotspot, increased naval patrols have led to a significant reduction in attacks. The dramatic reduction was the result of action taken by Malaysia and the neighbouring states that included multi-jurisdictional measures, such as coordinated patrols and 'eye-in-the-sky' programmes. Ten radar systems were supplied by the United States to Indonesia to improve security.

Instead, activity has moved towards the south or east, beyond patrols and in areas difficult to monitor, for example in the Anambas or Natuna Islands of the South China Sea or Batam, close to Singapore. Increased levels of poverty in the region, partly due to overfishing, have been amongst the factors behind the increase in piracy.

## Piracy in West Africa

Although Somali piracy is on the wane, this is certainly not the case in Nigeria, which has seen incidents soar. Attacks can occur up to 120 miles offshore, and gangs of pirates are often well armed and violent. Attacks have also occurred in neighbouring countries such as Ivory Coast, Benin and Togo.

In one instance, Nigerian pirates managed to board a chemical tanker. Having hijacked the vessel, it was sailed to another location, where part of its cargo was transferred to another tanker. This suggests significant levels of organization and planning, compared with many other attacks, which involve the theft of valuables and personal effects.

## Conclusion

What is clear is that although the recent efforts by the international community to reduce piracy in Somalia have been very successful, the underlying cause of the problem has not gone away. It has been seen that when anti-piracy initiatives such as on-board security personnel are ended, the number of attacks again increases. Consequently, rebuilding the Somali state must be at the forefront of policymakers' efforts.

According to the One Earth Future Foundation, the only long-term solution for the problem of piracy is investment on land rather than in short-term mitigation initiatives at sea. In 2013, five shipping lines – 'K' Line, Maersk Line, Stena, NYK Line, Mitsui OSK Line – teamed up with Shell and BP to donate $1 million in support of job-creation and capacity-building projects in Somalia.

This is a fact recognized by the shipping lines, maritime organizations and shippers. A joint statement issued by the International Chamber of Shipping, BIMCO, the Oil Companies International Marine Forum, the International Association of Independent Tanker Owners, the International Association of Dry Cargo Shipowners, the International Parcel Tankers Association and the International Shipping Federation warned that increased anti-piracy measures were required to fight the long-term threat of piracy:

> [We] remain convinced that the only long-term solution to piracy is to establish effective government and implement the rule of law ashore in Somalia. However, until that is achieved, there can be no room for complacency. Any reduction in the level of protection of merchant ships could lead to a resurgence of pirate activities. Piracy must continue to be suppressed through the visible presence of, and robust action by, the world's navies, consistent with international law.

## Summary

Cargo crime is an increasing threat to supply chains, not least because valuable freight travels largely unprotected over longer distances and cross-border. At each stop trucks can be attacked and cargo stolen. Police have given this sort of crime a low priority in the past, as often it is reported long after the act; there may be uncertainty over where the theft took place and in many cases there is little proof the goods have been stolen rather than lost. Air cargo is also a prime target for criminals because of its high value. Piracy has been a problem in the past for shipping lines, especially off the coast of Somalia. Although the problem has not entirely gone away, strong international coordination and action has been effective, although there are increasing problems now in West Africa.

## Key points

- Cargo crime, as well as being important in its own right, often acts as a gateway crime for other forms of illegal activity.

- Hotspots are generally around ports, airports, truck stops and distribution clusters – anywhere, in fact, that freight stops moving.

- Cargo crime is endemic in certain parts of the world, such as Brazil and Mexico, where the inadequacy of law enforcement agencies makes crime a 'cost of business'.

- Cyber-crime is a growing threat. The increasing availability of data will make security even more important.

- Piracy has been effectively countered in Somalia, although underlying conditions for its resurgence exist. However, the situation off Nigeria is worsening.

# Political risks in supply chains  10

**OBJECTIVES**

This chapter will familiarize the reader with:

- the rise of populism and the waning fortunes of economic liberalism;
- the implications of Brexit for the UK economy;
- the various types of agreement that the UK may forge with the EU;
- the range of impacts that Brexit may have upon various vertical sectors;
- how President Trump's policies may affect global trade agreements;
- how China is using trade to increase its influence around the world.

So far this book has focused on risks to supply chains from factors such as climate change, security or economic change. However, in the past few years it has become increasingly clear that the established global trading network is under threat from political factors.

Much has been written about the changing fortunes of economic liberalism over the past two centuries. Free trade held sway until the economic depression of the 1930s, leading to great advances in industrial, technological and, indeed, political development. However, when governments around the world adopted ill-judged protectionist and interventionist policies in an attempt to counter the depression of the 1930s, the primacy of economic liberalism came to an end. Instead, the next 50 years saw countries introduce varying levels of controls on trade, capital and migration. At the same time the Soviet Union, China and the countries within their sphere of influence offered a completely different system from the free markets of the West.

It was only in the 1980s that the pendulum once more swung back in favour of those who promoted the concept of more integrated international markets. Although the organizations forged at the Bretton Woods summit had been effective in ensuring some elements of transnational cooperation and reform, it took many decades before politicians and central bankers (led by the UK and US) realized that structural reform was necessary to avoid economic collapse.

China's change of economic philosophy and the implosion of the Soviet Union added to this momentum. Throughout the 1990s, global trade grew strongly, creating economic value in many parts of the world and providing consumers in the West with cheap products. The loss of traditional heavy industries in the West and even higher-value manufacturing was seen as part of an essential rebalancing of economic structure.

Now, however, this last premise is being challenged. It has always been the case that globalization has created 'winners and losers'. The 'losers' in the West have been those formerly employed in the industries that have adopted the 'unbundling and outsourcing' approach to production – such as in the high-tech or fashion sectors, for example. Alternatively, they may have been employed in a steel mill or chemical plant that has become uneconomic because of cheaper supplies produced elsewhere. Or, indeed, their company could have been acquired by a foreign investor and shut down, as production is centralized on a regional basis elsewhere.

Although this may have been happening for the past 30 years, the discontent that it has created has largely been ignored by the political elite (of whatever political persuasion). However, the political and economic environment has now changed. There are many reasons for this, and it is not within the remit of this book to explore them all. However, some of the key issues include:

- migration policies that led to an influx of foreign workers willing to work for much lower pay, resulting, as some analysts believe, in depressing wage rates for the whole labour market;

- the banking crisis of 2008 and the subsequent bailout of the banks – this generated universal ill-will and sowed the seeds of lack of confidence in the establishment and the judgement of government ministers;

- the economic crisis that occurred in large parts of southern Europe as a result of pressures wrought by untimely and ill-judged entry into the eurozone and the lack of flexibility of fiscal policy this created;

- the development of the so-called Rust Belt in the USA, as established heavy manufacturing jobs migrated to Asia (predominantly China) and Mexico.

These factors exacerbated mistrust in the systems created by politicians, who themselves have been regarded as increasingly self-serving and remote from the voters. This discontent manifested itself in the vote for Brexit in 2016 and the election of President Trump in the US later that year.

Concerning Brexit, although there were undoubtedly many factors in the decision by the UK electorate to leave the EU, including the desire of many to forge better and freer links with countries outside of Europe, it would be naïve to think that this latter point influenced the majority. Therefore, it will be a difficult job to appease the large proportion of voters who were motivated by the desire to reduce the level of migration into the UK while at the same time not irrevocably damaging parts of the economy. For example, it will be impossible to meet the demand from the indigenous UK population for the thousands of jobs in the transport, warehousing, hospitality or agricultural sectors presently filled by immigrants. This would undoubtedly have a major impact on the UK's competitiveness on a global basis.

One of the problems for economic liberalism and globalization is that proponents have always faced a difficult battle against nationalism and interventionism. In 2015, when large elements of the South Wales steel industry were faced with closure due, in part, to the low price of steel on the international market, unions and opposition politicians immediately called for the protection and support of the manufacturing plants. Few politicians would be brave enough to argue the doctrine of comparative advantage or about 'leaving it to the market' (although, of course, in this example the situation is made more complex by Chinese state support of its steel mills). Rather, politicians prefer to talk about 'industrial strategy', which suggests that they are better than the market in predicting successful outcomes, and this will almost inevitably involve some element of protectionism.

Likewise in the US, the argument for free trade with Asian markets was lost to Trump's persuasive, populist rhetoric about 'bring back American jobs', despite the enormous value that global supply chains have brought to the country.

Industry has also been poor at demonstrating the benefits of globalization, even to the markets to which production has been relocated. Instead, many companies have been criticized over the pay and conditions of their outsourced labour force. This is covered in Chapter 7.

Under attack at home and abroad, it would seem that global supply chains are not as resilient as many people would like to hope. There is nothing inevitable in the development of economic liberalism or, in the context of this book, global supply chains. Business cannot rely on politicians to support their development and consequently must make the case themselves, demonstrating the benefits to a largely unconvinced electorate. Without such efforts, there is a major possibility that countries adopt isolationist policies that lead to the fragmentation of global supply chains – the ultimate risk.

# What will Brexit mean for the UK supply chain and logistics industry?

When measured on its openness to trade, capital flows, exchange of technology and ideas, labour movements and, of course, culture, the UK has one of the most globalized economies in the world (Ernst & Young, 2013).

Industry and consumers have benefited significantly from this level of globalization, not least in terms of cost, as supply chains have integrated with businesses throughout Europe, while at the same time extending to emerging markets around the world.

Will this position be enhanced or damaged by the decision taken by the British electorate in June 2016? From conversations with a number of senior industry figures, it is evident that there is no consensus over what Brexit will mean for the UK's supply chains or the logistics companies that serve them. Those people who voted to remain in the EU typically consider that Brexit will create more complexity and regulation in dealing with our largest trading partner. Others who voted for Brexit see an opportunity to increase trade volumes with faster growing markets in North America and parts of the developing world. Their conclusions are largely subjective, an entirely understandable state of affairs given the lack of data with which to make an informed decision.

When addressing the issue of the UK's future role in global supply chains, it would be easy to become preoccupied by trade relations. This would be ill-judged, as in many respects supply chains have already left trade policy a long way behind. When supply chain managers make decisions, tariffs and non-tariff barriers are not at the forefront of their minds. Inventory levels, risk, product quality, transport availability and even ethical and environmental factors are significantly more important.

Global supply chains operate effectively both within and outside free trade agreements. Having said that, speed and visibility are critical, and anything that threatens either would be very costly to UK industry. This could be a major risk if the frictionless trade systems that have been developed within the EU are dismantled.

However, such an outcome isn't inevitable or even likely. Around a third of UK trade takes place without a free trade agreement, and consignments from Japan, US, China, Brazil and India have all been successfully integrated within manufacturers' and retailers' ecosystems.

Modern supply chains are flexible and responsive to changing global dynamics. However, in order to enable long-term investment decisions to be made by the international business community, there is a consensus that the UK government now needs to push ahead with the negotiations to create an environment of confidence and certainty.

## Future trade scenarios and supply chain impact

Trade policy formed an important part of the debate in the run up to the referendum on the UK's membership of the European Union. Many manufacturers based in the UK are deeply integrated within multi-country value chains facilitated by Europe's transport infrastructure and unhindered by barriers to trade.

Many argued that leaving the EU would lead to the unravelling of these regional supply chains, with a subsequent impact on economic growth and investment. However, others argued that such a move would allow the UK to build closer trade partnerships with a range of developed and developing markets. Countries such as India, China and the US are all growing more quickly than their European counterparts and hence could stimulate demand for UK exports.

In an attempt to identify what a future relationship with the EU could look like, it is insightful to examine agreements that a number of non-EU members have been able to negotiate with the European Commission. This can be useful to some extent, but of course the UK is in a unique position.

The types of relationship models highlighted below involve a varying level of access to the EU's Single European Market (SEM). An integral aspect of the SEM is a Customs Union, to which every EU country (plus Turkey) belongs. As well as setting external tariffs, it also eliminates a range of non-tariff barriers (NTBs), which allows the seamless movement of goods throughout all member countries with a low level of regulation. The EU estimates that European GDP is 2 per cent higher than it would have been had the SEM not been implemented in 1993.

There are four main models of agreement that demonstrate the range of relationships in place:

1 membership of the European Economic Area (so-called 'Norwegian' model);

2 membership of the EU's Customs Union ('Turkish' model);

**3** free trade agreements (for example, Switzerland, Canada and South Korea);

**4** World Trade Organization rules.

## 1. The Norwegian model

Norway (and also Iceland and Liechtenstein) are members of the European Economic Area but are not full EU members. Norway has significant access to the SEM, but it has to pay for the privilege as well as being bound by a number of EU rules and regulations. For example, it has to accept the free movement of EU citizens. It also has no influence on the development of EU legislation by which, in many instances, it is still bound.

## 2. The Turkish model

Turkey has been a candidate country to join the EU since 1999 and has been part of the EU's Customs Union since 1995 (although this agreement excludes agricultural goods and services). The EU recognizes that there is considerable 'asymmetry' in the agreement as it requires Turkey to align its trade with European policy, although it has no say in its formulation (EC, 2015).

## 3. Free trade agreements

Another alternative would be to agree a deal with the EU that allowed tariff-free access to the EU for UK exporters, and likewise, access to the UK for EU exporters. Critics say that this would not wholly address the issue of non-tariff barriers (NTBs), such as consistent product standards or label-ling. In Switzerland's case, the free movement of people is also one of the conditions. This may not be acceptable to the UK government.

The trade deal with South Korea could be a better example to follow. Negotiations with South Korea commenced in 2007 and were completed in 2009. The deal was officially signed in 2010 and ratified by the European Parliament in 2011 – what many would consider a very short timescale given the complexity of the negotiations relating to tariffs and NTBs. Any negotiations between the UK and EU would commence from the basis of an already standardized market, which may reduce timescales further.

## 4. WTO scenario

If no agreement between the UK and EU can be brokered, trade relations would default to World Trade Organization (WTO) rules. The UK is not alone in this, of course, as many major countries trade with the EU using this model. WTO rules work on a 'most favoured nation' (MFN) basis. This means that the best deal on tariffs that is struck by two countries must apply to all others. This would mean, for example, that even if it wanted to, the EU would not be able to unilaterally impose a higher level of tariffs on the UK than it had agreed with any other partner.

However, as will be discussed later in this chapter, tariffs are a relatively unimportant trade barrier after years of negotiated reductions.

It should also be noted that about a third of the UK's trade is already conducted under WTO terms. Global trade has grown fast in the last 50 years, largely as a result of WTO agreements. In fact, the EU has few free trade agreements in place with major trading nations (although several are in the process of being negotiated, such as the Transatlantic Trade and Investment Partnership (TTIP) with the USA).

## Changes in trade patterns and the impact of trade barriers

Trade patterns have changed significantly over the past two decades as, despite membership of the EU, trade with the rest of the world has increased in its relative importance. UK exports to the EU comprised 55 per cent of all exports in 2002; by 2015 this figure had fallen to 44 per cent. The EU's share of imports to the UK fell from 58 per cent in 2002 to 50 per cent in 2011, although it has now increased slightly to 53 per cent in 2015. It seems likely that Brexit will only accelerate this existing long-term trend and increase the UK's trade with the rest of the world.

### Tariffs and supply chains

The issue of any future tariffs that may, or may not, be levied on UK exports to the EU (and vice versa) may not be as serious as some imagine. According to the World Bank, the average tariff levied on goods entering the EU is only 1.5 per cent (World Bank, 2014), although there are higher tariffs on goods such as finished vehicles.

According to research (Feinberg and Keane, 2009), the influence of tariffs on world trade is less important than ever before. Following the NAFTA deal in 1994, US–Canada trade grew by 100 per cent, although tariffs fell by only 3–4 percentage points. Much larger tariff reductions in the 1960s had not resulted in such gains, leading to the conclusion by the research-ers that cross-border vertical specialization and multi-stage fragmented manufacturing processes were responsible for the growth in trade rather than tariff reduction. Advanced supply chain management practices were the catalyst, although these practices could only occur within a low-tariff environment. Applying this model to the UK and EU, it seems evident that as long as tariffs do not increase significantly (and even under WTO rules this would not happen), extensive fragmentation of production and supply chain integration would continue across the region.

## The threat of non-tariff barriers (NTBs)

Non-tariff barriers are measures put in place by individual governments to indirectly reduce the competitiveness of other countries' exporters, thereby protecting their own domestic producers. Largely as a result of the successes of the WTO, tariffs have played an increasingly minor role in protectionism, with governments choosing more subtle ways to influence markets. The most important NTBs are addressed below.

One factor that may mitigate the impact of non-tariff barriers is the level of intra-firm trade within domestic and international supply chains. Often multiple movements of components can occur within a single multinational company, and in some cases barriers to trade can be completely avoided (Minford, 2016).

The best example of how supply chains have outpaced trade negotiations is in Asia. The development of the 'Factory Asia' concept has brought about integrated, intra-regional cross-border supply chains focused around assembly in China. Often the countries involved have no, or few, official trading agreements, although that is now changing with the increasing importance of the Association of South East Asian Nations (ASEAN). It could be concluded, though, that in this case the trade agreement has followed the development of supply chains and not the other way round.

## Rules of origin

A significant cost threat to the UK economy is any change to the status of 'rules of origin' regulations as applied to UK exporters. Rules of origin are defined by the WTO as, 'The criteria needed to determine the national source of a product. Their importance is derived from the fact that duties and restrictions depend upon the source of imports (WTO, 2016).

If a free trade agreement is concluded between the EU and UK, UK exporters would have to declare to EU customs authorities the proportion of their goods that include sub-components that have been imported from outside the EU: below a certain threshold and the goods would qualify for preferential treatment; above and they would face the full tariff.

The administration of rules of origin can be a complex process and its impact could vary according to the nature of trading agreements between the EU and the UK. The think-tank Open Europe suggests that applying 'rules of origin' could cost around 0.9 per cent of GDP over a 15-year period (Ruparel, 2016). The method of how these rules will be applied will be a major issue to any exporter and importer.

The UK government has estimated that the 'rules of origin' provision could costs traders anything from 4–15 per cent of the cost of goods sold. Consequently, it is likely that rather than pay these internal costs, exporters would choose to pay the EU's external common tariff, especially in cases of low-value goods and where tariffs are low.

It should be noted, of course, that EU exporters would be very keen to avoid having to provide 'rules of origin' information to the UK administration. It would therefore become another bargaining chip in the Brexit negotiations.

In fact, as in its agreement with South Korea, EU officials have attempted to make the rules of origin administration as simple as possible (EC, 2011). Major traders can be authorized to make self-declarations as to whether their products have been wholly obtained or sufficiently processed in the EU or South Korea. As an example, products such as machine tools or cars will be classified as of EU origin if they have no more than 45 per cent of their parts by value originating outside of the EU.

## Food hygiene and safety/labelling and packaging

These two NTBs relate to levels of product standardization. This is often a critical stumbling block when countries enter into free trade agreement negotiations (as seen in the TTIP process). The UK, however, is already compliant with all the standards required by the EU and the issues in the Brexit negotiation may be the converse: a deal will be dependent on relaxing levels of standardization rather than increasing them.

## Anti-dumping measures

Another issue that will be addressed in NTB negotiations is 'anti-dumping' (goods exported to a market at a price substantially below their normal value). Most anti-dumping disputes relate to developing markets and commoditized goods, and it is difficult to see a material impact on UK–EU supply chains. However, it should be noted that the EU imposed anti-dumping measures on Norway (16 per cent duty on imports of salmon) in 2005 despite its free trade agreement.

## Producer subsidies

Producer subsidies (including farming) will make it difficult for UK farmers to export to the EU, even if no tariffs are imposed. This will encourage British farmers to push for the continuance of their own support measures.

## Currency impact

The fall in the value of sterling by around 10 per cent immediately after the referendum acted as a stimulus to UK exports as products become more attractive to foreign buyers. More recently, the Bank of England's decision to cut the UK's rate of interest to a record low should depress the value of the pound for some time.

Sterling's weakness will help rebalance air and sea freight import/export volumes in the short term. This may have the effect of increasing rates for the backhaul of containers from the UK to Asia, helping a struggling shipping industry. At the same time, import volumes may be negatively impacted as manufacturers and retailers turn to domestic suppliers, thus acting as another stimulus for UK industry and its logistics service providers.

However, for many goods that cannot be sourced in the UK (such as most consumer electronics), input costs may rise, which could depress consumer demand and retail sales. The overall picture is likely to remain confused and the consequences for each company will depend individually on its mix of business and customers.

## *Impact of Brexit on supply chains*

Supply chains are very sensitive to increases in costs, and should Brexit create additional expense and delays in terms of sourcing goods from the EU (and vice versa), significant changes should be expected. To what extent and the timescale involved relies on whether the supply chains in question are vertically integrated, with owned production facilities across Europe, or whether they are made up of a 'virtual' network of third-party suppliers. If the former is the case, the time taken to change supply chain strategy will be longer than if a 'virtual' model is employed.

Although much has been written about the potential impact of Brexit on UK-focused supply chains, it must be noted that the UK already has some of the most globalized supply chains in the world. The country successfully integrates components sourced from non-EU countries into its assembly plants with little problem. As one logistics director commented:

Look at the ease with which goods from Asia arrive in the UK destined for our retailers and manufacturers. It is seamless, with most formalities completed electronically. This includes goods under bond with all the additional complexities that go with that and this will be the same [after Brexit] with Europe.

## Agriculture

The most clearly affected sector, and one that demands extensive logistics services, is that of agricultural products. Although farming accounts for less than 1 per cent of GDP in the UK, it makes up 11 per cent of inter-EU exports. It is also the focus of more than 40 per cent of the EU's budget and is protected by an extensive system of tariffs.

Removing such subsidies and tariffs from the UK market will inevitably have an impact. Many basic food commodities such as wheat, beef and sugar are available in quantity from world markets at much lower prices. Bearing in mind the UK's long-held preference for market-driven trade policies, it seems likely that in the long term the UK government will seek a change from the protectionism of the Common Agricultural Policy (CAP).

Britain imports around 40 per cent of its food requirements, with the Republic of Ireland and France being the leading beneficiaries of this trade. There are already some indications that UK grocery retailers and their food processor suppliers are thinking about the structure of their supply chains – and here the implications for logistics may be significant.

The appetite for refrigerated services ('reefers') is likely to grow, as will agri-bulk shipping. Air freight may also benefit, with greater opportunities for higher-cost fruit and vegetable imports. It would appear logical to assume food warehousing capacity would increase.

The losers may be fewer than might be imagined. Most agricultural products from continental Europe are imported by road, often in a processed form. Cross-channel road freight therefore may be hit, but overall the logistics sector may benefit as a more globalized food supply chain will be more demanding in terms of intensity of logistics services.

## Automotive

The automotive industry is of critical importance to the UK's economy, representing 10 per cent of the UK's trade in goods. The automotive sector in particular faces a degree of uncertainty. The suggestion is that the assembly plants in Britain will be vulnerable to tariffs imposed by the EU. However, some of the numbers suggest that this might not be such a problem.

According to a 2014 report by consultancy KPMG, around 37 per cent of the total value of spend in the automotive supply chain is sourced from the UK. The report asserts that, 'Depending on the manufacturer, between 20–50 per cent is imported from the EU and the rest from outside the EU' (KPMG, 2014). This would suggest that the UK's automotive supply chains already work efficiently, with perhaps a third of inbound components manufactured outside the EU, with more than a third (UK-based) not affected directly by Brexit at all.

There are, of course, strategic concerns over whether non-UK automotive manufacturers would maintain their production locations in the UK. However, even here worries may be overstated, as operationally, according to Eurostat, the UK's automotive industry is the most productive in the EU (KPMG, 2014), which suggests there seems little reason for pulling production out of the UK.

The UK runs a £10 billion deficit in terms of finished passenger cars. The largest beneficiary of this is Germany, with Poland, Hungary, Sweden, Slovakia, France and Spain also exporting heavily to Britain. Consequently, there are good financial reasons why the major European manufacturers would not want the EU to impose trade barriers on UK imports, if there was a chance that the UK would reciprocate. As a result, the incentive to all concerned to retain the status quo is great.

Possibly there may be changes in the area of finished vehicle imports from outside the EU, with the UK pursuing free-trade agreements with the likes of Japan and the US.

In the specific examples of Japanese manufacturers in the UK, Nissan and Honda, most parts are supplied locally and the second-tier suppliers that support the manufacturing plants have long ago established operations in the UK. The parts that come from overseas are as likely to come from the US or Japan as Europe. These plants manufacture for a global market, with Europe being just one region, albeit important.

## Retail (non-grocery)

With the exception of grocery retailing, which will be influenced by any changes to food production support and protection, the retail sector may be least affected by Brexit in relative terms. Commodities such as clothing, furniture or consumer electronics have long been sourced globally from countries such as China or Japan under WTO rules.

However, even in this sector, there may be changes that support the increased status of non-EU markets. According to research by Barclays, many UK retailers are already reviewing their supply chains as a result of the vote to leave:

- 45 per cent of respondents thought that sourcing from EU would fall;
- 32 per cent thought that sourcing goods from the UK would increase;
- 50 per cent thought that sourcing from India would increase;
- 38 per cent stated that there would be more sourcing from Africa;
- 43 per cent said there would be more sourcing from China.

Perhaps the biggest threat to the sector would come from a loss of consumer confidence impacting upon the purchase of 'big ticket' items such as cars or a longer-term slowdown in the housing market. However, as all recent reports indicate, this has not occurred, and a reduction of the interest rate by the Bank of England is likely to stimulate spending further.

Compared with the impact of trends such as e-retailing, it is hard to think that Brexit will have an enormous effect on supply chain geography, despite the likelihood of an increase in local sourcing and more imports from non-EU markets, an ongoing trend that has already been identified above.

## Customs and technology

While it is unclear what sort of trading relationship the UK will have with the EU following its decision to leave, it is likely that UK customs' processes will change significantly. A withdrawal from the European Union Customs Union will involve establishing a new system for classifying imports and exports and the tariffs that would be applicable.

The good news is that the UK appears to have a flexible administration for managing these procedures. Shippers importing goods into the UK operate within a dedicated IT system. Her Majesty's Revenue and Customs (HMRC) has a centralized information network that both manages the authorization of specific consignments and accepts the payment of any tariffs. Accessing this system requires software that is available to any accredited user. The data demanded by this system is largely available on the bills of lading, waybills or consignment notes. It is widely accepted that the UK has an adaptable system for administering imports into the country, and changing such a system ought to be very straightforward to cope with imports from the EU.

Similarly, the nature of data interchange between the UK and the economies of the EU should not be so demanding. The EU 'TRACE' system, or 'Excise Movement and Control System', is a means of tracking movements of consignments for purposes of levying taxes or monitoring the routing of goods. Their duplication outside the EU, if needed, would be straightforward using the existing customs' systems.

## *Impact of Brexit on the logistics market*

### Road freight

The UK road freight industry is largely regulated through European legislation, especially in terms of drivers' hours and operator competence. Although it will be possible to amend such legislation when powers are repatriated from Brussels, there would seem little appetite to make major changes, especially to health and safety regulations related to trucks or drivers.

However, there is potential to unwind some 'pseudo' quantitative regulations, such as corporate financial competence, which attempt to regulate market entrance (operators have to maintain a certain level of cash in their bank). This could increase market efficiency without impacting on safety.

The UK will also regain sovereignty over imposing charges for the use of roads by European freight operators, thereby creating a level playing field of costs. Should the government wish, 'cabotage' (access to the UK's domestic market by European freight operators) in the UK domestic market could also be regulated.

Other macro impacts could include:

- cross-channel road freight volumes may be negatively impacted as sourcing moves to intercontinental markets;
- UK international road freight exports to the EU boosted by weak sterling;
- port-centric road freight services and drayage to increase as sea and air freight volumes rise;
- domestic road haulage industry to benefit from increased local supply chains as EU imports become more expensive;
- UK road freight companies benefit from 'level playing field' because of road user charges imposed on foreign hauliers;
- hiring drivers becomes more difficult and expensive as Eastern European immigration reduced (especially parcels sector).

### International freight

Brexit will inevitably change the supply chain geographies of many industry-vertical sectors, as outlined above. This could have a major impact on the international freight market and the infrastructure needed to facilitate the movement of goods on an intercontinental rather than intra-regional basis. In summary:

- new trade deals will increase intercontinental volumes;
- deep-sea shipping services and air cargo will be main beneficiaries;
- inbound European volumes may decrease, especially if barriers raised;
- weaker sterling will see boost for export/outbound volumes;
- 'reefer' services benefit from increased intercontinental food imports;
- deep-sea ports and airport-based distribution to gain;
- cross-channel roll-on, roll-off (RORO) to lose out;
- added complexity in terms of documentation processes will increase demand for freight forwarders' services.

## Warehousing and distribution

There will also be changes to the UK warehousing and distribution markets, although overall impact will be negligible in relative terms when compared with other major trends, such as e-commerce:

- gateway logistics (port-centric) facilities to benefit from increase in sea and air freight volumes;
- challenges to hiring supply chain employees due to limits on immigration;
- increase in warehousing for national distribution if Single European Market rolled back and local supply chains increase;
- migration of pan-European distribution centres to mainland Europe.

## *Recommendations and conclusion*

To meet the challenge of the Brexit negotiations, the UK government should look to the supply chain industry to second experienced and expert opinion. Modern supply chains are complex ecosystems, consisting of sophisticated, evolving and interdependent networks. Trade negotiations must take into account that flows of finished goods and intermediate components are rarely linear or easily understood.

Consequently, negotiators should understand the true costs of a supply chain. This may mean less emphasis on tariffs, for example, and more on the trade barriers that have the potential to delay the movement of cross-border shipments. For UK businesses to remain competitive, they will need to retain their agile and lean inventory supply chains.

It is likely that throughout the period of negotiation, there will be considerable uncertainty until the final structure of UK–EU trade relations are agreed. It is in the interest of all parties to keep this period to a minimum, and there would seem to be little reason why negotiations should be protracted (unless for political aims). After all, a new trade partnership was agreed with South Korea within a relatively short timescale.

Meanwhile, the over-riding message from the UK logistics and supply chain industry is one of 'business as usual'. As one senior executive who voted to remain put it, 'There is no intention for us to sit in a corner and sulk. Now the decision has been made, we need to get on and negotiate the best outcome.'

For UK manufacturers and retailers, the prize will be enhanced links with many of the world's fastest growing economies, such as China and India, while maintaining their integrated European supply chains.

# De-globalization and the Trump administration

For decades the trend towards globalization has seemed unstoppable. However, there has been growing unease in many parts of the developed world – especially in the United States – over the perceived detrimental effect that globalization has had on the job prospects of many workers. The outsourcing of a large proportion of manufacturing to low-cost labour markets, predominantly in Asia, has led to a surge of discontent that has manifested itself in the rise of 'populist' parties and politicians, by far the most important and influential being Donald Trump. Blaming outsourcing for the loss of jobs is only partly true, as automation is also a major factor. However, Trump's rhetoric touched a chord with a large number of US voters, who had seen traditional manufacturing decline throughout the 1990s and 2000s and whose standards of living had declined throughout this period.

It would be wrong to suggest that Trump has created this growing protectionist sentiment. The US, according to the Centre for Economic Policy Research, implemented over 1,000 discriminatory trade measures between November 2008 and September 2016, about twice as many as India and Russia, in second and third position in the rankings of G20 nations. Many of these measures involve the development of 'industrial policies' (a term also used by the incoming May administration in the UK) that justify the subsidy of local companies, 'local' standards that discriminate against foreign competition and, of course, tariffs and duties.

It is very difficult at such an early stage of Trump's presidency to say whether or not many of his populist policies will be implemented. It has yet to be seen whether Trump will actively develop protectionist policies rather than withdraw support for free markets. However, his approach to the following trade issues will be critical.

## Terminating TPP

One of President Trump's first acts when coming to power was to sign an executive order to withdraw from negotiations with 11 Asian countries, effectively ending the development of the Trans-Pacific Partnership (TPP). The accord had been likened by some as an attempt to create a single market in the same mould as the EU and had been widely supported by US businesses. Although the TPP does not include China (in fact, the initiative was seen as a way of challenging China's power in the region), it does include countries making up 40 per cent of the world's economy. Trump says he would rather make bilateral trade agreements with the countries involved.

## Trump and China

President Trump swept to power on a largely anti-globalization ticket promising to repatriate outsourced jobs back to the USA. In one tweet he stated, 'China is stealing our jobs', although he saw Asia as a whole as a threat to US domestic employment. Since meeting the Chinese President, Xi Jinping, his rhetoric seems to have changed, not least because of the role China must play if the North Korean crisis is to be solved.

## Mexico and NAFTA

The role that Mexico has played as a low-cost near-sourcing market for US manufacturing has long been of concern to Trump. However, any efforts to roll back the free market created by NAFTA will have significant consequences to the region. More than a quarter of Mexico's economy is accounted for by exports to the US, and in order to facilitate this trade, companies have invested billions in upgrading port, road and rail infrastructure.

The automotive sector could be particularly hard hit, although, at this stage, it is hard to estimate what Donald Trump's Twitter statements will mean for the industry and cross-border trade. However, already the impact of his comments about the importation of vehicles from Mexico appear to have alarming implications for supply chain management.

If vehicle manufacturers were to feel under pressure to start changing their supply chain policies, global trade and logistics markets would come under substantial pressure. To take the Mexican example, much of production in Mexico relies on major components – including items such as engines and gearboxes – made in the US. The reverse is also true, with Mexican plants acting as sources for parts for US production. Unravelling this supply chain structure would be possible but expensive and would have a major impact on rail and road freight across the US.

The effects on the South Korean, Japanese and German economies would also be immense even if the US levied only modest increases in import taxes. The logistics sectors of all three economies are heavily dependent on automotive-related demand. Most of the big manufacturers have diverse production facilities in Mexico and are planning to expand them.

---

**CASE STUDY**  Argentina's attempts to clamp down on
cross-border e-commerce

Argentina has faced many challenges to its economic stability over the past few years, and in 2014 its currency came under sustained pressure. Argentina had been using its currency reserves to pay foreign debt since its economic collapse in 2001–02, and found it difficult to attract international loans at market rates.

To keep currency reserves from falling further, Argentina announced yet additional restrictions on imports, including a 35 per cent tariff on credit card transactions abroad and on online shopping. Anyone who purchases items through international websites such as Amazon or eBay will now need to sign a declaration and produce it at a customs office, where the packages have to be collected. Individuals are allowed to buy items up to the value of $25 from abroad tax-free every year. Once the $25 level is reached, online shoppers in Argentina will then pay a 50 per cent tax on each item bought from international websites.

Instead of helping Argentina's economic situation, restrictions such as these will instead exacerbate an already difficult situation, and as the country turns further inward and embraces further protectionist measures, Argentina's status as an 'emerging market' could even be questioned.

Included in the definition of an 'emerging market' is the emergence or expansion of a middle class. According to the Economic Commission for Latin America and the Caribbean, while Latin America's middle class has collectively increased by 56 million people since 1999, Argentina's middle class dropped from 56 per cent to 52 per cent of the country's total population. A declining middle class combined with import restrictions bodes for limited, if any, growth for Argentina's e-commerce market.

According to eMarketer, Argentina's business-to-consumer e-commerce market is still in its early stages and is estimated at about $3.3 billion for 2012, with growth expectations of 15 per cent to $3.8 billion for 2013. Cross-border online shopping is also beginning to increase in Argentina, with about 1.5 million Argentinians purchasing items from foreign websites in 2013, about double the number in 2012. However, as we saw earlier in this case study, cross-border online shopping will likely come to a halt thanks to recent government restrictions. This is unfortunate, particularly as product selection is already cited as a hurdle to e-commerce.

Why is e-commerce important? Countries such as China see it as a means to not only encourage domestic spending and to help balance its trade more evenly between exports and imports, but also to encourage the growth of small to medium-sized businesses. Likewise, the same can occur in Argentina, where its exports outweigh imports and its small to medium-sized businesses must battle government restrictions that are prohibitive to such growth.

## China's use of trade to secure political aims

When a direct rail freight service arrived in Barking, East London, from China via the ancient 'Silk Road', there was a flurry of speculation about the potential for this new route. However, the truth and implications of this event are more complex and potentially far-reaching.

China has always been interested in the ancient trading routes heading west towards Europe; consequently there has been a massive amount of government investment in infrastructure in the west of the country and, increasingly, in countries en route between China and Europe.

In the autumn of 2013, Chinese President Xi Jinping announced the 'One Belt, One Road' project. This is both a strategy and framework to revitalize the trading routes from the East to the West. The scale is massive, the estimated total value of the project will be in the region of $4 trillion and ultimately involves up to 65 countries along four major corridors.

This project has involved the adjacent countries of Central Asia (Kyrgyzstan, Tajikistan, Kazakhstan, and so on), with much of the investment and construction going into refurbishing and re-energizing the routes that criss-cross the region. Opening these routes into Eurasia and European markets is a natural extension.

However, this is not just about the flow of trade from East to West. The goal is also to boost regional trade and establish an economic zone supported by China. Unlike the existing China–Europe maritime trade flows from the seaports of the east coast, China is investing in trade routes over which it can establish a reasonable amount of direct control. It does this by managing (controlling) how these investments are financed.

Almost all of their investments in Central Asia are in the form of Chinese Yuan loans and come with strict conditions. The primary one is for the borrowers to avoid acting in a manner that is contrary to the views of Beijing. In return, roads, rail and energy pipelines are constructed or refurbished and modernized. Export deals for energy from the oil- and gas-rich nations into China are agreed alongside the construction of pipelines and power grids.

Logistics operators with expertise in these areas should review these developments as opportunities, as in some countries the lack of logistics expertise is holding back the exploitation of the revitalized routes. But, as with any investments in areas with 'interesting' political structures and overtones, one should not be naïve in why this is happening. China is quite clear that investment in new projects can be stopped or loans renegotiated on less favourable terms if the recipients appear to be operating contrary to the interests of China. This is subtly different from trade loans and investments from other pan-global institutions such as the IMF, UN, EU and sovereign countries such as the USA.

Alongside the colossal investments in the so-called 'One Belt, One Road' programme, as it has been termed, the maritime 'Silk Road' trade routes are also the subject of intense investment – not least in terms of the dramatic expansion of the Chinese navy (PLA(N)) in both size and capability. Informed observers believe that by 2025 they will match, if not exceed, the size, scope and capability of the US Navy – currently the world's largest. Western governments have consistently underestimated the rate of development of the PLA(N) and, while they claim to be doing this to protect existing trade routes, it is obvious that other motives are at work.

On a more positive note, the expansion of the Chinese Navy has helped to assist and augment the humanitarian and anti-piracy efforts in the Indian Ocean, the Middle East and the Horn of Africa, which is to be welcomed. They have also invested heavily in the development of ports along the route for trade as well as naval support.

In summary, China is expanding trade routes via the development of the ancient pathways and networks of the past. It is also establishing a maritime footprint to support trade flows back into China. It is doing this via direct investment and views these developments as critical parts of the strategy to develop Western China and trade into Eurasia, the Middle East and Europe.

Logistics operators can, with caution, provide expertise and assistance in this effort and also exploit these revitalized trade routes to improve supply chains and global business.

One cautionary note, though. Information flows will be key to all of these things, and as most people are aware, China has interesting views about the free flow of data and information. Unless they accept that transparency of information is necessary for efficient and effective trade flows, these new roots may struggle to reach their potential.

**SOURCE** Lyon (2017)

# Conclusion

Political factors, because of the overarching nature of government legislation, obviously affect many other issues already discussed within this book. For example, decisions made by ministers at intergovernmental conferences on climate change impact upon the environmental regulatory framework in which logistics companies operate. Likewise, geo-political decisions influence the security situation, potentially leading to instability in certain regions, such as Crimea or Syria, with all the attendant threats to the supply chains that touch these areas.

It could be argued that supply chain management theory, which has influenced manufacturing and retailing practice since the early 1980s, ignored the political dimension. It assumed that the benefits that accrued from, say, the outsourcing of production processes to low-cost markets in Asia would be shared in both the developed and developing world.

## Summary

For many years, globalization was regarded as an unstoppable force transforming the world's economy. However, this belief has been challenged by two major demonstrations of populist sentiment: the vote for Brexit and the election of President Donald Trump in the US. Even before this, politicians have been quietly enacting hundreds of new protectionist laws. It is not yet clear whether either Brexit or Trump will result in the fragmentation of supply chains. In fact, economic growth that has occurred since both votes has led to shipping and air cargo volumes increasing (in some cases dramatically). It is clear, though, that globalization and internationally integrated supply chains are at risk as never before.

## Key points

- Global supply chains are at threat from a rising tide of protectionism.
- Political sentiment has turned against economic liberalism, as many people feel threatened by free movement of capital, workers and goods.
- Brexit provides opportunities for greater levels of trade between the UK and non-EU countries, but labour-intensive logistics companies are threatened by the reduction of immigrant workers.
- The impact of Brexit on some supply chains (such as automotive or consumer goods) may not be as great as feared as a large proportion of imports already comes from non-EU countries.
- The election of Donald Trump has seen the end of US negotiations to create a trans-Pacific free trade agreement, and a similar deal with Europe is also under threat.
- China is using trade and investment as a political tool to project its power in regions such as Central Asia.

# Illicit supply chains  11

## Value chains in illicit goods

So far this book has discussed the threat posed to supply chains by those who wish to cause economic loss or further their own political ambitions (terrorism), as well as by those who wish to steal from them for their own economic gain (cargo crime).

In the abstract of his thesis on the subject, Ekwall characterizes these threats as follows:

> The thieves are after the monetary value that the cargo represents, therefore they prefer to steal high-value, untraceable and highly demanded products.

> The ideological perpetrator or terrorist wishes to make a statement with the attack, therefore he will sabotage products which will give the statement attention and (if possible) understanding for it (Ekwall, 2007).

There is a third possibility: the subversion of existing supply chains and transportation networks for illegal purposes. Whereas cargo crime is related to theft (exiting) from the supply chain, smuggling can be viewed as 'entering' a supply chain.

Ekwall also identifies the different effects of theft from smuggling. One destroys value in the supply chain by causing disruption, the other (smuggling) is not designed to create disruption at all. Criminals are as interested as legal shippers in ensuring their consignments reach the destination in a timely fashion. However, countermeasures designed to intercept illicit goods have the impact of disrupting logistics systems for both legal and criminal parties.

Illicit supply chains resemble their legal equivalents in many ways, except of course the status of the goods being moved. As the goods move along the supply chain, 'value' is added as they pass from intermediary to intermediary. This can involve processing of the product, as in the case of drugs, or it can be what is termed a 'crime tax', which relates to the level of risk (and hence remuneration) required to move the product across borders to the destination market.

For example, according to Tom Wainwright's book *Narconomics*, 1 tonne of coca leaf is required to make 1 kilogramme of cocaine. The value that the farmer will receive for the coca leaf is about $400, but in the US the kilogramme of cocaine will fetch $100,000 (Wainwright, 2016).

This is one reason, according to Wainwright, that efforts to disrupt the production of coca leaf have failed. Even if large areas of coca leaf production are degraded through the extensive use of aerial-dropped weed killer, for example, and the per tonne price is doubled, this will have a negligible impact on the street value in the US. Wainwright believes that a 100 per cent increase in production price would result in less than a 1 per cent increase in street price.

Very little of the final price paid by the recipient for the illicit good (whether drugs or any other contraband) relates to the cost of production. The end-user is paying for the risk incurred by the many intermediaries in the supply chain.

The value chain for species and species products (see page 254 below on trade in endangered species) shows a similar increase, although not necessarily due to the 'crime tax' effect (although this may well be a factor for illicit trafficking). A snake may be sold by a local hunter for just $30 in a developing country. However, by the time the skin has been transformed

**Figure 11.1**    The cocaine value chain

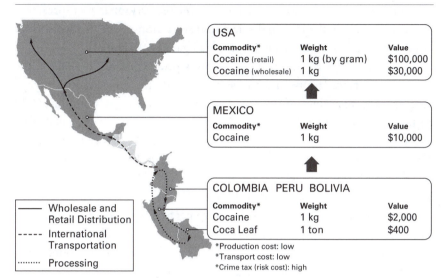

into a handbag in Europe or North America, it may fetch up to $10,000. The importing country therefore captures the vast majority of the value. The price of ivory in Africa is just 5 per cent of what it fetches in Asia.

In fact, risk is even more of a factor in illicit supply chains than it is in their 'white' equivalents because of the threat of interception by law enforcement agencies. Hence, highly organized criminal gangs may even offer their own insurance policies to members of the downstream extended crime networks (or, as they have often been referred to, 'franchises') against such eventuality.

# Types of illicit supply chains

In his report on illicit supply chains, Mackenzie (2002) identifies four different types:

1 illicit at source, transport and destination;

2 illicit at source and transport, but licit at destination;

3 licit source, but illicit transport and at destination;

4 licit source, but illicit transport and then licit at destination.

The first type of supply chain is straightforward. A commodity, such as narcotics, that is illegally held or traded in the origin market is also transported illegally and, through international convention or domestic law, is also illegal in the destination market. The transportation (smuggling), and potential bribery of customs officials, border security or law enforcement officers, as well as the eventual sale and distribution of the products, is all conducted underground through organized gangs of criminals.

The second type of supply chain involves products that are illicit in the origin market and transport, but that in the destination country enter a legal market. Examples of these goods could be diamonds, antiquities and certain types of minerals (see Chapter 7 on conflict minerals). Legitimate markets exist around the world for these goods and it is often impossible for consumers to tell legal from illegal. Consequently, attempts have been made by authorities to develop audit systems, providing certification of the provenance of the goods and their legality.

A third supply chain involves the movement of legal goods that become illicit when moved across borders or become used illegally. Firearms can fall into this category, as they can be legally held in the source country but exported illegally or become illegal because of the domestic laws of the destination market. People smuggling is also included in this 'supply chain'. Individuals can have the right to live and work in their own country, but their movement and then insertion into a new country can, of course, be illegal.

Finally, there is the licit–illicit–licit supply chain. Here the goods themselves are not illicit in either source or destination market. Rather, the export/import regulations have been contravened. So, for example, cigarettes are legal in all countries around the world, but their importation is often subject to duty, leading to a wide variety of price points. This variance has led to the development of a large-scale cross-channel smuggling market between France and the UK. Although the consumption of such cigarettes is not illegal, the movement and sale of them is.

Of the four categories, only the first is what could be termed completely 'black'. As all the others involve the goods being legal at some point in the supply chain, certain grey areas exist. It is these that can lead to certain amounts of confusion in the response of authorities in how to deal with these illicit supply chains. It also allows organized criminals to exploit and prosper from the complexity.

## Illicit transport networks

Whatever the goods being trafficked, there is a very strong likelihood that they will be moved using transport networks that have been designed and operated for legal products. With only 5 per cent (more likely 1 per cent) of containers being inspected by border authorities, criminals understand the chances that their consignments will be intercepted as small and the costs can be absorbed within their overall business.

In many cases, the organized criminals behind the smuggling are agnostic to the type of goods that they deal with. They will engage with commodities that offer the highest returns, whether these are drugs, ivory, endangered species, counterfeit electronics or illicit antiquities. However, drug smuggling is the most popular activity, with this being supplemented by one or more subsidiary operations.

Law enforcement agencies have realized that rather than focus on one type of illegal commodity, they should identify illicit supply networks that are used to move a variety of products. So, for example, an operation involving the trade of illicit cigarettes (the physical movement as well as potentially the leverage of corrupt officials) can just as easily be used for the movement of drugs, antiquities, and so on.

## Narcotic supply chains

Narcotics are what is termed 'controlled substances' under the United Nations Single Convention on Narcotic Drugs, 1961. According to the International Narcotics Control Board (INCB), the convention '…codified all existing multilateral treaties on drug control and extended the existing control systems to include the cultivation of plants that were grown as the raw material of narcotic drugs.'

The aim of the convention, which has been signed by 185 countries, was to limit the possession, use, trade in, distribution, import, export, manufacture and production of drugs exclusively to medical and scientific purposes and to address drug trafficking.

Consequently, for the narcotics covered by the convention, which include products derived from the opium poppy, coca bush, and cannabis plant, it is clear that supply chains are almost entirely 'black'. Production (except for medicinal purposes), transportation, distribution and sale are entirely illegal.

Narcotic supply chains can resemble those of legal counterparts. Wainwright (2016) compared the cartels that exist in Central America with major retailers, such as Walmart, because of the exclusive relationships they are able to build and control with suppliers. This has helped the cartels keep the price of drugs, such as cocaine, stable on the international market even when production is disrupted.

For the US, Mexico has become a huge centre for value-adding process-ing and production for the narcotics industry; in fact, it would be termed near-sourcing in any legitimate manufacturing industry. One example is methamphetamine, which has been growing in popularity in the US. Chemical ingredients for the drug – largely ephedrine – were imported legally in large quantities through the Mexican container ports Lázaro Cárdenas and Manzanillo from Asia. When the Mexican authorities banned ephedrine, the recipe was changed to use still unbanned substances.

This latter point clearly shows an example of a supply chain where commodities can be sourced legally and then transformed downstream into illicit products. From an economic point of view, it makes more sense to produce narcotics close to the end-user market.

In terms of logistics, the operations required are extensive and need to be agile. In the 1980s US law enforcement agents managed to shut down routes from South America to the US via the Caribbean. Instead, new routes opened up transiting Mexico, which coincidentally helped to move the balance of power from Colombian drugs cartels to those in Mexico. According to the *New York Times*, anywhere between 5 and 16 flights would be landing in remote Mexican airstrips a night from Colombia. The consignments would then pass over the border for distribution throughout the US, for example through Arizona (Keefe, 2012).

**Figure 11.2**   Main trading routes of major drug types

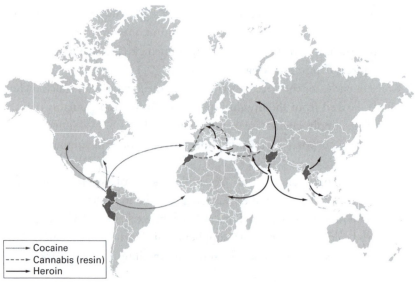

Many ways have been developed to cross the US–Mexico border. These include using established (and 'white') logistics systems such as railroads, refrigerated truck networks and the major air express operators. One drugs baron established a factory, ostensibly for canning chillis but actually for packaging cocaine. The cans would then be distributed through Mexican-owned stores in California.

As with any supply chain, there is a reverse flow of money up the supply chain. In the drugs world this tends to be in cash and often uses the same routes as the drugs on the return journey. One of the problems faced by organized crime is the 'laundering' of the money, and this has been estimated at 15 per cent of the amount moved.

## European narcotics trafficking

Europe's narcotics supply chains are complex and vary dependent on the type of drug being trafficked.

Cannabis is the most popular drug consumed in Europe and it is believed by the European police organization, Europol, that 22 million people use it on an annual basis. Spain, the Netherlands and Belgium are the major import hubs for cannabis resin, a large proportion of which emanates from Morocco. A smaller market for resin imported through Turkey from Afghanistan also exists. There are fears that instability in North Africa could present opportunities for smugglers to use new routes through Southern Europe (Europol, 2016).

Heroin has traditionally been supplied to Europe through what is known as the Balkan route. This links Afghanistan to Iran and then into Turkey. From Turkey, heroin can then proceed into Europe:

- south through Greece, Albania and Italy by ferry;
- westwards through Bulgaria and the former Yugoslavia states into Austria or Italy by land;
- northwards through Bulgaria, Romania into Eastern Europe and Germany by land;
- air links are also used from Turkey to the EU.

As in the Americas, there are complex networks of organized crime gangs overseeing the supply chain to Western Europe. Turkey is believed to be the main hub, with Turkish gangs managing the sourcing and supply, including the distribution of the drug through legitimate businesses along the trafficking route, including in Germany, the Netherlands and the UK.

In terms of the modes used to move the drugs, although road (concealed in cars and lorries) is still the most popular, it is believed that use of shipping containers is becoming more frequent. The size of consignment is also believed to be getting bigger, and this favours sea freight.

Cocaine is imported into Europe from South America, with Brazil growing in importance as the transit hub, handling product from Bolivia and Peru. Other routes involve the Caribbean as well as West Africa.

Cocaine is transported using a range of different types of mode and service provider. These include air express/air freight, post and parcels services, and sea containers. The latter proves the most worrying to authorities, with cocaine accounting for 75 per cent of all drugs seizures from containers in 2013. With Rotterdam and Antwerp being the largest ports in Europe, they also are the most popular gateways for cocaine to Europe.

# Trade in endangered animals

There is a global market in endangered species, animal parts (such as rhino horn or ivory) and forestry products from protected areas. Such trade is in contravention of a number of national and international laws and conventions. Not only is the activity illegal in its own right, but trafficking is often carried out by the same organized crime groups moving drugs, antiquities, firearms, and so on. Consequently, the crime is of interest to a range of law enforcement agencies.

The United Nations has actively encouraged all countries to adopt domestic laws that establish this type of illicit trade as a criminal offence. The United Nations Security Council (UNSC) resolutions 2134 and 2136 'require all states to adopt sanctions, namely freezing assets and restricting travel, on any individual or entity involved in wildlife and forest trafficking' (UN, 2015). This was prompted by a desire of the members to put a halt to ivory trafficking from the Democratic Republic of the Congo and in the Central African Republic, the proceeds of which were being used to finance armed rebel groups.

The Convention on International Trade in Endangered Species of Wild Fauna and Flora, better known as CITES, is fundamental to the coordination of national governments to prevent the trade in these types of products. The international nature of the trade requires a transnational response to prevent organized crime groups from exploiting variances in national legislation.

The trade in endangered species of both flora and fauna is extensive, amounting to several billions of dollars, according to CITES. It includes not only live animals and plants but the products derived from them, such as ivory, medicines, food, leather goods and tourist souvenirs. There are currently 35,000 species of protected animals and plants on the CITES register. The species are divided into three 'appendices' depending on their level of rarity and the fragility of their environments:

- Appendix I – (species threatened with extinction) trade is generally prohibited;
- Appendix II and III – (species not necessarily threatened but at risk) trade is permitted under certain circumstances.

Trade in species that fall within Appendix II is very considerable. CITES estimates it to range from $350–530 million a year (CITES, 2011), with reptiles (alive and skins) accounting for almost two-thirds of this amount.

The supply chain for each species varies considerably. The trade in Appendix II species is not necessarily illegal and probably gives a good indication of the illicit flows of species contained in Appendix I. For example, the biggest exporters of reptile skins are Indonesia, Colombia, Malaysia, Argentina and the US. The biggest importers are Singapore, Italy and Mexico, with Singapore re-exporting much of its imports, presumably throughout Asia (CITES, 2013).

Examples of Appendix I species include:

- Asian elephant (Elephas maximus);
- monkey-puzzle tree (Araucaria araucana);
- arowana (Scleropages formosus);
- Peregrine falcon (Falco peregrinus);
- Queen Alexandra's birdwing butterfly (Ornithoptera alexandrae).

Sanctions can be severe for smuggling Appendix I species. For example, in Canada, if intercepted, the goods will be seized, and fines of up to $150,000 levied with up to five years in jail for individuals, and fines of up to $300,000 for businesses.

However, the trade continues. Nowhere is more evident and high profile than the trade in illicit ivory, which, according to the Born Free Foundation, is at record high levels. In 2013, 50 tonnes of ivory were seized. It is estimated that seizures run at just 10 per cent of the total, and therefore, a total volume of about 500 tonnes of ivory seems reasonable. Between 2009 and 2014, Born Free believes that 229,729 elephants were killed (Vira, Ewing and Miller, 2014).

As with many other illicit commodities, smugglers use legal logistics networks to move ivory to consumer markets, largely in Asia and specifically in China. Three main ports are involved in the traffic – Mombasa, Dar es Salaam and Zanzibar – and three main airports – Nairobi, Addis Ababa and Johannesburg. However, the most important routes by far are from East Africa to East Asia, in particular to ports in the Strait of Malacca, Vietnam and Pearl River Delta Region. The ivory trade can be said to be becoming more 'vertically' integrated. Asian organized crime groups have an increasing presence in Africa to oversee the whole process.

According to the Born Free Foundation's report *Out of Africa* (Vira, Ewing and Miller, 2014), the supply chain works as follows:

- Elephant tusks moved from African interior ('African local transport') to port – this occurs rapidly to prevent interception.

- Consolidation with other ivory shipments at the port – shell companies are used to conceal the nature of the shipment and owners.

- Bribes paid to customs officials and freight forwarders to falsify and forge documentation.

- Ivory can be concealed in shipping containers under other materials such as fish, nuts, decorative stones, and so on. In other cases, false compartments are utilized.

- Shipping routes used will involve a number of hubs to make detection more difficult.

- Asian import and local transport is likely to involve numerous hand-off points and false companies to obfuscate the supply chain. Ivory may be stockpiled in warehouses to control the sale price.

# Counterfeit goods

A recent report by the OECD and the European Union Intellectual Property Office, *Trade in Counterfeit and Pirated Goods*, estimates that counterfeit goods accounted for 2.5 per cent of the world's trade in 2013 (EUIPO, 2016). For the EU it is an even bigger problem, with counterfeit and pirated goods accounting for as much as $116 billion, or 5 per cent of international trade. In each of the three years that were analysed (from 2011 through 2013), there were over 100,000 customs seizures.

One of the major drivers of opportunity for counterfeiters, it seems, has been the growth of international e-commerce. The report identified that this type of trade is mainly facilitated by the international postage system, which is the primary mode of choice because of the small shipment size involved. Between 2011 and 2013, just under two-thirds of all seizures worldwide were postal shipments. This category was followed by air (20 per cent), sea (9 per cent) and road (7 per cent).

The supply chains involved in moving the counterfeit goods are complex. As well as the largest logistics hubs, such as Hong Kong and Singapore, other intermediary transit points include countries where there is weak governance and where criminal and terrorist networks are able to operate at will. Supply chains are very dynamic, with criminals able to make routing decisions based on the quick identification of vulnerable logistics nodes.

Even though counterfeit goods originate from every country and region, China is by far the biggest culprit. Around 85 per cent of goods seized originated in either China or Hong Kong, with Turkey being the third most frequent country of origin, albeit with a much smaller proportion (around 5 per cent). In terms of the commodities most likely to be counterfeited, footwear and clothing stood out as the most important categories, although electrical machinery and equipment and watches were also frequent targets. The report only measured the numbers of seizures in terms of volumes, not in terms of value. Hence, although pharmaceuticals was one of the smaller categories, in financial terms it is far more important.

Obviously counterfeit and pirated goods are major sources of risk to supply chains. They represent not only a cost to the legitimate manufacturers through lost sales, but, in the case of pharmaceuticals and electrical goods, present a material threat to consumers' health and safety. An interesting aspect of the illicit trade is that many of the supply chains are legitimate, that is, established to move legal goods. However, these supply chains can be 'hijacked' for criminal purposes, either by the manufacturers themselves who set them up in the first place or by third parties substituting counterfeit goods for real ones. Either way, it seems inevitable that government attention will be intensified on this problem, not least because of the security risk that counterfeit supply chains present.

## Counterfeit medicines

Counterfeit drugs are a major security risk to pharmaceutical supply chains. These are defined by the World Trade Organization as:

> A counterfeit medicine is medicine that is deliberately and fraudulently mislabelled with respect to identity and/or source. Counterfeiting can apply to

both branded and generic products. Counterfeit products may include products with the correct ingredients or the wrong ingredients, lacking active ingredients, with incorrect quantities of active ingredients or fake packaging.

According to the World Customs Organization, worldwide trade in counterfeit medicines could be as much as £1 billion.

The drug's importation history and country of origin may affect the safety of a product. Based on a survey of pharmacists, a drug's country of origin influences the quality of that drug and is also a major factor for pharmacists when choosing one company's product over another.

There is a growing recognition of the need for stricter security measures, especially in the United States. Most of the key ingredients used in the drugs prescribed by US doctors are produced overseas, as are about 40 per cent of finished drugs, from more than 150 countries. In addition to the volume of imports and foreign facilities, there has been an increase in the variety of sources, shippers, methods of transportation and supply chain complexity of imported products.

The US Food and Drug Administration (FDA) has undertaken a wide range of activities aimed at addressing the challenges of globalization, including efforts to harmonize scientifically rigorous standards internationally; to share scientific and technical expertise with fellow regulators; to provide training around the world in crucial regulatory disciplines; to strengthen detection, surveillance and assessment systems; and to design innovative risk-modelling systems.

Permanent FDA overseas posts are based in:

- Beijing, Shanghai and Guangzhou, China;
- New Delhi and Mumbai, India;
- San Jose, Costa Rica;
- Mexico City, Mexico;
- Santiago, Chile;
- Brussels, Belgium;
- London, England;
- Parma, Italy;
- Amman, Jordan;
- Pretoria, South Africa.

These offices enable the FDA to have a regional presence around the world and serve as important hubs for improved coordination with regulatory authorities and industry in other nations. They also conduct and facilitate inspections with foreign counterpart agencies to share inspection reports and other non-public information.

States in the United States have taken steps to increase the security of pharmaceuticals. For example, since 2015 California has required all medications to have a serial number and be accompanied by electronic records detailing every instance the product changes hands. The total cost for companies within California to implement this requirement is estimated at $3.5 billion. Other states have different requirements, which has created a situation of confusion within the industry, as well as adding costs and opportunities for thefts and counterfeiting to occur between states.

As such, the US government is taking steps to establish a national track and trace programme requiring companies to track drugs among supply chain partners, including wholesalers, distributors and packagers. The FDA also operates a licensing programme for third parties that provide outsourced logistical services to support pharmaceutical manufacturers, wholesalers and dispensers.

## Illicit trade in antiquities

The market for licit and illicit antiquities has been characterized in the *American Journal of International Law* as follows:

> [T]he world divides itself into source nations and market nations. In source nations, the supply of desirable cultural property exceeds the internal demand. Nations like Mexico, Egypt, Greece and India are obvious examples. They are rich in cultural artefacts beyond any conceivable local use. In market nations, the demand exceeds the supply. France, Germany, Japan, the Scandinavian nations, Switzerland and the United States are examples. Demand in the market nation encourages export from source nations. When, as is often (but not always) the case, the source nation is relatively poor and the market nation wealthy, an unrestricted market will encourage the net export of cultural property (Merryman, 1986).

Therefore, it is immediately evident that there will be flows of historic items from mainly (but not exclusively) developing countries in the Middle East, Latin America, Africa and Asia to Europe and North America.

Some terrorist groups, such as so-called Islamic State (also known as ISIS or ISIL), have sought not only to disrupt supply chains by attacks on transport infrastructure, but to exploit them in order to profit from looted antiquities ('blood antiquities'). This has been referred to as cultural racketeering and forms part of 'heritage crimes', which include not only the theft of archaeological items but also the destruction of many historical and culturally significant sites.

Although the role of ISIS in this trade has had the highest media profile, it is by no means unique. For years (in fact centuries), tombs have been robbed across the Mediterranean. There is even an Italian word for the thieves who broke into and robbed Roman tombs – *tombaroli*.

Egypt has also been badly affected. Following the Arab Spring protests in 2011, the resignation of President Hosni Mubarak, the overthrow of President Mohammed Morsi in 2013 and the general breakdown of law and order throughout the country, many heritage sites were attacked and pillaged.

The success that Islamic State had in taking over large parts of Syria and Iraq provided it with the opportunity to rob valuable artefacts from sites of historic interest. The organization even went as far as establishing its own 'Natural Resources' department and, according to the US State Department, has raised several hundred million dollars since 2014 through the sale of these antiquities, with the Iraqi Ambassador to the UN claiming that it could be as much as $100 million a year (Gladstone, 2015). The sale of antiquities is only second in terms of revenue-raising to the sale of plundered oil.

ISIS was not the first to plunder historical items from this region. Even before they took control, there were accusations that Syrian government officials had been complicit in the theft and sale of antiquities. In fact, when ISIS arrived, one of their first acts was to tax locals who had been selling these items. The difference was that ISIS turned an ad hoc activity into an industry, systematically excavating sites with heavy machinery and establishing a network of people to steal, handle and sell on the goods.

The process of facilitating the movement of illicit antiquities to Europe and North America is not difficult for those who know how to do it:

- Obtain fake documentation in the knowledge that either civil service officials would show little interest in checking or could be bribed.
- The same could be said for the shipping company.
- Use the busiest ports, where there is very little chance of containers being searched.

- Trans-ship goods at major hubs (such as Hong Kong or Dubai) to make searching of containers less likely; direct sailings to Western ports from high-risk origins are more likely to raise suspicion.

- Misdeclare the goods – terms used can include words such as 'handicraft' or 'handmade'.

- Bribe port workers to allow access to containers and goods and/or release contraband.

## Ethical arguments over the trade in antiquities

As with many ethical issues related to supply chains, the arguments over the trafficking (itself an emotive term) are never straightforward. As defined by the Australian Institute of Criminology (AIC), there are three main bodies of opinion (Mackenzie, 2002). They are:

- cultural 'nationalists', who believe that the sale and trade of historical artefacts represents the outflow of their heritage and cultural diminution – in effect, they believe that such items are the property of the state and that it is reasonable to exert controls over their trade;

- cultural 'internationalists', who believe that these artefacts belong wherever the market dictates;

- and, the local populations (often poverty-stricken), who believe it is their right to dig up and sell antiquities to the highest bidder.

It is not the role of this book to examine the relative merits of these arguments, although it is clear that the pillaging of historic sites by terrorist organizations to fund their activities is obviously an alarming development. The ethics of the export of an antiquity by a private trader to a collector (or even a museum) in a developed country are less clear-cut. After all, without such trade in the past, many of the world's most important museums would not have been founded and consequently understanding of other countries' cultures would have been harmed. Likewise, it is difficult to blame local people for attempting to augment their income by selling items that they see as theirs, rather than belonging to the state.

Nevertheless, governments have sought to exert controls over the trade in antiquities, either through export prohibitions, or by transferring ownership to the state. Neither mechanism has been particularly effective, and many people believe that they have only succeeded in creating a black market in these goods.

Many countries have developed 'control lists' that regulate, in theory, the international sale of goods. These may relate to specific cultural items (African or Australian indigenous art, for example) or to items over a certain age, or both. Some lists will include derogations that allow for the sale of some artefacts that were made historically for the export market (some Chinese and Japanese pottery has, for several centuries, been aimed at either the tourist or export market). However, these derogations also make it more complicated to differentiate the legal trade from the illicit.

A further problem relates to the enforcement of international law. Often the mechanisms do not exist that enable the country where the artefact originated from to recover it from the 'market nation'. It may be perfectly legal to buy a historic item in one country, even though it was illegally exported. As the AIC puts it:

> The non-enforceability of export restrictions abroad can be seen as an
> application of the principle of private international law that courts of one
> nation will not enforce claims based on the public law (as distinguished from
> claims based on private rights, like ownership) of another nation (Mackenzie,
> 2003).

Organizations such as UNESCO have sought to remedy this by enacting a convention (in 1970, indicating that the problem has been recognized for several decades) that signs members up to preventing museums in their jurisdictions acquiring illegally exported cultural property. However, this does not apply to private collectors. In addition to this, only property that has been properly catalogued as belonging to a museum, religious or secular monument is covered. Given the immensity of such a task and the fact that many artefacts are dug up by local citizens and do not pass through official systems at all, this is obviously a major weakness.

Consequently, a complementary convention was developed by UNIDROIT (1995) for UNESCO that did not require the source country to prove ownership through cataloguing. However, it did allow for the collector in the market country who bought the item to be compensated. Given the huge amounts of artefacts in circulation, this would be an unjustifiable cost for a developing country.

The root cause of the problem (very similar to that of piracy) is the levels of poverty that exist in many developing countries. The sale of antiquities through a network of intermediaries to an eager international market may only finally be addressed by:

- creating stable economic, social and political structures in developing countries from where the artefacts are sourced;

- improving the living standards of local populations so they do not rely on the sale of antiquities to augment their income;

- creating a register of antiquities and making possession of non-registered antiquities illegal (although this may be only possible in richer countries).

At the same time, there are steps that are being encouraged in the market countries – the other end of the supply chain:

- developing legislation that would make the purchase of plundered antiquities illegal;

- making it socially unacceptable to buy antiquities where there is ambiguous or no provenance;

- focusing border and customs authorities on the trade by highlighting the tax/duty loss through illegal, undeclared trafficking.

# Human trafficking in Europe

Pictures of refugees trying to cross European borders have become commonplace following the crisis in Syria and long-running instability in Iraq, Afghanistan and other Middle Eastern and North African countries. Whether at Calais trying to jump trains or trucks bound for the UK, or on a much larger-scale crossing en masse into Hungary, Austria or Croatia, the migrant crisis has dominated the political agenda. Whereas the media has rightly highlighted the humanitarian consequences of the movement of thousands of people across the continent, little attention has been paid to the impact of the political response on European trade and transport.

One of the most successful results of greater European integration has been the free movement of goods and people throughout the Single European Market. For many countries in the region, a separate treaty – the Schengen Agreement – has meant the total abolition of border controls. This means that trucks can travel anywhere in mainland Europe without being required to stop by authorities. The pressure that the mass movement of migrants has placed on European governments, especially those in Eastern and Southern Europe, means that this agreement is under threat as never before.

In total, 26 countries have signed the agreement – 22 EU members and 4 non-EU. Only 6 of the 28 EU member states are outside the Schengen zone – Bulgaria, Croatia, Cyprus, Ireland, Romania and the UK.

However, the agreement includes a clause that allows countries to temporarily re-impose border controls in certain situations. This is exactly what

Germany has done because of the influx of migrants across the border from Austria. Austria itself imposed controls on its border with Hungary and has carried out spot-checks on trucks since the deaths of 71 migrants in a refrigerated vehicle in August 2015. On occasion these have resulted in queues up to 30km in length.

The costs for Europe's economy are twofold. First, re-applying border restrictions would undermine the supply chain strategies of manufacturers and retailers. The Single European Market was a critical element in the efficient distribution of goods around the region and the unrestricted movement of trucks was a fundamental part of this. Inventory costs would rise, making Europe even less competitive compared with markets in Asia, for example. With delays at borders sometimes running into days and an inability to effectively schedule just-in-time deliveries, the whole foundation of European retail and manufacturing strategy would have to be re-assessed.

Second, transport costs would also rise. Dutch-based logistics provider Jan de Rijk has been one European road freight operator to comment on the disruption the crisis is causing the industry. Its managing director, Sebastiaan Scholte, stated that it was faced with increased waiting times at border crossings due to checks by authorities: 'In an industry with very thin margins, these additional costs are not sustainable in the long run.' In order to offset these costs, his company would be charging waiting costs because of border checks or Channel Tunnel disruptions. Of course, ultimately these will be passed on to European consumers.

It is clear that, to date, European governments have been influenced by political factors relating to fears over uncontrolled, mass migration. Economic considerations are much lower down the agenda, and the supply chain and logistics industry must lobby hard to make sure that governments understand the full consequences of their decisions on border controls.

# Illegal trade in cigarettes

The main reason for the existence of illegal tobacco smuggling, which is of particular importance in the EU, is the price differential between member states. It has been estimated that 99 billion cigarettes are smuggled annually in the EU, of which 20 per cent are counterfeit. This costs EU governments in the region of €10 billion. Not only is this undertaken by 'shuttle trade', that is, the movement of contraband typically in small vans, but also in large-scale smuggling operations. Counterfeit cigarettes are imported by container, largely from China. In the UK it is believed that over a quarter of all cigarettes smoked have been smuggled.

The vast sums of money available have obviously attracted organized crime. Long-held links between gangs in the former Soviet Bloc countries still exist, and this has opened up distribution channels between Russia, Ukraine and Belarus and the new Central and Eastern European member states of the EU. Once in the EU, it is easy to move the cigarettes to the UK and Germany, where they can fetch many times the price they can in most of the rest of Europe.

An enormous logistics operation exists to support the movement of these illegal cigarettes, including networks of warehousing that are focused on trade lanes where the highest price differential exists.

On certain of these land border crossings, wide-scale customs corruption certainly exists – especially in Eastern Europe. However, at the major port gateways this is less likely, as with only 2 per cent of containers being checked by customs, smugglers are happy to take their chance that a consignment of cigarettes will not be found. According to one report, cigarette smugglers only need one in seven containers to get through in order to break even. In reality, they do much better than this.

Customs are not the only parties that are prone to corruption from organized crime gangs. Transport companies' employees have also been bribed to carry consignments of illegal tobacco, as well as transport managers. Port workers have also been implicated in the past, moving consignments outside of the duty-free zones, for instance.

# Vehicle theft and exportation

The stolen vehicle supply chain is entirely managed by organized crime. In the 1990s, thousands of cars, agricultural and construction machinery were stolen in the developed EU for export to the new members of the EU in Central and Eastern Europe. A huge demand for cheap cars fuelled the activity of car crime rings, and gangs were highly effective in shipping stolen vehicles to these markets.

Developing car security measures in Western Europe, and increasing disposable income in the East, resulted in much lower demand in the 2000s and criminals instead targeted high-end vehicles or those that could be broken down for spare parts. Eastern European EU members became less of a market in their own right and more of a trans-shipment point for onward delivery to Russia and former CIS countries.

If many manufacturers have evolved their production strategies towards build-to-order, it is possible to describe organized criminals' strategies as having evolved to steal-to-order. One estimate suggests that the 'logistics' costs of delivering a stolen car to its new owner outside of the EU could amount to €10,000. However, this compares with a resale value of €50,000 and upwards to be split amongst the criminals. In fact, 'black market' and legal supply chains may not necessarily be totally separate. In some cases, either knowingly or unknowingly, transport companies and second-hand car dealers may be involved in the distribution process. In the case of exporting stolen vehicles to outside of the EU, there may additionally be an element of customs corruption, bribing officers to turn a blind eye to the clearance of the car.

# Conclusion

The development of global transportation networks and the logistics services that support them has ironically resulted in a highly efficient conduit for illegal goods of all types. The sheer volume of shipping containers, air cargo and road freight transiting borders means that it is impossible for security agencies to prevent smuggling – only a tiny proportion of contraband is intercepted each year.

The situation is made worse by the 'grey' areas in international legislation that exist in certain markets. The movement of goods that can be legally consumed in one market but not another creates uncertainty and confusion – a state of affairs that can be exploited by criminals.

Price differentials in entirely legal products (such as cigarettes) caused by diverse taxation policies has also created a market for organized criminals, who often use the proceeds to fund other criminal activities or for laundering money.

How does this affect licit supply chains? Obviously it is of major concern that supply chains are being misappropriated for illegal purposes, even if unknowingly. There is no suggestion that the vast majority of companies active in the supply chain and logistics industry are party to these activities. However, many of their employees will be involved in falsifying paperwork or allowing access to the illicit goods that are in transit or being stored.

In addition, as was shown at the height of the refugee crisis in Europe, governments have the ultimate option of disrupting the free movement of goods and vehicles across borders, if only for a short time. It is critical for the industry that it ensures that it does everything in its power to reduce the level of illicit goods within global supply chains.

## Summary

Legitimate supply chains have been hijacked by criminal gangs to move illicit goods around the world. Air cargo carriers, express operators, shipping lines, and road freight companies and freight forwarders are all unwittingly involved in a multi-billion-dollar industry. Whether cocaine from Central America, antiquities from the Middle East or ivory from Africa, criminals operate highly efficient and complex value chains, relying on the authorities' inability to check the sheer volume of shipments moved. However, legitimate supply chains are at risk from intervention by border and other government agents as well as increased levels of regulation. The most visible example of this is the high cost of fines levied on road freight operators who, even unwittingly, carry migrants from Europe into the UK.

## Key points

- Supply chains can be under threat from attack, from theft, from substitution, but also from subversion for illegal purposes.
- Illicit supply chains 'piggyback' on mainstream transport networks using legitimate carriers and freight forwarders.
- There are many 'grey areas' within legal frameworks of international commerce that criminals are very proficient at exploiting.
- Narcotics supply chains are complex and well-organized, spanning the world and specific to each type of drug.
- Trade in endangered animals and their products is being driven by Asian criminal gangs, which are operating ever more 'vertically integrated' supply chains, with their own operations in Africa.
- Counterfeit medicines are introduced into legitimate supply chains, with trade now estimated at around $1 billion, presenting a major threat to public health.
- Instability in the Middle East has led to a surge in illicit trade in antiquities.

# Terrorism and security    12

**OBJECTIVES**

This chapter will familiarize the reader with:

- the different approaches to risk and security in air cargo supply chains;
- the difficulties involved in scanning 100 per cent of shipments;
- the vulnerability of airports to terrorism and political disturbance;
- why shipping was prioritized by regulators following the 9/11 terrorist attacks;
- processes established to screen sea freight shipments;
- the regions most vulnerable to terrorist attack.

Since the 9/11 terrorist atrocity in New York and Washington, DC, administrators around the world have focused heavily on air and sea freight as a potential source of risk to national security. Given that the events of 9/11 were in no way connected to the breach of the integrity of supply chains, this is perhaps slightly surprising. However, to those involved in security, the ease with which criminals are able to infiltrate supply chains (as evidenced by the illegal trafficking of narcotics and by cargo crime) also makes the air and sea freight sector an obvious target for terrorists. To date there have been few instances of such action (see page 271 for case study of the Yemeni bombs), although this in itself is not necessarily an endorsement of the efficacy of security agencies' initiatives. However, it is possible to say that there have been significant costs imposed on shippers and taxpayers from the security initiatives taken by authorities around the world. Regulators must be aware that by adding in layers of complexity and delays, they risk undermining the fundamental business model of air cargo, which is speed. This consequently has an impact on economic growth and prosperity.

# Risk and security in air cargo supply chains

## Risk-based or comprehensive security screening?

More than 15 years after the 9/11 events, threats to air travel and air cargo are as great as ever, although the source of the threats is continually changing. In 2016, the United Nations Security Council passed a resolution that stressed:

> the vital importance of the global aviation system to economic development and prosperity, and of all States strengthening aviation security measures to secure a stable and peaceful global environment, and further recognizing that secure air services in this regard enhance transportation, connectivity, trade, political and cultural links between States, and that public confidence in the security of air transport is vital (UN, 2016).

The resolution went on to say that there was 'particular concern that terrorist groups are actively seeking ways to defeat or circumvent aviation security, looking to identify and exploit gaps or weaknesses where they perceive them'. The response should be, according to the resolution, strengthened security screening procedures, new technologies that are better able to detect explosives, as well as better collaboration and cooperation related to the sharing of data about threats, risks and vulnerabilities.

The vulnerability of the global air cargo system was demonstrated in October 2010 when two US-bound shipments containing explosives were intercepted on cargo planes in the United Kingdom and Dubai. The parcels had originated in Yemen, where they had managed to avoid security measures.

This security breach highlighted the dilemma that the authorities and the air cargo industry face. Should they adopt an approach with a risk-based strategy that relies on characteristics of a shipment to identify packages for increased scrutiny, or one in which all shipments are subject to some form of physical inspection?

Backers of comprehensive physical screening argue that this approach is the only way to ensure adequate security, while advocates of risk-based approaches argue that comprehensive screening is too costly and time-consuming. Not only is it massively expensive, but it also creates delays, adding even more costs to the overall system.

Despite this, the latter approach has powerful proponents. In November 2011, a US Senator introduced the 'Air Cargo Security Act', which required screening of all cargo transported on freighters. The bill did not go far as it was referred to the House Homeland Security Committee, which took no further action. However, given the power of its political lobby, the bill could potentially be reintroduced at some stage, especially if the air cargo system is compromised again in the future.

Under the current air cargo security regime, a number of risk-based strategies have been implemented and expanded to evaluate the security risk of air cargo shipments. Existing programmes such as the 'Known Shipper Program' and the 'Certified Cargo Screening Program', both of which have been in place for several years, are being studied for potential enhancements and expansions.

Other 'comprehensive' initiatives rely on technology. The US Transportation Security Administration (TSA) had approved a number of x-ray, bulk explosives detection systems and explosives trace detection machines for screening air cargo. However, these were variations of technologies used for screening checked baggage and carry-on items. Unfortunately none of these devices was capable of effectively screening palletized or containerized cargo, which makes up 75 per cent of all cargo carried on passenger planes. Instead, screening would have to have been done on individual cargo items, which would have meant excessive delays. As a result, the TSA was forced to look at various new technologies, which led to several delays in the project.

Comprehensive air cargo scanning on passenger planes had been scheduled to begin at the end of 2011. However, a number of airlines lobbied hard against this, asserting that meeting the deadline with an unworkable scanning solution would cause massive disruption to air cargo supply chains. The agency also noted the difficulty in verifying the accuracy of self-reporting screening data from passenger air carriers, as there were no requirements for all-cargo carriers to report comparable data. The Department for Homeland Security responded by suggesting a new compliance deadline of December 2012.

In the end, as a result of costs and concerns raised by the air cargo industry, the plan was scrapped. Another problem had been the lack of support from foreign governments, which would have had to have been involved in scanning all shipments bound for the United States. In theory, although the TSA lacked the direct authority to dictate screening requirements at foreign airports, it could potentially impose regulations on both foreign and US carriers. However, enforcement overseas would have been up to authorities in other countries and disagreement was becoming potentially damaging.

The US administrators have had more success in agreeing a common approach to security standards with many of its biggest partners. In 2012 the US entered into a mutual recognition agreement on aviation security, streamlining transatlantic cargo operations. Before this, shipments had to be broken down, inspected and then repacked because of the inadequacy of screening technology. This deal has been regularly extended on a short-term basis and authorities on both sides of the Atlantic have been looking at agreeing a longer-term arrangement. Similar agreements are in place between the EU, the USA and South Africa, Canada and Australia.

By working with cargo and customs associations, US Customs and Border Protection (CBP) appears to have introduced a more simplified way to identify potential risks earlier as well as simplify the merchandise release process and reduce transaction costs. It seems that the merits of a risk-based approach to dealing with air cargo security have been judged to outweigh those of the 'comprehensive' alternative.

## CASE STUDY  The Yemen air cargo plot

In 2010, UK security agencies found an improvised explosive device on board a UPS cargo aircraft at East Midlands Airport. A second bomb was discovered at a cargo facility in Dubai, United Arab Emirates, both of which originated in Yemen and were destined for the United States. The packages were carried on board passenger and freighter flights before being discovered.

The placing of the devices on a Qatar Airways plane between Sana'a, Yemen, and Dubai as belly-hold freight amplified the issue of security for the air freight sector. While it was disturbing that terrorists were able to penetrate the networks of FedEx and UPS, the Qatar Airways incident demonstrated that the whole of the air freight industry is affected by the problem.

In the aftermath of the failed bomb attempts, individual countries immediately implemented emergency security measures, such as banning flights from Yemen as well as limiting the types of commodities allowed on cargo planes. For example, cargo originating from cities in India, Qatar, Pakistan, Iran, Bangladesh, Thailand, the Maldives, Sudan and Libya had to be re-screened after arriving in Britain before being loaded onto onward flights.

Although freight industry organizations cautioned against an excessive security clamp-down, politicians in Britain and the United States committed to security reviews. The reaction by the authorities resulted in calls for more inspection and scanning, and the wider use of 'explosive detection systems'.

Germany requested that the European Union devise a bloc solution and recommended a five-point plan, which included:

- greater coordination of measures at a European level;

- evaluation of security at airports outside the European Union;

- increased scrutiny for airports with high-danger security concerns;

- closer tracking of suspicious consignments;

- greater cooperation among officials working on air transport and aviation security.

Agreeing to Germany's request, the EU Transport Commissioner of the time, Siim Kallas, said:

> We should remain smart. Simply adding more layers of cargo screening would be hard to implement and cause great operational difficulties. We need an approach based on risk assessment, better integrated with intelligence and we need to use a range of control methods in combination. To be effective, Europe has to work closely with the United States: there is no point developing different and incompatible approaches on both sides of the Atlantic for addressing the same problem. That would not be good for transatlantic trade.

Like Europe, the United States immediately implemented a series of security measures, including the banning of all air cargo from Yemen and also Somalia. High-risk cargo on passenger aircraft was prohibited and toner and ink cartridges over 16 ounces were no longer allowed in carry-on and checked bags. The stricter rules also applied to international mail packages, which must be individually screened and certified to have come from an established postal shipper.

Individual airports have also introduced additional security measures. Dubai Airports, which owns Dubai International and Al Maktoum International, have introduced a series of procedures and processes to be used by ground handlers, security police, authorities and other carriers. Dubai Airports has recommended that its staff:

- rely on the technology available to profile cargo coming from countries or airports that are less efficient in their security measures;

- work on the implementation of the regulated agents' philosophies and empower them to ensure the safety and security of cargo;

- rely on the intelligence provided on each shipment, shipper and country of origin;

- have a clear understanding of the roles of customs, security and intelligence services;

- screen all cargo on passenger aircraft 100 per cent – no exceptions;
- screen all mail 100 per cent on acceptance and transferring through bilateral agreements between airports and authorities.

In the latest cases the core problem is that the primary systems put in place to prevent the loading of explosive devices failed. Both the surveillance technology being used at present and the 'known consignor' system were either deceived or bypassed. It is worth observing that it was the express providers who were targeted, as these systems are possibly more open to the general public and therefore may offer greater opportunity to hide the identity of the person placing the package in the system.

The lesson that the incidents appear to give is that the nature of the threat is dynamic rather than static. The individuals placing the bombs into the freight systems designed the devices to deliberately evade the security systems. This displayed both a knowledge of the security systems used and the ability to design a device capable of evading these systems. Therefore, any effective new security systems put in place by the air cargo sector are going to have to be both proactive and continually adaptive.

Although terrorists managed to penetrate the security of an express carrier, the ability of customers to track their packages every step of the way through the FedEx and UPS networks helped investigators pinpoint the location of the parcel bomb packages in Britain and Dubai, and intercept them before anyone was harmed. According to Michael Mullen, executive director of the Express Association of America:

> Already the express industry sets the gold standard in terms of information management and the security of their supply chain. The business model itself is so information intensive that they know where these packages are every minute of the day. That might be one of the lessons out of this. There probably has to be a better information sharing regime between the government and the private sector so the threat information is disseminated a little more rapidly.... That means information sharing needs to be a two-way street in which government does a better job of letting businesses know what to look out for and when.

In truth there was nothing particularly original about the approach taken in planting these devices. The bomb on Pan Am 103, which blew up over Scotland in 1988, had strong similarities in design. However, the innovation of disguising explosive as printer toner illustrates an evolution in the nature of the problem. The air freight business systems must in turn evolve to anticipate such developments. It must achieve this while not crippling the operations of the business, either in terms of time to scan each consignment or cost. Either way, the cost penalty of developing such a response quickly and across the whole air cargo system is likely to be substantial.

## Political disturbances

Air cargo is not only vulnerable to disruption from terrorist sources. Its reliance on major nodes or gateways means that it is inherently inflexible and therefore exposed to other forms of political activity (as well as criminal and meteorological events detailed elsewhere in this book). One example of this was the occupation of Bangkok's Suvarnabhumi Airport by anti-government protestors in 2008. The protests affected cargo operations at the airport and this impacted on flows right across South East Asia.

The airport is the nineteenth largest cargo-handling airport in the world, with a throughput of over a million tonnes of freight. That is only slightly less than the major UK gateway of London Heathrow. Suvarnabhumi is also the second largest air freight hub in South East Asia, behind Singapore. Its effective closure therefore had a big impact on the economies of the region as well as on Thailand itself.

Freight forwarders in Thailand re-routed cargo being moved into and out of the country via Penang International Airport in Malaysia, about 800 kilometres south of the Thai capital. One source suggested that this option was costing 50 per cent more than using normal services through Suvarnabhumi (Transport Intelligence, 2008). Other smaller Thai domestic airports, such as Don Mueang, which is also in Bangkok, were closed too, further reducing the options for air freight services.

Most concern was expressed about the impact of the protest action on Thailand's tourism sector. However, it also threatened other types of businesses in that country. Thailand has experienced rapid economic growth in recent years, with electronics assembly and the automotive sector driving the development of manufacturing. Electronics, in particular, relies on the import of components and the export of product by air freight. Fresh produce and flower shipments, which remain an important aspect of the Thai economy, were also being affected.

Since Suvarnabhumi was designed to act as a hub airport for South East Asia, handling the distribution of cargo to/from Malaysia and other developing economies such as Vietnam, the impact of its problems rippled out across the region.

## The future for air cargo security

The years ahead will inevitably see increased scrutiny of air cargo security. Cooperation will increase as the US, EU and other administrations meet to discuss global air cargo security standards. At the same time the TSA will continue to test new procedures and technologies in order to develop solutions as quickly as possible. The air cargo industry will also play an important role by sharing its expertise and knowledge of movement and tracking of goods.

The events of 9/11 caused the United States to take a serious look at its security processes at sea ports, border entry points and airports. While the US government has seen some success in its implementations, it has proved costly for many transport providers, who have been required to add additional manpower, scanning equipment, upgrade IT systems, and so on, to be in compliance. As a result, much of these additional costs end up being passed down to customers in varying forms of 'surcharges'.

While it is unlikely that there will be a fundamental change in security procedures in the near future, it is recognized that processes can become more efficient. In a document calling for proposals from private sector companies (CDE, 2016), the UK government asked for proof-of-concept proposals for solutions that help improve existing aviation processes through maximizing:

- reliability and confidence – in the detection of threats, particularly through the ability to screen dense goods and small areas of high density in large consignments;
- throughput levels – improving the speed and volume of baggage and cargo security;
- improved automation – reducing false positives and the need to manually break down containers and baggage;
- cost benefits – reducing cost (purchase, maintenance and operation) of security screening.

# Sea freight security

## C-TPAT and AEO

One of the cornerstones of the US response to terrorism in the early 2000s was the Customs-Trade Partnership Against Terrorism (C-TPAT) programme. The initiative was designed as a partnership between government and business aimed at increasing the protection of cargo into and out of the country while not restricting the flow of trade.

C-TPAT was established by US Customs and Border Protection (CBP) in November 2001, in response to the US terrorist attacks two months earlier (9/11). The programme has increased border security with respect to goods imported into the United States by all transport modes, while not slowing down the flow of trade. In this respect, C-TPAT complements and supports the CBP's Free and Secure Trade (FAST) programme, which has increased security for goods imported into the United States via land border crossing points.

C-TPAT began in 2001 with seven major US importing companies as members. In exchange for C-TPAT importer members providing the CBP with detailed information covering their door-to-door global supply chain (including information on all their suppliers and factories), the CBP provided them with a number of major advantages in their logistics operations. The benefits that accrue, and which are listed below, accelerate and simplify C-TPAT members' import procedures.

Since C-TPAT began, its membership has grown rapidly, and continues to do so. Also, membership has been expanded to the service providers and suppliers of US importers. Today, C-TPAT has more than 11,400 so-called 'certified partners', which include US importers, US/Canadian trucking companies, US/Mexican trucking companies, rail operators, ocean carriers, customs brokers, US port authorities and terminal operators, freight forwarders/3PLs (third-party logistics providers), and overseas manufacturers. These companies account for more than 50 per cent, by value, of US imports.

To apply for C-TPAT membership, a company must conduct a self-assessment of its supply chain with respect to security, using guidelines developed jointly between the company and the CBP. These guidelines cover the following areas: procedural security; physical security; personnel security; education and training; access controls; manifest procedures; and conveyance security.

In return importers are provided with the following benefits:

- a reduced number of CBP goods inspections for imports, resulting in reduced border delay times;
- priority processing with respect to CBP goods inspections for imports, including front of the line processing for inspections when possible;
- assignment of a C-TPAT Supply Chain Security Specialist (SCSS), who will work with the company to validate and enhance security throughout the company's global supply chain;

- potential eligibility for the CBP's importer self-assessment programme (ISA), with an emphasis on self-policing rather than CBP audits;
- eligibility to attend C-TPAT supply chain security training seminars.

The CBP is currently working towards giving highly compliant importers, in terms of stringent supply chain security procedures, further benefits, in the form of a higher-level service. Referred to as C-TPAT plus, such higher-tier importers will obtain 'green lane' import clearances in the future, which entail no inspections on arrival and immediate goods release. A requirement of the 'green lane' facility is the deployment of a so-called 'smart' container, which is secured on all six sides.

To comply with the code, freight forwarders and logistics companies must have comprehensive supply chain security processes involving freight security procedures, personnel screening and training as well as inventory control measures in all of their locations used to process freight. On a practical level, as well as the confidence this provides, customers also benefit from faster customs clearance and fewer inspections of their shipments. Forwarders are able to segregate shipments into dedicated C-TPAT-only containers, minimizing the chance of potential delay from non-C-TPAT shippers, and allowing these cargoes to be 'green-laned' by US Customs and Border Protection.

In the EU a similar initiative was implemented – the Authorized Economic Operator (AEO) programme. It was one of a series of measures being coordinated by the World Customs Organization as part of a multi-layered approach to facilitating trade and making supply chains more secure and controlled. The goal of these arrangements is to link the various international industry partnership programmes, so that together they create a unified and sustainable security posture that can assist in securing and facilitating global trade. A system would be created whereby all participants in an international trade transaction are approved by the various customs bodies as observing specified standards in the secure handling of goods and relevant information.

In May 2012, US Customs and Border Protection (CBP) and the European Union (EU) signed a Mutual Recognition Decision between the CBP's Customs-Trade Partnership Against Terrorism (C-TPAT) programme and the EU's AEO, which recognized their compatibility. The decision on the mutual recognition of the trade partnership programmes was hailed as saving time and money for trusted operators on both sides of the Atlantic while allowing customs authorities to concentrate their resources on 'riskier' consignments.

The decision means that certified trusted traders enjoy lower costs, simplified procedures and greater predictability in their transatlantic activities. The agreement allows companies registered under either scheme to enjoy fast-track customs clearance into the United States. The EU has also concluded and implemented Mutual Recognition of AEO programmes with Norway, Switzerland, Japan, Andorra and China.

## Container screening

One of the most contentious issues at present in the US security debate is the perceived threat from terrorists of penetrating the country's borders with weapons of mass destruction transported in shipping containers. Containers have for some time been regarded as a major gap in the United States' defences against terrorism, not least because smugglers have been exploiting the inability of security services to search the huge volumes handled. Logically terrorists should be able to make use of the same vulnerability.

In 2002 US Customs, now part of the Department of Homeland Security (DHS), launched its Container Security Initiative (CSI). Under this initiative, bilateral partnerships with foreign customs authorities were established, whereby containers destined for the United States that are considered high risk in terms of being a potential terrorist threat, undergo x-ray and radiation scans at the overseas port of loading (or trans-shipment). This involves US Customs officers being stationed at the overseas ports. The CSI is operational in 58 foreign ports, which between them cover 86 per cent of maritime containerized cargo destined for the United States. The participating ports are located in Europe, Asia, Africa, the Middle East, and North and South America.

The CSI also includes the '24-Hour Manifest Rule', under which, since 2003, exporters of containerized cargoes to the United States have been required to provide detailed shipment information to their ocean carrier or logistics service provider prior to the container being loaded onto the vessel at the port of origin. This enables the ocean carrier to submit its vessel cargo manifest to US Customs 24 hours before the vessel sails, as required by this ruling.

To facilitate the agency's targeting of high-risk shipments, US Customs requires 10 pieces of information to be provided by shippers and two by ocean carriers, in addition to the data currently provided on the cargo manifest. The additional data elements include information on the manufacturer and/or seller of the goods, country of origin of the goods, and a more detailed product description than shown on the manifest, amongst others.

A considerably more ambitious – and contentious – US government project concerned the plan for 100 per cent of US-bound containers to undergo scanning. This requirement was signed into US law in August 2007, as the 'Implementing Regulations of the 9/11 Commission Act of 2007', amidst criticisms that, with the technology available at the time, it was unworkable without slowing down the flow of goods in the supply chain. Critics said the economic impact of this would be a huge 'own goal'.

The 100 per cent scanning of US-bound containers has been opposed by many industry associations, including the National Retail Federation (NRF), which issued the following statement: 'We do not believe the "scan-all" requirement improves supply chain security,' the NRF said. 'As the US Customs Border Patrol and Protection has indicated in several congressional reports, there have been continued technological problems, significant costs, resistance from foreign governments and delays at some ports' (MMH, 2012).

A letter in 2014 from Secretary of Homeland Security Jeh Johnson laid bare the problems:

> [T]he use of systems that are available to scan containers would have a negative impact on trade capacity and the flow of cargo. Additionally, systems to scan containers cannot be purchased, deployed, or operated at ports overseas because ports do not have the physical characteristics to install such a system (DHS, 2014).

As such the DHS announced it would delay the cargo-scanning requirement, and this decision has been extended in two-year increments since. According to the agency, expanding checks at international seaports would be expensive and cumbersome to implement from a diplomatic, administrative and technical standpoint.

It is estimated in the industry that only about 5 per cent (if that) of all cargo containers heading to the United States are screened. The DHS's risk-based approach, which it now favours for screening of cargo, calls for extra scrutiny on freight imported from 58 of the most active international shipping hubs, such as Dubai and Hong Kong.

The effect of the heightened security regime will be a big push towards creating more secure transport networks that use superior visibility to monitor the behaviour of specific cargoes, tracking them in real time. The C-TPAT conventions and the tighter operation of bills of lading are the first step in improving information flows. However, these systems are 'historical' and usually based on paper systems. In the near future the logistics sector is likely to see pressure to adopt real-time monitoring systems – probably based around RFID surveillance of all cargoes – feeding into much more powerful databases held by shippers, freight forwarders and transport operators. If this is not enough, the trends in air passenger monitoring suggest that such systems will be accessible in real time to law enforcement and security organizations. Of course, these systems will cost substantial amounts of money.

The problem is that even where these systems already exist, they are not secure. For example, FedEx faced severe embarrassment when its own secure billing systems were breached by criminals buying information from FedEx employees. The Nigerian drug smugglers were able to use this information to pass material through the UK and into the United States. The quality of the workforce is fundamental to all security systems, and here the logistics sector is very vulnerable.

## Shipping – vulnerability to terrorism and security threats

Around the world there are several logistics 'pinch points' that act as vulnerabilities in the global trading network. These can be affected either by piracy (for example off the Somali coast or the Strait of Malacca) or by geo-political conflict and terrorism.

There is considerable fear amongst Western governments around the world that terrorists – most likely Islamic extremists – could target these locations to inflict severe economic damage. Attacks could take the form of sinking a ship through either bombing or assault (boarding, hijacking and scuttling), setting off a 'dirty' bomb smuggled on board or compromising the integrity of the transport infrastructure (for example, by damaging locks, canals, bridges, tunnels, and so on). In reality, the geographic scope of some of these pinch points is so vast that defending them is almost impossible. The only robust defence relies on intelligence work that can stop an attack at the planning stage.

In addition to terrorism, there is also the threat to these transit ways from 'rogue' states, such as North Korea. 'Failing' states, into which category Somalia, Yemen and Syria can be placed, create a security vacuum in which insurgents, terrorists or warlords can thrive.

### The Suez Canal

The volatile political situation in Egypt, first with the overthrow of President Mubarak and then President Morsi, has increased risks to one of the world's busiest waterways, the Suez Canal. The canal handles about 7 per cent of the world's trade and in 2015 it was transited by 17,483 ships. After the Strait of Hormuz, the canal is the second most important pinch point for oil and liquefied gas heading from the Middle East to Europe and North America.

Any geo-political or security event that resulted in the closure of the Suez Canal would have major implications for shipping and world trade. It would force ships bound to and from Asia to instead use the Cape of Good Hope in South Africa, adding several days to the transit time. Whereas ships using the Suez Canal only travel 12,000 kilometres from the Arabian Gulf to London, those choosing the Cape of Good Hope would travel 20,900 kilometres. In terms of days, such a transit would be 24 days compared with 14.

**Figure 12.1**   Map of the Suez Canal

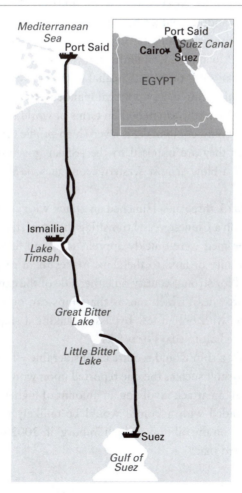

Going via the Cape would increase not only operational costs such as fuel, chartering and crewing (impacting on rates charged to shippers), but also add significantly to inventory costs as shippers would have to bear an additional 10 days of capital.

Threats to the Suez Canal come from a number of sources:

- ongoing civil unrest in Egypt;
- international terrorist organizations;
- a wider Middle Eastern conflict.

Each of these threats has a varying level of probability. The present poor security situation in Egypt is perhaps the most pressing, as the Suez Canal would become a valuable strategic asset to both sides in a civil war. At present the Egyptian military has provided sufficient security, ensuring that operations were not affected even during the uprising against Mubarak. However, the longstanding conflict between the Muslim Brotherhood and the Egyptian army risks becoming far more serious to the long-term stability of the country. Providing $5.1 billion in revenue from tolls, there is an obvious interest to all sides to keep the canal open. However, it could also be used as a bargaining chip in any political manoeuvring that may occur.

The economic value of the canal, both in terms of world trade and impact on the Egyptian economy, could make it a very high-profile target for Islamic extremists, whether they are opposed to the secular government in Cairo or looking to strike a blow against Western economies via the disruption of world trade.

In September 2013, three men launched an attack with guns and a rocket propelled grenade on a Chinese vessel transiting the canal, the COSCO Asia. Although the three men were quickly apprehended and little damage was inflicted, the proximity of land to the ships makes them easy targets, and highlights the need for strong security on either side of the canal. Part of the problem is its narrowness, which means that ships can only travel in one direction at a time, with only a few bypasses. Sinking a ship would bring traffic to a complete halt for days or weeks.

However, to sink a ship would require a considerable effort from a landborne attack. An assault such as the one reported upon would be completely ineffectual and even an attack involving an amount of high explosive (using perhaps a boat loaded with a bomb) would be unlikely to succeed. The unsuccessful attack on the oil tanker the 'Limburg' in 2002 off the coast of Yemen demonstrated that.

## The Strait of Hormuz

Tensions between Iran and the West increased in 2011 when sanctions imposed as a result of Iran's nuclear programme started to bite. In response to the United States' and the EU's further plans to block exports of Iranian oil exports, Iran retaliated by threatening to close the Strait of Hormuz. This is the narrow passage between Iran and Oman, linking the Gulf with the Indian Ocean. Twenty per cent of the world's oil supplies pass through the Strait as well as container vessels using the UAE's and other Gulf countries' ports.

Since that time tensions between Iran and the West have eased and some sanctions have been lifted. However, with the arrival of the new Trump administration in the US, the relationship seems to have soured once again.

Many analysts believe that Iran's threats to the Strait are baseless, and that closing the Strait would be economically and politically damaging, not only to relations with the West, but with its powerful neighbours Saudi Arabia and the UAE.

The consequences of any sort of military action in the Strait of Hormuz would be severe. Dubai is the ninth largest port in the world, and the region has in recent years developed as a major hub for shipping, supplying Indian, Central Asian and African destinations with Asian-originating products. International sea–air business would also be affected, not to mention end markets in the Gulf itself.

**Figure 12.2**   Map of the Strait of Hormuz

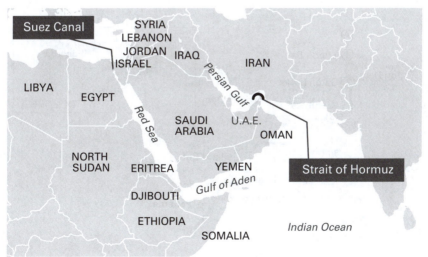

## The Panama Canal

In 2016 there were 13,114 transits of the Panama Canal carrying 204 million tonnes of cargo. As well as container vessels, the canal is used extensively by reefer vessels, liquid bulk carriers, car carriers, dry bulk carriers, and military and passenger ships. It is believed that about 5 per cent of world trade is transported through the canal. Any disruption to this trade would have a major impact on the global economy, and specifically that of the United States, which accounts for two-thirds of the canal's traffic.

Given the world's attention on the unrest in the Middle East, it might be considered that the Panama Canal is less of a security risk. This may be partly true; however, if the full historical context of the canal is taken into account, a slightly different risk profile appears.

For most of the last century the Panama Canal was under the control of the US authorities, who were responsible for looking after its security. Thousands of US troops were stationed in the country in order to secure what was regarded as a highly valuable asset. In 1977, the then president of the United States, Jimmy Carter, signed an agreement with Panama's president General Omar Torrijos handing over the Canal, with the condition that it must remain managed neutrally. The handover took place at the end of 1999.

The security situation in Central America is in one way far more stable than it has been over the past few decades, when the region was gripped by a number of insurgencies and civil wars. Now, however, the problem faced

**Figure 12.3**   Map of the Panama Canal

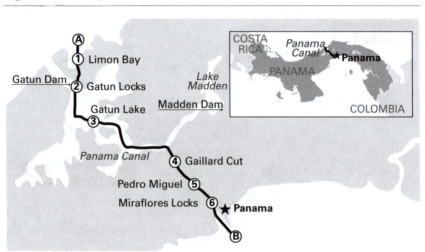

by various countries to the north and south of the canal is the lawlessness created by the strength of the drugs cartels.

Joint exercises are regularly held between United States, Panama and other countries to develop and test the command and control of forces at sea, involving participants in maritime, air, land, space and cyber operations. Scenarios include open water diving operations, counterdrug interdictions and simulated river operations. One specific vulnerability that the Panama Canal has compared with the Suez Canal is its locks. According to one security expert, these locks could be disabled with a small amount of explosive.

Despite this, perhaps the biggest threat to supply chains is not the closure of the canal but its use as a conduit for drug and illegal arms smuggling. Following the expansion of the canal, considerable investment was made in the security systems that are used to identify and track ships.

One of the initiatives being put in place is the creation of a digital ship registry, which will allow authorities to see ships' licences, country of origin, cargo and ports of call for all vessels transiting the canal. Tracking systems are able to flag up deviations from schedules, and hence assess which levels of risk a ship presents.

## Conclusion

It is obviously impossible to assess the likelihood of a major terrorist event that targets the global air network or one of these major shipping transit points. However, it is clear that there is considerable potential for massive disruption should an attack be successful.

The huge volumes carried by air and sea networks make 100 per cent screening of containers and consignments impossible. Even if the technology were put in place, which would be very costly, the potential to circumvent security procedures by bribery and corruption would be considerable. Transport networks are used on a daily basis by organized crime to smuggle narcotics and illegal arms around the world – it is highly likely that their integrity could be compromised by a committed terrorist organization using a similar technique to that employed by the Yemeni bombers.

In terms of shipping, with the security situation in the Middle East becoming increasingly of concern, the Suez Canal would seem to be most at threat, not only from terrorists potentially based in Yemen and Somalia, but also insurgent groups in Egypt and even further state-sponsored terrorists emanating from Iran or Syria.

It is not just shipping or air cargo that is at risk. According to documents obtained from Osama Bin Laden's Pakistani compound, Al-Qaeda was planning an attack on the US railroad network. The US government believes that this could lead to catastrophic loss of life because the system often travels through densely populated urban areas carrying hazardous materials.

Terrorism and geo-political sources of risk are not the only security threats to transportation. As was seen in Thailand, political and civil disturbances brought a busy air cargo hub to a halt, impacting on volumes around the region and adding considerable cost to shippers.

Another example of this type of disruption was the London riots of 2011. Following a shooting by police in Tottenham, riots broke out across London and other cities in the UK. At the height of the violence, a mob descended on the Sony warehouse in Enfield, setting it alight. The fire raged for 10 days and resulted in damage of £60 million, involving stock and the destruction of property. The 200,000-square-foot, three-storey distribution facility provided around a quarter of the UK's home entertainment media, including CD, DVD and Blu-ray discs, all of which were destroyed in the fire. The impact on Sony's logistics was severe. It took 13 months to rebuild a replacement facility.

## Summary

The 9/11 terrorist attacks on New York and Washington, DC, changed the security environment for international movements of goods. Following the event, there were calls from US politicians to implement 100 per cent screening of shipments to the US, both air and sea. However, the impracticalities of such a move and the overwhelming cost to world trade meant that security agencies pursued alternative 'risk-based' approaches. Transport networks are still highly vulnerable to attack, with nodes and pinch points such as the Suez Canal and Strait of Hormuz at greatest risk.

## Key points

- It is impractical and costly to scan 100 per cent of international shipments.

- A 'risk-based' approach is the only feasible method by which to prevent terrorist attacks.

- Air cargo security was breached by the Yemen bomb plot, although fortunately no one was harmed.

- Political disturbances can also disrupt air cargo operations.

- Shippers and sea freight forwarders are now required to comply with a host of regulations designed to identify potential threats, although the process allows special dispensation for regular, large shippers.

- The technology still does not exist to allow authorities to scan containers swiftly or efficiently.

- Key transport routes that travel through nodes or pinch points are most at risk from terrorist attack because of the economic disruption it would cause.

# Conclusion

As this book has demonstrated, risk comes in many forms. It can have a direct impact in terms of financial loss, or can be more indirect in its consequences through a detrimental effect on reputation. Its impact can range from operational and containable to systemic and catastrophic.

It is impossible for supply chain managers to predict low-probability, high-impact events such as natural disasters. However, it is possible for supply chains to be made more resilient – 'risk agnostic' – by adopting a series of measures:

- Implement international standards of risk awareness and response.
- Ensure that there is clear responsibility for managing risk.
- Start measuring risk so that decisions on appropriate levels of inventory can be made more accurately.
- Improve visibility to tier 2 suppliers and beyond.
- Improve inventory visibility and increase levels of agility and velocity.

Risk is not just about the catastrophic and business-critical 'Black Swan' event. Criminality, for example, tends to be regarded by many companies outside of the high-tech and pharmaceutical sectors as a low-level threat, seen by many as almost another operational cost. In fact, as has been described, cargo crime and corruption costs industry and governments billions a year, and much more attention should be focused on the issue. Companies can play a role in this through implementing a range of sensible and basic checks on their logistics providers' operational and security procedures. Governments need to prioritize the crime and stop treating it as 'victimless'.

Terrorism (and, indeed, governments' fear of terrorism) is another pressing issue facing the logistics industry. Undoubtedly air and sea freight supply chains are highly vulnerable, demonstrated by the ease with which criminals seem able to breach security. Therefore it is perhaps surprising that incidence of terrorist activity is very low. The introduction of comprehensive x-ray screening would seem to present a greater threat in terms of costs to the efficiency of supply chains (and the wider economy) than terrorist activity itself.

Corruption is another risk that is either ignored by many shippers and logistics companies, or swept under the carpet. Yet, it is an issue that will only increase in importance as supply chains move into second- and third-tier emerging markets. As UK and US legislation makes it more difficult for companies to turn a blind eye to bribery, governments and private sector must work together to ensure that economic growth is not held back.

Physical disruption to supply chains is only part of the problem. The very nature of modern 'virtual manufacturing networks' means that production often takes place in remote and emerging markets, where labour is cheap and environmental standards are low. Manufacturers and retailers have a responsibility to ensure that they balance the commercial benefits of such a strategy with their own social and corporate responsibilities. As companies such as Hewlett-Packard have shown in the way they have approached sourcing conflict-free minerals in the Democratic Republic of Congo, this is perfectly possible.

# REFERENCES

BAN (2002) *Exporting Harm: The high-tech trashing of Asia*, Basel Action Network, Seattle, USA

Ben Barka, H (2012) *Border Posts, Checkpoints, and Intra-African Trade: Challenges and solutions*, African Development Bank, Tunis

Bowen, F and Kennedy, J (2010) *Accounting for Toyota's Recalls*, Foster School of Business, University of Washington, USA

Bunkley, N and Maynard, M (2010) With recall expanding, Toyota gives an apology (29 January) [online] www.nytimes.com/2010/01/30/business/30toyota. html [accessed 6 December 2016]

CDE (2016) *Competition Document: The future of aviation security*, November, Centre for Defence Enterprise [online] www.gov.uk/government/publications/cde-themed-competition-the-future-of-aviation-security/competition-document-the-future-of-aviation-security [accessed 23 December 2016)

Christopher, M and Peck, H (2004) Building the resilient supply chain, *International Journal of Logistics Management*, 15 (2), pp 1–13

Cisco (2011) *Annual Report*, Cisco Systems Inc, San Jose, CA [online] https://www.sec.gov/Archives/edgar/data/858877/000119312511247394/d202951d10k.htm [accessed 7 May 2016]

CITES (2011) *CITES Trade: A snapshot*, CITES, Geneva [online] https://www.cites.org/sites/default/files/common/docs/CITES-trade-snapshot-eng.pdf [accessed 13 September 2016]

CITES (2013) *Trade: Recent trends in international trade*, in Appendix II-Listed Species (1996–2010) CITES [online] https://cites.unia.es/cites/file.php/1/files/CITES-trade-recent-trends.pdf [accessed 15 September 2016]

Committee on Climate Change and US Transportation (2008) *Potential Impacts of Climate Change on U.S. Transportation*, Transportation Research Board, Washington, DC

CSD (2010) *Examining the Links between Organised Crime and Corruption*, CSD, Sofia

CTA (2015) CTA comments on growing cargo crime problem (2 December), Canadian Trucking Authority [online] http://cantruck.ca/cta-comments-on-growing-cargo-crime-problem-on-w5/ [accessed 17 September 2016]

Davies, P (2015) *Growing the Automotive Supply Chain*, Automotive Council, London

Department of Commerce Bureau of Industry and Security (BIS) Office of Technology Evaluation (2010) *Defense Industrial Base Assessment: Counterfeit electronics*, BIS, Washington, DC

Department of Health (2013) *Pandemic Flu 02/13* [online] https://www.gov.uk/
guidance/pandemic-flu [accessed 3 May 2017]

Despoudi, S, Papaioannou, G and Dani, S (2012) Supply chain collaboration (SCC)
to reduce postharvest food losses (PHFL), in *17th Logistics Research Network
Annual Conference*, pp 1–8, Cranfield University, UK

Dhingra, S and Sampson, T (2016) *Life after Brexit: What are the UK's options
outside the European Union?* Centre for Economic Performance/LSE, UK

DHS (2014) *Letter to Chairman Carper, 5 May 2014*, Department of Homeland
Security, Washington, DC, USA

Dittman, J Paul (2014) *Managing Risk in the Global Supply Chain*, University of
Tennessee, USA

Dolfman, M, Wasser, S and Bergman, B (2007) The effects of Hurricane Katrina on
the New Orleans economy, *Monthly Labor Review*, June [online] https://www.
bls.gov/opub/mlr/2007/06/art1full.pdf [accessed 6 July 2017]

Dranginis, H (2016) *Point of Origin: Status report on the impact of Dodd-Frank
1502 in Congo*, Enough Project, Washington, DC, USA

Duhigg, C and Barboza, D (2012) In China, human costs are built into an iPad,
*New York Times* [online] www.nytimes.com/2012/01/26/business/ieconomy-
apples-ipad-and-the-human-costs-for-workers-in-china.html?_r=0 [accessed 14
December 2016]

EC (2011) *The EU–Korea Free Trade Agreement in Practice*, European
Commission, Brussels

EC (2015) *Enhancement of EU–Turkey Bilateral Trade Relations* [online] http://
ec.europa.eu/smart-regulation/roadmaps/docs/2015_trade_035_turkey_en.pdf
[accessed 6 July 2017]

Ekwall, D (2007) *Antagonistic Gateways in the Transport Network in a Supply
Chain Perspective*, University of Borås, School of Engineering, Sweden

Environment, Food and Rural Affairs Committee (2013a) *Contamination of Beef
Products, Eighth Report of Session*, House of Commons, London

Environment, Food and Rural Affairs Committee (2013b) *Food Contamination,
Fifth Report of Session 2013–14*, House of Commons, London

Ernst & Young (2013) *Globalization and New Opportunities for Growth* [online]
http://www.ey.com/gl/en/issues/driving-growth/globalization – looking-beyond-
the-obvious [accessed 6 July 2017]

Escaith, H (2009) *Trade Collapse, Trade Relapse and Global Production Networks:
Supply chains in the Great Recession*, OECD, Paris, France

EUIPO (2016) *Trade in Counterfeit and Pirated Goods*, EU Intellectual Property
Office, Brussels

Europol (2009) *Cargo Theft Report: Applying the brakes to road cargo crime in
Europe*, Europol, The Hague

Europol (2016) *EU Drug Markets Report 2016*, Europol, The Hague

FCO (2016) *Alternatives to Membership: Possible models for the UK outside the EU*, Foreign and Commonwealth Office [online] https://www.gov.uk/government/publications/alternatives-to-membership-possible-models-for-the-united-kingdom-outside-the-european-union [accessed 6 July 2017]

Feinberg, S and Keane, M (2009) Tariff effects on MNC decisions to engage in intra-firm and arm's-length trade, *Canadian Journal of Economics*, **42** (3), pp 900–29

Ford (2014) *Ford Sustainability Report* [online] http://corporate.ford.com/microsites/sustainability-report-2013-14/default.html [accessed 6 July 2017]

FreightWatch International (FW) Supply Chain Intelligence Center (2013) *Global Cargo Theft Threat Assessment*, FW, USA

GLA (2010) *Determining the External Costs of Road Freight Activity in London*, GLA Economics, London

Gladstone, R (2015) UN resolves to combat plundering of antiquities by ISIS, *New York Times*, 28 May

Good Corporation (2012) *Anti-Corruption Procedures in Freight Forwarding*, Good Corporation, London

Guardian (2016) Four of world's biggest cities to ban diesel cars from their centres, *Guardian*, 2 December [online] www.theguardian.com/environment/2016/dec/02/four-of-worlds-biggest-cities-to-ban-diesel-cars-from-their-centres [accessed 17 January 2017]

Harvard T.H. Chan School of Public Health (2016) Air pollution killing 3.3 million people a year worldwide, 16 September [online] www.hsph.harvard.edu/news/hsph-in-the-news/air-pollution-killing-3-3-million-people-a-year-worldwide/ [accessed 7 April 2017]

Heyndrickx, C and Breemersch, T (2012) *ECCONET: Climate change and adaptation to inland waterways*, Transport & Mobility, Leuven

House of Commons (2016) *Brexit: Impact across policy areas*, House of Commons Library, London

IBM (2009) *The Smarter Supply Chain of the Future*, IBM, New York

ICC International Maritime Bureau (IMB) (2016) *Piracy and Armed Robbery against Ships*, ICC IMB, London

IHS Markit (2012) Pitfalls of counterfeit-part epidemic exposed at ERAI/IHS event [online] https://technology.ihs.com/406787/pitfalls-of-counterfeit-part-epidemic-exposed-at-eraiihs-event [accessed 12 February 2017]

Improved Road Transport Governance Initiative (IRTG) (2011) *Fourteenth Improved Road Transport Governance Report*, UEMOA, Burkina Faso

Institute of Development Studies (2009) *Screening for Climate Change Adaptation: Managing the potential impacts of climate change on water sector in China* [online] www.ids.ac.uk/publication/screening-for-climate-change-adaptation-managing-the-potential-impacts-of-climate-change-on-water-sector-in-china [accessed 17 November 2016]

Intel (2012) *Intel Corporate Responsibility Report* [online] http://www.intel.com/
content/www/us/en/corporate-responsibility/corporate-responsibility-report-
overview.html [accessed 6 July 2017]

Intergovernmental Panel on Climate Change (2014) Annex II: Glossary, in *Climate
Change 2014: Synthesis Report. Contribution of Working Groups I, II and
III to the Fifth Assessment Report of the Intergovernmental Panel on Climate
Change*, eds KJ Mach, S Planton and C von Stechow, pp 117–30, Geneva,
Switzerland

International Chamber of Commerce (ICC), Transparency International, United
Nations Global Compact, World Economic Forum (2011) *RESIST: Resisting
extortion and solicitation in international transactions*, UN Global Compact
Office, New York

International Road Transport Union (IRU) (2008) *Attacks on Driver of
International Heavy Goods Vehicles*, IRU, Geneva

Keefe, P (2012) Cocaine Incorporated, *New York Times*, 15 June [online] http://
www.nytimes.com/2012/06/17/magazine/how-a-mexican-drug-cartel-makes-its-
billions.html [accessed 13 December 2016]

KPMG (2014) *The UK Automotive Industry and the EU*, KPMG, London

Lee, B and Preston, F, with Green, G (2012) *Preparing for High-impact,
Low-probability Events: Lessons from Eyjafjallajökull*, Chatham House, London

Leonard, D (2005) The only lifeline was the Wal-mart, *Fortune Magazine*,
3 October

Leviäkangas, P and Saarikivi, P (2012) *European Extreme Weather Risk
Management – Needs, Opportunities, Costs and Recommendations*, EWENT,
Brussels

Lyon, K (2017) *China's 'One Belt, One Road' Project Provides Opportunities and
Rules*, Transport Intelligence [online] www.ti-insight.com/briefs/chinas-one-belt-
one-road-project-provides-opportunities-rules/ [accessed 11 July 2017]

Mackenzie, S (2002) *Organised Crime and Common Transit Networks*, Australian
Institute of Criminology [online] http://www.aic.gov.au/media_library/
publications/tandi_pdf/tandi233.pdf [accessed 6 July 2017]

Mackenzie, S (2003) *Regulating the Market in Illicit Antiquities*, Australian Institute
of Criminology [online] http://traffickingculture.org/app/uploads/2012/07/
regulating-the-market-in-illicit-antiquities.pdf [accessed 28 April 2017]

Mason-Jones, R and Towill, D (1998) Shrinking the supply chain uncertainty cycle,
*Control*, September, pp 17–22

McKinnon, A (2006) Life without trucks: the effects of the disruption of road
freight transport on a national economy, *Journal of Business Logistics*, 27 (2)

Merryman, J (1986) Two ways of thinking about cultural property, *American
Journal of International Law*, 80 (4), pp 831–53

Minford, P (2016) *Understanding UK Trade Agreements with the EU and Other
Countries*, Cardiff Business School, Cardiff

MIT (2011) *Global Risk Survey, Phase II*, MIT, Boston

MMH (2012) NRF voices support for the SMART Port Security Act, *Modern Materials Handling*, June [online] http://www.mmh.com/article/nrf_voices_support_for_the_smart_port_security_act [accessed 14 November 2016)

Mongelluzzo, B (2012) How California's ports cleared the air, *Journal of Commerce*, 23 January [online] www.joc.com/port-news/how-californias-ports-cleared-air_20120123.html [accessed 7 May 2017]

OECD (2015) *Due Diligence Guidance: Towards conflict-free mineral supply chains* [online] http://www.oecd.org/daf/inv/mne/EasytoUseGuide_English.pdf [accessed 6 July 2017]

One Earth Future (OEF) Foundation (2016) *The State of Maritime Piracy*, OEF, Broomfield, Colorado

Reason, J, Hollnagel, E and Paries, J (2006) *Revisiting the Swiss Cheese Model of Accidents*, EUROCONTROL Experimental Centre, Brussels

Regmi, M and Hanaoka, S (2009) Impacts of climate change on transport and adaptation in Asia, *Proceedings of the Eastern Asia Society for Transportation Studies*, 7

Ruparel, R (2016) *Post Brexit, leaving the customs union is a no-brainer*, Open Europe [online] http://openeurope.org.uk/today/blog/post-brexit-leaving-customs-union-no-brainer/ [accessed 6 July 2017]

Savage, K, with Jackollie, MS, Kumeh, DM and Dorbor, E (2007) *Corruption Perceptions and Risks in Humanitarian Assistance: A Liberia case study*, Humanitarian Policy Group (HPG), ODI, London

Shang-Jin, W and Smarzynska, B (1999) *Pollution Havens and Foreign Direct Investment: Dirty secret or popular myth?* World Bank, New York

Shiers, V and Manners-Bell, J (2016) *Food Supply Chain Vulnerability*, Transport Intelligence, London

Ship and Bunker (2013) Drewry: bunker surcharges should fall, *Ship and Bunker*, 16 September [online] https://shipandbunker.com/news/emea/957736-drewry-bunker-surcharges-should-fall [accessed 18 February 2017]

Swanekamp, K (2010) Toyota expects recall to cost $2 billion, *Forbes*, 4 February [online] https://www.forbes.com/2010/02/04/toyota-earnings-recall-markets-equities-prius.html [accessed 3 May 2017]

Swiss Re (2016) Total losses from disaster events rise to USD 158 billion in 2016, December [online] http://www.swissre.com/media/news_releases/preliminary_sigma_estimates_total_losses_from_disaster_events_rise_to_USD_158_billion_in_2016.html [accessed 3 May 2017]

Taleb, N (2007) *The Black Swan: The impact of the highly improbable*, Random House, New York

Tesco (2012) *Corporate Responsibility Review 2012*, Tesco PLC [online] https://www.tescoplc.com/assets/files/cms/Resources/Reporting/CR_Report_2012.pdf [accessed 15 September 2016]

Tesco (2016) Saving water in the garment industry, Bangladesh [online] www.tesco-plc.com/tesco-and-society/sourcing-great-products/working-in-collaboration/saving-water-in-garment-industry-bangladesh/ [accessed 6 July 2017]

Transparency International (2016) *Corruption Perceptions Index 2016*, Transparency International, Berlin

Transparency International India (TII) (2007) *Corruption in Trucking Operations in India*, TII, New Delhi

Transport Intelligence (2008) Bangkok airport closure has significant implications for air cargo [online] http://www.ti-insight.com/briefs/14629-2/ [accessed 6 July 2017]

Transport Intelligence (2011a) Japan earthquake had little impact on high tech supply chains, says consultancy, 18 July [online] http://www.ti-insight.com/briefs/15132-2/ [accessed 6 July 2017]

Transport Intelligence (2011b) US floods impact on barge, truck and rail traffic, 23 May [online] http://www.ti-insight.com/briefs/15096-2/ [accessed 6 July 2017]

Transport Intelligence (2012) The shrinking mighty Mississippi River, 1 August [online] http://www.ti-insight.com/briefs/15404-2/ [accessed 6 July 2017]

Tyrie, A (2016) *Giving Meaning to Brexit*, Open Europe, UK

UN (2015) *UNODC Legal Mandates for Wildlife and Forest Crime*, UNODC, Geneva [online] www.unodc.org/unodc/en/wildlife-and-forest-crime/mandates.html [accessed 16 September 2016]

UN (2016) *Adopting Resolution 2309 (2016), Security Council Calls for Closer Collaboration to Ensure Safety of Global Air Services, Prevent Terrorist Attacks*, 22 September, UN, New York [online] https://www.un.org/press/en/2016/sc12529.doc.htm [accessed 18 December 2016]

UNCTAD (2016) *Review of Maritime Transport 2016*, UNCTAD, Geneva [online] http://unctad.org/en/PublicationsLibrary/rmt2016_en.pdf [accessed 29 April 2017]

US House of Representatives Subcommittee on National Security and Foreign Affairs Committee on Oversight and Government Reform (2010) *Warlord, Inc: Extortion and Corruption along the U.S. Supply Chain in Afghanistan*, Congressional Research Service, Washington, DC

Van der Lugt, L and Streng, M (2013) *Slow Steaming in de containerlijnvaart kost meer dan het oplevert*, Erasmus Universiteit, Rotterdam [online] www.erim.eur.nl/centres/smartporterasmus/publications/smart-port-opinion/detail/2958-slow-steaming-in-de-containerlijnvaart-kost-meer-dan-het-oplevert/ [accessed 11 July 2017]

Vander Stichele, M *et al* (2011) *Bitter Fruit*, Centre for Research on Multinational Corporations/SOMO, Netherlands

Vira, V, Ewing, T and Miller, J (2014) *Out of Africa*, Born Free Foundation, Horsham, UK

Wainwright, T (2016) *Narconomics: How to run a drugs cartel*, PublicAffairs, New York

Washington, R (2016) Long-haul trucking's billion-dollar cargo theft problem, *Pacific Standard*, 4 February

Wiggins, J (2008) Unilever recall over China milk, *Financial Times*, 1 March

Wilcox, D (2011) *Hard Disk Drive Prices and Supplies Impacted by Thailand Flooding* [online] http://www.dataspan.com/blog/post/hard-disk-drive-prices-and-supplies-impacted-by-thailand-flooding [accessed 3 November 2016]

World Bank (2013) *The Pirates of Somalia: Ending the threat, rebuilding a nation*, World Bank, Washington, DC

World Bank (2014) EU tariff rate, applied, weighted mean, all products (%) [online] http://data.worldbank.org/indicator/TM.TAX.MRCH.WM.AR. ZS?locations=EU [accessed 6 July 2017]

World Economic Forum (WEF) (2012) *New Models for Addressing Supply Chain and Transport Risk*, WEF, Geneva

World Economic Forum (WEF) (2013a) *Building Resilience in Supply Chains*, WEF/Accenture, Geneva

World Economic Forum (WEF) (2013b) *The Global Competitiveness Report 2012–2013*, WEF, Geneva

World Trade Organization (WTO) (2016) *Technical Information on Rules of Origin* [online] https://www.wto.org/english/tratop_e/roi_e/roi_info_e.htm [accessed 6 July 2017]

# FURTHER READING

ALPA (2013) *Cyber Threats: Who controls your aircraft?* International Federation of Air Line Pilots' Associations, Montreal

Bailey, S (2008) *Need and Greed: Corruption risks, perceptions and prevention in humanitarian assistance,* Humanitarian Policy Group (HPG), ODI, London

Brenton, P and Isik, G (2012) *De-Fragmenting Africa,* World Bank, Washington, DC

Brown, J (2012) *Risk Management Defined,* CSCMP, Illinois

Canis, B (2011) *The Motor Vehicle Supply Chain: Effects of the Japanese earthquake and tsunami,* Congressional Research Service, Washington, DC

Carbon Disclosure Project (2013) [online] www.cdp.net

CargoNet (2012) *2011 United States Cargo Theft Report,* CargoNet, Jersey City, NJ

Center for the Study of Democracy (CSD) (2004) *Transportation, Smuggling and Organized Crime,* CSD, Sofia

Chang-Gui Gu, Sheng-Rong Zou, Xiu-Lian Xu, Yan-Qing Qu, Yu-Mei Jiang and Da Ren He (2011) Onset of cooperation between layered networks, *Physical Review E-Statistical, Non-linear and Soft Matter Physics,* **84** (2)

Cozzolino, A (2012) Humanitarian logistics and supply chain management, in *Cross-Sector Cooperation in Disaster Relief Management,* Springer, Berlin

Criminal Justice Information Services (CJIS) Division Uniform Crime Reporting (UCR) Program (2013) *Cargo Theft User Manual,* Law Enforcement Support Section (LESS) Crime Statistics Management Unit (CSMU), USA

Dean, J, Lovely, M and Wang, H (2009) Are foreign investors attracted to weak environmental regulations? Evaluating the evidence from China, *Journal of Development Economics,* **90,** pp 1–13

Department of Homeland Security (DHS) (2006) *A Performance Review of FEMA's Disaster Management Activities in Response to Hurricane Katrina,* DHS, Washington, DC

Dolfman, M, Wasser, SF and Bergman, B (2007) The effects of Hurricane Katrina on the New Orleans economy, *Monthly Labor Review,* June, pp 3–18

DOT Center for Climate Change and Environmental Forecasting (2002) *The Potential Impacts of Climate Change on Transportation,* DOT, Washington, DC

Federal Financial Institutions Examination Council (FFIEC) (2006) *Lessons Learned from Hurricane Katrina,* FFIEC, Virginia, USA

FW APAC (2013) *Global Cargo Theft Threat Assessment,* FW, Malaysia

Global Risk Miyamoto (2007) *Niigata Chuetsu-Oki Japan Earthquake Reconnaissance Report,* Global Risk Miyamoto, Sacramento, CA

Hearson, M (2006) *Who Pays for Cheap Clothes?,* Labour Behind the Label, Norwich

Helferich, O (2012) *Catastrophic Events: The ultimate supply chain resiliency test*, CSCMP, Illinois

Horwitz, S (2009) Private enterprise's response to Hurricane Katrina, *Independent Review*, **13** (4) pp 511–28

Khan, O (2005) *Managing Risk by Internalising Product Design in Fashion Retail: An exploratory case of Marks & Spencer*, Indian Institute of Materials Management, Mumbai

Koetse, M and Rietveld, P (2009) The impact of climate change and weather on transport: an overview of empirical findings, *Transportation Research Part D*, **14**, pp 205–21

Kramek, J (2013) *The Critical Infrastructure Gap: US port facilities and cyber vulnerabilities*, Center for 21st Century Security and Intelligence at Brookings, Washington, DC

Lezhnev, S and Hellmuth, A (2012) *Taking Conflict out of Consumer Gadgets*, Enough Project, Washington, DC

OECD (2007) *The Economic Impact of Counterfeiting and Piracy*, OECD, Paris

Renaud, P (2012) *The DHL Supply Chain (DSC) BCM10-Step Plan*, CSCMP, Illinois

Sony DADC (2011) Rebuilding the UK Supply Chain, in *The Insider*, Sony DADC, London

Steele, J (2012) *Leading Practices in Action with Cisco's Japan Earthquake Response*, CSCMP, Illinois

Supply Chain Risk Leadership Council (SCRLC) (2011) *Supply Chain Risk Management: A compilation of best practices*, SCRLC, San Jose, CA

TenBarge, T (2012) *Operational Risk Management*, CSCMP, Illinois

Wong, M (2005) *The ICT Hardware Sector in China and Corporate Social Responsibility Issues*, SOMO, Netherlands

# INDEX

Note: The index is filed in alphabetical, word-by-word order. Numbers within main headings and 'St' are filed as spelt out. Acronyms are filed as presented. Page locators in *italics* denote information contained within a Figure or Table; locators as roman numerals denote material contained within the preliminary pages.

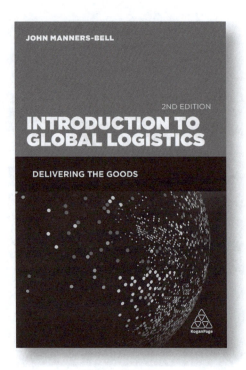